Charles John Vaughan

Epiphany, Lent, and Easter

A selection of sermons preached in St. Michael's Church, London

Charles John Vaughan

Epiphany, Lent, and Easter
A selection of sermons preached in St. Michael's Church, London

ISBN/EAN: 9783741193514

Manufactured in Europe, USA, Canada, Australia, Japa

Cover: Foto ©Lupo / pixelio.de

Manufactured and distributed by brebook publishing software (www.brebook.com)

Charles John Vaughan

Epiphany, Lent, and Easter

EXPOSITORY SERMONS,
&c.

Cambridge:
PRINTED BY C. J. CLAY, M.A.
AT THE UNIVERSITY PRESS.

EPIPHANY, LENT, AND EASTER:

A SELECTION OF SERMONS

PREACHED IN

ST. MICHAEL'S CHURCH, CHESTER SQUARE, LONDON.

BY

C. J. VAUGHAN, D.D.

VICAR OF DONCASTER.

THIRD EDITION, REVISED.

London and Cambridge:
MACMILLAN AND CO.
1868.

[All Rights reserved.]

DEDICATED

TO THE

CONGREGATION OF ST. MICHAEL'S

WITH AFFECTIONATE RESPECT.

PREFACE

TO THE FIRST EDITION.

THE first of these Sermons will be found to contain a sufficient explanation of the circumstances which led to their delivery. In consenting to publish them[1], I yield to the desire of those who had the best right to express a wish on the subject.

I would that this little Volume might be regarded as a token of the gratitude which I shall always feel for the kindness of a Congregation to which it has been a privilege to be permitted even temporarily to minister.

Expository Sermons labour under many disadvantages both in the hearing and still more in the reading. It is difficult to make them lucid: it is still more difficult to make them

---

[1] The whole course consisted of thirty Sermons, eighteen of which have been selected for publication. (*See Preface to Second Edition.*)

attractive. But are they not needed? Do they not lay the most solid basis of Christian instruction? Do they not contain the best antidote to error? Are we not then most sure that we are rightly proportioning the Word of truth, when we take it as it stands in the pages of Revelation, and seek only to illustrate, to enforce, and to apply it?

In so doing, we shall find it necessary to vary in many cases the language of the Authorized Version. Sometimes for the sake of precision, sometimes for the sake of clearness, sometimes for the very purpose of arresting the attention by a change of terms, by a departure from the too familiar form even where it is impossible to improve it, the expositor of Scripture must claim and exercise the right of immediate access to the original, and bear the responsibility, always a grave one, of declaring to his Congregation that the sense of God's Word is, to the best of his judgment, this and not that. They will be thankful for any honest effort to make the language of Inspiration more real to them, and certainly neither the preacher nor the hearer will feel the less admiration or the less thankfulness for that "form of sound words" which

Preface. ix

has been familiar to them from childhood in the English Version of the Bible.

No one can be more conscious of the incomparable force and beauty of that Translation than one who makes the attempt to vary it. The gain of an authorized Revision of it could scarcely equal the loss. Beyond a very few passages, in which all scholars would agree in sanctioning the correction, it may be doubted whether an ordinary reader would be benefited by change, whether indeed the meaning of the change itself would be readily intelligible to him.

Yet, while leaving the Authorized Version almost or altogether intact, as substantially correct, as uniformly grave and simple, as eminently graceful, harmonious, and beautiful, as invested by the associations of two centuries and a half with a sanctity scarcely inferior to that of the original itself, we may still hail with gratitude any subsidiary elucidations, whether in the more fragmentary form of expositions from the Pulpit, or in the more systematic and elaborate shape of a retranslation of the whole.

I have prefaced each of the following Sermons with a careful Version of the whole passage in which the text is found[1]. In so doing, I have aimed at nothing but exactness. I have introduced expressions, not only far less beautiful than those of the Authorized Version, but, in some cases, quite inconsistent with its style. My one object has been faithfulness to the original text. And, in the hope that my purpose would not be misconceived, that, at all events, this protest against such misconception would be received as sincere, I have aimed only at the benefit of those who may be willing to accept a very careful and anxious effort of this nature—how careful and anxious none can know without making the experiment—as a help, slight and inadequate, I know, but not, I trust, quite superfluous, in the patient study of the revealed mind of God.

Perhaps a similar translation (with brief explanatory notes) of continuous portions, or of the whole, of the New Testament, might not be without its use, if it were distinctly understood to be designed only as the companion of the Authorized English Version, not as a substitute for it. To those who are unac-

---

[1] The text which I have usually followed is that of Tischendorf's second edition.

quainted with the language of the original, it might be a satisfaction to have in their possession as close and accurate a rendering of the text of the Greek Testament as the English idiom, with some sacrifice of taste and beauty, could be made to bear. The portions of Scripture here presented may be regarded as specimens of such a work. But the labour of the undertaking would be far beyond anything that an inexperienced person could suppose. To do it as, if done at all, it ought to be and must be done, would be a task not of weeks or months, but of some devoted years. And at last it would disappoint those who might expect in it such a result as cannot be produced by man for his brother. The Bible, to be understood, must be searched, pondered, and prayed over: with this, an imperfect translation will suffice for illumination; without this, no version can give it.

SOUTHBOROUGH,
June 25, 1860.

PREFACE

TO THE SECOND EDITION.

EIGHT Sermons have now been added to the series. These were preached in the month of July, the former course having ended in April. The title of the Volume has thus been rendered somewhat less appropriate; but it could scarcely have been altered without risk of confusion. The additional Sermons are also published separately, for the convenience of those who may be in possession of the former Edition.

I am grateful for many kind notices of this little Volume in its earlier form; and I can only hope that its present enlargement will not be found unseasonable.

DONCASTER,
May 4, 1861.

PREFACE

TO THE THIRD EDITION.

IN preparing this Volume for a third Edition, I have endeavoured to supply some of its many deficiencies, so far as this could be done without rewriting the whole.

It is, however, only in one Sermon, that I have found it necessary to make any important change in the interpretation of the text. Two paragraphs in the 12th Sermon (*On the Efficacy of the Blood of Christ*) have been altogether altered. The explanation of the words *offered Himself* (in Heb. ix. 14), as expressing not the actual Sacrifice of Christ, but the subsequent presentation of Himself to God after Resurrection, has been felt, on further consideration, to be scarcely consistent with the use of the same word in the 28th verse of the same Chapter (ἅπαξ προσενεχθεὶς εἰς τὸ πολλῶν ἀνενεγκεῖν ἁμαρτίας). And the change of this interpretation carried with it also the whole context in reference to *the Eternal Spirit*. I have the more willingly parted with this passage, because my later study of Rom. i. 4, on which I had chiefly rested my argument, has led me to a different view of that text also.

DONCASTER,
April 15, 1868.

CONTENTS.

SERMON I.

First Sunday after Epiphany, January 8, 1860.

CONFORMITY AND TRANSFORMATION.

               PAGE
ROMANS XII. 2.—Be not conformed to this world 1

SERMON II.

Second Sunday after Epiphany, January 15, 1860.

SYMPATHY AND CONDESCENSION.

ROMANS XII. 15, 16.—Rejoice with them that do rejoice, and weep with them that weep . . . Mind not high things, but condescend to men of low estate 17

SERMON III.

Fourth Sunday after Epiphany, January 29, 1860.

THE DOCTRINE OF OBEDIENCE.

ROMANS XIII. 7.—Render therefore to all their dues: tribute to whom tribute is due; custom to whom custom; fear to whom fear; honour to whom honour 35

SERMON IV.

Septuagesima Sunday, February 5, 1860.

VAGUE RUNNING AND INEFFECTIVE FIGHTING.

1 CORINTHIANS IX. 26.—I therefore so run, not as uncertainly: so fight I, not as one that beateth the air 53

SERMON V.

Sexagesima Sunday, February 12, 1860.

GLORYING IN INFIRMITIES.

2 CORINTHIANS XI. 30.—If I must needs glory, I will glory of the things which concern mine infirmities 69

SERMON VI.

Quinquagesima Sunday, February 19, 1860.

PRESENT KNOWLEDGE AND FUTURE.

1 CORINTHIANS XIII. 12.—For now we see through a glass, darkly; but then face to face: now I know in part; but then shall I know even as also I am known 87

SERMON VII.

First Sunday in Lent, February 26, 1860.

THE PROTECTIVE POWER OF CONSISTENT HOLINESS.

2 CORINTHIANS VI. 7.—By the armour of Righteousness on the right hand and on the left 105

SERMON VIII.

First Sunday in Lent, February 26, 1860.

CHRIST THE STRENGTH OF THE TEMPTED.

ST. MATTHEW IV. 1.—Then was Jesus led up of the Spirit into the wilderness, to be tempted of the devil.

HEBREWS II. 18.—For in that He Himself hath suffered being tempted, He is able to succour them that are tempted . . 123

SERMON IX.

Third Sunday in Lent, March 11, 1860.

ST. PAUL TO PHILEMON.

PHILEMON 15.—For perhaps he therefore departed for a season, that thou shouldest receive him for ever 141

SERMON X.

Third Sunday in Lent, March 11, 1860.

CHRIST IN HIS WORD.

St. Luke xi. 28.—But He said, Yea rather, blessed are they that hear the word of God, and keep it 161

SERMON XI.

Fourth Sunday in Lent, March 18, 1860.

THE ELDER TO THE ELECT LADY.

2 John 8.—Look to yourselves, that we lose not those things which we have wrought, but that we receive a full reward . 179

SERMON XII.

Fifth Sunday in Lent, March 25, 1860.

THE EFFICACY OF THE BLOOD OF CHRIST.

Hebrews ix. 14.—How much more shall the blood of Christ, who through the eternal Spirit offered Himself without spot to God, purge your conscience from dead works to serve the living God? 195

SERMON XIII.

Fifth Sunday in Lent, March 25, 1860.

THE DISINTERESTEDNESS OF CHRIST.

St. John viii. 50.—I seek not mine own glory 213

SERMON XIV.

Easter Sunday, April 8, 1860.

THE MYSTERY OF THE CHRISTIAN LIFE.

Colossians iii. 1.—If ye then be risen with Christ, seek those things which are above, where Christ sitteth on the right hand of God 233

SERMON XV.

Easter Sunday, April 8, 1860.

THE RETURN FROM THE SEPULCHRE.

ST. JOHN XX. 10.—Then the disciples went away again unto their own home 251

SERMON XVI.

First Sunday after Easter, April 15, 1860.

THE VICTORY OF FAITH.

1 JOHN V. 4.—Whatsoever is born of God overcometh the world: and this is the victory that overcometh the world, even our faith 271

SERMON XVII.

Second Sunday after Easter, April 22, 1860.

THE WANDERING AND THE RETURN.

1 PETER II. 25.—For ye were as sheep going astray; but are now returned unto the Shepherd and Bishop of your souls . 289

SERMON XVIII.

Second Sunday after Easter, April 22, 1860.

ONE FLOCK, ONE SHEPHERD.

ST. JOHN X. 16.—And other sheep I have, which are not of this fold: them also I must bring, and they shall hear my voice; and there shall be one fold, and one Shepherd . . . 307

SERMON XIX.

Fourth Sunday after Trinity, July 1, 1860.

THE EXPECTATION OF THE CREATION.

ROMANS VIII. 19.—The earnest expectation of the creature waiteth for the manifestation of the sons of God 325

Contents.

SERMON XX.

Fifth Sunday after Trinity, July 8, 1860.

GOD THE SANCTUARY OF MAN.

1 PETER III. 15.—Sanctify the Lord God in your hearts . . . 343

SERMON XXI.

Fifth Sunday after Trinity, July 8, 1860.

WISDOM TOWARDS THOSE WITHOUT.

COLOSSIANS IV. 5.—Walk in wisdom toward them that are without, redeeming the time 361

SERMON XXII.

Sixth Sunday after Trinity, July 15, 1860.

THE MAN OF SIN.

2 THESSALONIANS II. 8.—And then shall that wicked be revealed, whom the Lord shall consume with the spirit of His mouth, and shall destroy with the brightness of His coming 379

SERMON XXIII.

Seventh Sunday after Trinity, July 22, 1860.

THE WAGES OF SIN AND THE GIFT OF GOD.

ROMANS VI. 23.—The wages of sin is death: but the gift of God is eternal life through Jesus Christ our Lord . . . 403

SERMON XXIV.

Seventh Sunday after Trinity, July 22, 1860.

THE MATURITY OF CHRISTIAN EXPERIENCE.

2 TIMOTHY I. 12.—I know whom I have believed 421

SERMON XXV.

Eighth Sunday after Trinity, July 29, 1860.

THE SPIRIT OF BONDAGE AND THE SPIRIT OF ADOPTION.

ROMANS VIII. 15.—Ye have not received the spirit of bondage again to fear : but ye have received the spirit of adoption, whereby we cry, Abba, Father 439

SERMON XXVI.

Eighth Sunday after Trinity, July 29, 1860.

GOD SPEAKING IN HIS SON.

HEBREWS I. 1, 2.—God, who at sundry times and in divers manners spake in time past unto the fathers by the prophets, hath in these last days spoken unto us by His Son . . . 457

SERMON I.

CONFORMITY AND TRANSFORMATION.

EPISTLE FOR THE FIRST SUNDAY AFTER THE EPIPHANY.

ROMANS XII. 1—5.

1 *I BESEECH you therefore, brethren, by the mercies of God, to present your bodies a living sacrifice, holy, acceptable to*
2 *God, which is your reasonable service. And be not fashioned according to[1] this age; but be ye transformed by the renewing of the mind, that ye may prove what is the will of God, even*
3 *that which is good and acceptable and perfect. For I say, through the grace which was given me, to every one that is among you, not to be high-minded beyond what he ought to be minded, but to be minded so as to be sober-minded, according*
4 *as God dealt to each one a measure of faith. For as in one body we have many members, and all the members have not*
5 *the same office; so we, the many, are one body in Christ, and, regarded one by one, each other's members.*

---

[1] 1 Pet. i. 14.

SERMON I.

CONFORMITY AND TRANSFORMATION.

ROMANS XII. 2.

Be not conformed to this world.

THE work of a Christian minister, my brethren, is not easy. He has the common difficulties of all men in maintaining a right conversation and a clear conscience, and he has others all his own. That public ministry which is often regarded as a mere matter of course; those sermons to which his hearers often give little heed; that exposition of revealed truth, and that application of the truth to practical life, which is often treated as if any one could utter, as if every one knew it; these things cause no little anxiety, involve no little exertion, to one who would make full proof of his ministry, and desires not only to be instant in season and out of season, but also to be wise in the choice of subjects, and successful in the enforcement of the truth upon the consciences of those who hear.

The will of God has deprived you for a time—I hope and believe but for a time—of the public exercise of that faithful ministry which you have long and, I am sure, thankfully enjoyed. Most unexpectedly, and in some senses most unwillingly, I have been called to stand before you in another's room. In all sincerity and in all humility I would ask you, my brethren, to join your prayers this day with mine, as for the restoration to health and activity of him who is now laid aside, so also for an especial blessing on that subsidiary and temporary ministry by which it is sought to fill the void.

In many respects, the teaching of a temporary instructor must be most deficient. He cannot know, in detail, the cases and the circumstances of those to whom he is to minister. He must, to a great extent, draw his bow at a venture. But there are two considerations which may lawfully encourage him.

First, the human heart is not many, but one. *As in water face answereth to face, so the heart of man to man* (Prov. xxvii. 19). If a man knows one heart well, even his own; much more, if he have had any enlarged intercourse with other minds and lives, though it may have been elsewhere and under different circumstances; he may hope that, by God's blessing, his words will not be altogether vague, nor his aim wholly missed: let him speak as a man to men, let him speak to them that are bound as bound with them, to them that suffer adversity as being himself also in the body, to them that are tempted as himself liable to temptation, to them that are struggling as himself in the conflict, to them that would win heaven as having himself also that hope and aim, to them that are sinful and weak and often stumbling as himself also in like case with them; and he may rely upon it that an echo will come back to him from the souls addressed, they will recognize a brother's voice, and give it entrance into their hearts.

The other encouragement is this, that the Word of God suits all cases, and is the same in every place. The office of the Christian instructor is to preach the Word; not his own word, but God's. Let him do that —with all plainness of speech, with all closeness of interpretation, with all explicitness, with all fulness; let him explain it, let him apply, let him aim, let him enforce it; and He from whom the Word comes will carry it home: God desires the edification, the progress, the comfort, the salvation, of the souls here present before Him; He desires these things, and He has given His own Word, in all its variety and in all its compass, to effect them: therefore, if a man mistrusts himself, let him turn there; let him throw himself upon the purpose as well as the promise of Him in whose name he speaks; and he may be assured that some fruit will follow, something which is real and shall be permanent, as well as much to remind him that both he and his hearers are sinful men, and that all which is man's only must waste and fail and perish.

It is my purpose to stand as much aside as possible,

and to let the Word of God have free course and be glorified. The Scriptures which furnish the regular instruction for each Sunday, more especially the Epistle and the Gospel for the day, shall be brought before you in due order, and we will seek to learn together out of them. We will begin to-day. The Epistle for this day shall be our morning subject, and the Gospel for this day our evening subject. And may God Himself by His Holy Spirit be the inward teacher and light of each one of us.

I will read you the Epistle once again, with a brief word or two of elucidation, and then turn your thoughts to the especial topic suggested by the text.

We are celebrating at this season the Epiphany or Manifestation of Christ, typified by the visit of the wise men from the east to the lowly cradle of the infant Saviour; realized in fact by that proclamation of His name to all nations, which began in the conversion of the first Gentile, Cornelius, and is still (though too faintly and intermittently prosecuted) the work and office of the age in which we live; hereafter to be perfected and consummated in that glorious season to which faith looks forward, when the earth shall be full of the knowledge of the Lord as the waters cover the sea.

At this season it is appropriate that we should be reminded, as we are in the chosen services of our Church, what Christ Himself was in His earthly life, and what we must be who would hereafter see Him as He is. The Gospel for each Sunday, speaking generally, gives us the one, in some special phase of its manifestation; the Epistle gives us the other. Listen to its teaching.

I beseech you therefore, brethren. The words follow, in the place from which they come, a large disclosure of the truth of Redemption; its basis, a work of propitiation and atonement; its condition, a hearty acceptance by faith in Christ; its compass as coextensive with the world; its effect, in each individual who receives it, a life of inward peace, of inward strength, of assured hope, of final glory. Such is the force of the word *therefore.* Since God has done these great things for us; since such is the safety, such the happiness, such the hope, such the present and such the future, of every one who will have Christ for his Saviour; *I beseech you,* as the first and natural consequence of these things, and *by the mercies of God,* as my argument and your motive, *to present your bodies a living sacrifice;* to set yourselves, your living selves, with every power of action and service, as it were beside the altar of God, for Jesus Christ your great High Priest to offer up daily to His Father, making that surrender acceptable through His own most precious blood. A *living* sacrifice; not, like those offered under the Law, one of dead victims: *holy,* that is, consecrated and set apart from all profane uses for God's use only: and further, *acceptable unto God,* through His Son: *which is your reasonable service. And be not fashioned according to this age*—we will return to this clause presently—*but be ye transformed by the renewing of the mind:* that is where the work must begin, with the mind; the act will follow: *the renewing of your mind;* the renovation, as by an act of new creation, of your whole spirit and inward being by the indwelling of the Holy Spirit of God. *That ye may prove,* put to the test of personal trial and experience, *what the will of God is, even that which is good, and acceptable, and perfect;* that you may not only know, as a matter of theory or of sound doctrine, what God would have you to do and to be, but may put it, as it were, to the test, by setting yourselves to do it.

The Apostle proceeds to illustrate this will of God in some special points of duty. *For I say, through the grace which was given me,* in virtue of that undeserved favour of God which made me an Apostle, *to every one that is among you, not to be high-minded beyond what he ought to be minded, but to be minded so as to be sober-minded; according as God,* in the distribution of His gifts—and the especial reference is to the gifts of His Holy Spirit following upon Baptism and the laying on of the Apostles' hands—*dealt to each one a measure of faith:* that is, according to that measure of faith which God assigned to each. Each one of us is to see in himself, not an isolated being, possessed of independent gifts, which he may boast of as his own and vaunt as superior to those of another: such a view of our Christian standing is as false as it is mischievous. *For as in one body,* in one natural human body, *we have many members, and all the members have not the same office; so we, the many,* we collectively, *are one body in Christ, and, regarded one by one,* individually, *each other's members;* fellow-members, that is, of the same body. Instead of being all isolated, independent, and self-contained, we are mutually related, mutually dependent, mutually interested and concerned, even as a human body, in which the eye and the hand, the foot and the head, have indeed each one its own work and function, but cannot exercise that function, any one of them, without the energy and cooperation of all the rest.

. There the Epistle for this day ends, and certainly not without having suggested matter enough for reproof and for correction, as well as for doctrine and instruction in righteousness.

But of all the topics here suggested, could I have selected one more suitable to the wants of this congregation than that read as the text, *Be not conformed to this world?*

How familiar the words! The world, conformity to the world, are phrases often on the lips of religious teachers: and well they may be. But let us be quite sure that we first understand them.

There are two terms in the original language for this expression, *the world.* One of them regards the things that now are in reference to time, the other in reference to space. The one means the things that are seen, this material world, with all its enjoyments and gratifications, its riches, pleasures, and honours;

the other means the time or age to which these things belong, and by which they are limited and circumscribed; the period, longer or shorter—we know not its duration, but God knoweth—previous to what we are taught to designate as the end of all things; that consummation of the old, that introduction of the new, which shall be the concomitant of the second Advent of Jesus Christ, the consequence of that second and greater Epiphany for which the Church on earth and in heaven is ever waiting and watching.

The two terms are often employed separately, and once at least in the Scriptures they are combined. The phrase, *according to the course of this world* (Eph. ii. 2), is an example of that combination. *Ye walked in sin, according to,* following the rule and direction of, *the age,* or *period, of this present world.*

In the passage before us, the term rendered world means properly the period or age that now is. The same word, and its opposite—the contrast of the two being always implied where it is not expressed—are found in direct opposition in a single passage to which I will refer you, in St Luke's Gospel (xx. 34): *The children of this world,* of this age or period, *marry and are given in marriage: but they that shall be counted worthy to obtain that world,* that age or period, what we designate as eternity in contrast with time, *and the resurrection from the dead, neither marry nor are given in marriage; neither can they die any more, for they are equal with the angels, and are the children of God, being the children of the resurrection.*

I call your attention to this passage, because it sets so clearly before us what is really intended by the world spoken of in the text; namely, the period of time prior to the resurrection; the duration of earthly interests and of earthly life as a whole; the age of things temporal, as opposed to the age of things eternal.

Now therefore, *Be not conformed to this world*, becomes equivalent to, *Be not conformed to time, but rather to eternity.* Wear not the fashion of persons who belong to time, and have nothing to do with eternity. Let not the garb of your souls, let not the habit of your lives, be that which befits persons whose home, whose dwelling-place, whose all, is in the passing unreal scene which we call human life, and who have no part nor lot in the permanent unchanging realities of the new heaven and new earth, which shall come into view with the return of Christ and the resurrection of the just. Wear not the garb of time, but invest yourselves already with the fashion of eternity.

O, my brethren, how large, how elevating, how magnificent a view is here opened! How different from those poor narrow rules which would prescribe to a Christian exactly what he shall allow himself of human pleasure, and from what particular kinds of recreation he shall of necessity turn aside! The world here does not designate particular circles of society, or particular modes of occupation or of amusement. The text says to each of us, Brother, sister, made of God for Himself, redeemed of Christ for glory, object of Divine love, temple of the Holy Spirit, live not for time, live for eternity. Let it not appear from your manner of life, let it not be inferred from your tone of conversation, let it not be gathered from your evident frivolity, your prevailing vanity, or self-indulgence, or eagerness after the pleasures or advantages of this world, that you are one of those for whom this life is all, and who are not looking for any blessed hope beyond the grave to which you are hastening. Do not so great an injustice to yourself, do not so great an injury to others, as to leave it in any doubt where your real home is, your heart, your treasure. When two things come into competition, the opinion of men and the will of God, let it be well seen which you prefer. If any particular occupation or any particular amusement, if any particular friendship or any particular affection, be found by you, on trial, to be unfavourable to your growth in grace, to have a direct tendency to make you forget your soul, forget heaven, forget your Saviour, forget your God, suspect that thing, forego it if you can, not as a painful sacrifice, but with a cheerful and a willing heart, as one who loves something else far above all. When any question arises of right and wrong, of reverence or of irreverence, of charity or harshness, of faith or unbelief, let none doubt for one instant on which side you are. When others look to you for the sanction, by word or by silence, of an ungodly principle, of a worldly maxim, of an un-

Conformity and Transformation.

charitable judgment, show them, instantly and boldly, that you withhold it out of love to God. When the advantages of this life are spoken of as all-important, when the chastisements of God are regarded as unmixed evils, when His providence is set aside or His mercy doubted in your hearing, when the death of the Christian is too much lamented, or the death of the unbeliever treated as a happy release; when in any of these or the like ways Christ's brightest promises are virtually denied, and His most solemn warnings dealt with as if they were not; then be not conformed to this world: let not your part be taken with time, but show yourself to belong to the eternity beyond.

Be not conformed to time. How brief a rule, yet how wide, hôw difficult, in its application!

Alas! my brethren, many things might be said against us untruly, or truly perhaps of one and not truly of another, or of the same person truly at one time and not truly at another; but this too truly, though it be in different degrees, of all, that we are too much conformed to time. Is it not the very latest of all Christian attainments, that a man shall really and consistently live, act, speak, and feel, as if he belonged not to time but to eternity? Where is he who constantly keeps in view his connection with that within the veil? Where is he whose affections are really set on the place where Christ dwells, and who really feels, and lives as if he felt, that his life, his true life, *is hid with Christ in God* (Col. iii. 3)? If we did this, could we be thus vexed with life's cares?

could we be thus sensitive to the world's opinion? could we be thus hurt by a slight, thus agitated by a rumour, thus upset and shattered by an adverse incident? should we not have at once an interest and a safeguard independent of chance and change; a humble yet sure looking for of a rest already secured, only waiting to be disclosed, to be revealed, to be unveiled?

But we are honest with ourselves, and therefore we cannot say that we have yet felt this. We confess, some of us sadly and sorrowfully, that we are still conformed to time. We see how the Apostles, how the first Christians, felt about earth and heaven; how they were marked out from all else by the brightness of their hope, no less than by the purity of their life; how they made it one half of their whole practice, *to wait for the Son of God from heaven* (1 Thess. i. 10); how they had even *a desire to depart and to be with Christ*, which they knew to be *far better* (Phil. i. 23). But in all this we cannot resemble them. And the first question for us all is, Why not? And the second question for us all is, How can we learn to do so? We will end with a brief answer to each of these.

No one can be conformed to, can fashion himself according to, that which he knows not. We are conformed to this world, not because it satisfies us, not because it makes us happy, not because we find rest or peace in living by its rules and principles, but because it is the only world that we know, the only world (let me say) in which we know any one. The early Christians were conformed to the other world because One whom they knew well, and whom they loved above all, lived there; because they had a Friend, trusted in and ever communed with, in that other world; and because, where He was, there their hearts were. The way to escape from our worldliness is not so much to struggle with it hand to hand, but to supersede it, as it were, by the entrance into us of a new affection; by giving our hearts to another, even to Him who has already entered for us within the veil, and who now and ever liveth to be our intercessor and our life. In proportion as we enter more deeply into the knowledge of ourselves by careful self-examination, we shall more deeply feel our need of a Saviour out of ourselves; and in proportion as we more simply and more humbly throw ourselves upon the mercy and help of God in Christ, we shall be more strongly drawn towards Him in whom alone we find real relief, real rest, real strength, and real peace. As soon as ever the moments which we spend on our knees before God in prayer become, as they surely will become to all who try the experiment, the most refreshing, the most invigorating, and the most comforting, of the whole day; as soon as we begin to look forward to them as our chief help, and back to them as our chief solace; we shall have learned one great part of the lesson of non-conformity to the world, because we shall have begun to take a personal interest in, and to feel a personal connection with, the world above and the world beyond. We shall have begun to learn something, though it be as yet but little, of the mind of those who belonged to eternity, not to time, because Jesus, their hope and their life, had passed already through death into the world of resurrection and of immortality.

Thus it is written, *Be not conformed to this world, but be ye transformed by the renewing of your mind.* Intercourse with Christ, and with God through Him, by the Holy Spirit, is the infusing of a new element, a new character, into the heart which practises it. It is this which is to transform us from the likeness of the one world into the likeness of the other. It is this which must make us unworldly. It is this which must make us heavenly. God grant us this; this renewing of the mind by communion with Christ, by the communication of His Spirit; and then all will be ours. No amount of exertion in the cause of benevolence or of charity will do anything for us without earnest, frequent, cherished intercourse with God through Christ in prayer. No degree of scrupulosity in avoiding worldly society or denying ourselves worldly pleasure, will do anything for us without this positive access, as of mind to mind, and spirit to spirit, to the presence of Jesus Christ Himself, and of God with whom He is one. *Through Him we both have access by one Spirit unto the Father* (Eph. ii. 18). *Abide in me, and I in you. As the branch cannot bear fruit of itself, except it abide in the vine, no more can ye except ye abide in me. Without me ye can do nothing* (John xv. 4, 5).

SERMON II.

SYMPATHY AND CONDESCENSION.

EPISTLE FOR THE SECOND SUNDAY AFTER THE EPIPHANY.

ROMANS XII. 6—16.

6 *AND having gifts different according to the grace which was given to us, whether prophecy, let us use it according*
7 *to the proportion of the faith; or ministry, let us be*[1] *in our*
8 *ministry; or he that teacheth, in his teaching; or he that exhorteth, in his exhorting: he that imparteth, let him do it in liberality; he that ruleth, in earnestness; he that showeth*
9 *mercy, in cheerfulness. Let your love be without hypocrisy: abhorring that which is evil; cleaving to that which is*
10 *good: in brotherly love affectionate one to another; in*
11 *honour esteeming each other before yourselves; in earnestness not slothful; in spirit fervent; to the Lord doing ser-*
12 *vice; in hope rejoicing; in affliction enduring; in prayer*
13 *persevering; to the wants of the saints communicating;*
14 *hospitality pursuing. Bless them that persecute you; bless,*
15 *and curse not. Rejoice with men rejoicing;*[2] *weep with men weeping: being of the same mind towards each other: not minding high things, but condescending to those that are humble.*

[1] In 1 Tim. iv. 15, the words, *give thyself wholly to them*, are literally, *be in them*.

[2] *If any rejoice, rejoice with them: if any weep, weep with them.*

SERMON II.

SYMPATHY AND CONDESCENSION.

ROMANS XII. 15, 16.

Rejoice with them that do rejoice, and weep with them that weep . . . .
Mind not high things, but condescend to men of low estate.

IN the prosecution of a plan proposed last Sunday, we reach to-day a portion of Scripture which almost baffles us. So various are its topics, so important, so attractive, yet requiring so much of explanation, and admitting so much of enforcement, that the compass of one sermon is wholly inadequate to the task now presented to it. Let us give our whole minds, my brethren, to the work before us. And let us not, by God's help and blessing, be left altogether poor in the midst of such abundance.

We have, as before, first to sketch rapidly the meaning, and to express briefly the force, of the whole passage read as the Epistle for this Second Sunday after the Epiphany; and then, in the second place, to dwell somewhat more fully upon the two topics suggested by the text for special exhortation.

The close of last Sunday's Epistle had introduced one of St Paul's favourite and characteristic doctrines, that of the unity in variety, the one and the many, in what he has taught us to speak of so familiarly as *the Christian body*, to which we all belong. *As in one body we have many members, and all those members have not the same office, so we collectively are one body in Christ, and individually members one of another.* The human body is a whole made up of parts, each one of which parts has a different function from all the rest, and which yet form in their completeness, not a number of discordant units, but a harmonious and efficient unity. Even so is it with that community, that society, that assembly of the faithful, which Christ came upon earth, died, and rose again, to gather and to cement. The Christian congregation, whether viewed in each of its local organizations, or regarded as existing on the face of the whole earth, is a body; a body composed of members, designed to work together without jar or confusion, for a great common end, the manifestation of God's glory, and the highest, the eternal, happiness of God's creatures.

To-day the subject is further illustrated. I read from the sixth verse, slightly varying the authorized version where it appears in any respect to fall short of the sense or force of the original.

And having gifts, different according to the grace which was given to us; according to the measure of that Divine favour and blessing which was bestowed upon each of us in the assignment of our several posts and offices. And then these are exemplified from the various duties and functions of the Church of Christ in those earliest times. *Whether prophecy:* a spiritual gift of which we read much in the First Epistle to the Corinthians, and especially in the fourteenth chapter of that Epistle; from which we gather with much certainty that it was not a power of prediction, but (to express it in modern phraseology) rather of preaching; not of foretelling, but of forthtelling: and St Paul speaks of it as the most desirable of all supernatural gifts, because, unlike the gift of tongues, it conveyed instruction, exhortation, and comfort to the congregation; was a sign, not to the unbelieving, but to the believing, hearer; was the means of disclosing to a listener the very secrets of his heart, and thus of bringing him to conviction and faith: adding, that, although exercised under a direct and special revelation, it was yet capable of control by the possessor, and might therefore be made the subject of such a caution as is here given. *If prophecy be our gift, let us exercise it according to the proportion of the faith;* with due regard, that is, to the proportion and, if we might so paraphrase it, the balance of the Gospel: let our instructions be so shaped, and timed, and ordered, as that each part and each side of the truth may have its turn in our hands; let us, to use an expression found in one of St Paul's Epistles, *rightly divide the word of truth* (2 Tim. ii. 15); let us have no favourite doctrines, to the exclusion or neglect of others, but let *the whole counsel of God* (Acts xx. 27), not a few isolated fragments of it, be our study and our subject. Need I say, my brethren, how deeply important a rule is here laid down, applicable at least as much to modern preaching as to primitive prophesying? Is it not, in fact, from the disregard of this divine maxim, in this direction or in that, that all heresy, all fanaticism, all error, has sprung?

Or ministry. In contrast with *prophecy*, we shall understand this more particularly to refer to ministrations to the poor in the distribution of the alms of the congregation; perhaps even to that office which in the original language bears the name here employed, that of the deacon, the institution of which is recorded in the sixth chapter of the Acts of the Apostles. If this, then, be our office, *let us,* to use the forcible phrase of the Apostle's own language, *be in it;* let us exist in and for that office, be absorbed in and engrossed by it, as though it were the whole of life to us. *Or he that teacheth,* he who exercises any office of teaching, whether public or private, whether for young or old, in the Christian body, *let him be in his teaching,* in the sense already explained; *or he that exhorteth,* he whose duty it is to cheer others on to the attainment of grace or the execution of duty by his ministry as an exhorter, *let him be in that exhorting: he that imparteth* to the necessities of others, let him do it *in liberality;* literally, *in simplicity* or *singleness* of aim and motive, with self-forgetfulness, and therefore also with ungrudging bounty: *he that ruleth,* whether as the head of a congregation or the master of a family, let him do it *in earnestness*, with zeal, not with indifference; with exertion, not in languor of spirit: *he that sheweth mercy*, he who exercises compassion towards the suffering, let him do it, not with distaste, not in a spirit of bondage, but *in cheerfulness*.

There follow several brief but comprehensive principles of Christian feeling and conduct.

Let your love be without hypocrisy; genuine, not affected; according to St John's charge in his first Epistle, *My little children, let us not love in word, neither in tongue, but in deed and in truth* (1 John iii. 18). *Abhorring that which is evil; cleaving to that which is good.* Do not trifle or tamper with anything wrong; do not go to the edge of temptation; do not only refrain from sin, but abhor, hate, abominate it, because it is sin. On the other hand, do not sit loose to what is right; do not coldly and tamely practise it as a thing to which you are in heart indifferent, but cleave to it; *be glued to it*, is the original expression; grasp it as a thing from which nothing shall part or sever you. *In brotherly love affectionate one to another; in honour esteeming each other before yourselves;* as it is elsewhere written, *in lowliness of mind let each esteem other better than themselves* (Phil. ii. 3). That is the extent of the charge here: not only *prefer one another*, as by an act of voluntary self-denial, when anything is to be enjoyed by one which cannot be enjoyed by both; but really and honestly think others better than yourselves, more deserving, more worthy of honour or advancement: begin there, with the thought, and then your humility will be, not assumed —for sometimes what is called humility is only masked pride—but ready, consistent, and as it were natural.

In earnestness not slothful; in spirit fervent; to the Lord doing service. I pass over unwillingly the many remarks which suggest themselves upon this combination of weighty maxims, this threefold cord of Christian duty. *In hope rejoicing; in affliction enduring; in prayer persevering; to the wants of the saints* (that is, *of Christians*) *communicating; hospitality pursuing. Bless them that persecute you; bless, and curse not. If any rejoice, rejoice with them; if any weep, weep with them: being of the same mind towards each other: not minding high things, but condescending to those that are humble.*

It is to two of these latest directions that I desire now for a few moments to turn your thoughts.

1. *Rejoice with them that do rejoice, and weep with them that weep.*

The words are very familiar to us; but is the thing which they signify?

It is a call, you observe, to sympathy. That lies on the surface. But notice what St Paul meant by sympathy; how he describes it. Was any definition of sympathy ever equally perfect?

Take it in its two parts. *Rejoice with them that do rejoice.* It is an old remark, that this is more difficult than to weep with them that weep. Human nature, fallen and unrenewed, is said to find even in the misfortunes of friends something not wholly unpleasing. And, without dwelling upon that worst development of the feeling, at least we may say that the prosperity of others is sometimes difficult to rejoice in; that, though congratulation, more or less formal, more or less hearty, is generally ready, it does not always imply *fellow-joy*, community of rejoicing; and that there is a point beyond which the happiness of others becomes actually provoking to us; there is a joy, the sight of which wearies and at last irritates; a fulness of success, and honour, and wealth, which we either compare invidiously with our own lot, or else grudge to its possessor.

My brethren, let us practise ourselves in this rule, that we rejoice with them that do rejoice. It is as much a Christian duty as the maxim which follows it. Let us endeavour, in little matters, within our own doors first of all—for there the grace is best learned—to be glad when another is glad, to feel another's joy as our joy, to be not willing only, but thankful, that another should have, even though that other's gain may be outwardly our own loss. Try this, and, I do not say we shall find it easy—no Christian grace, as distinguished from natural disposition, is easy—yet, on the other hand, to them that believe in Christ and in the Holy Spirit every Christian grace is possible, and it is their happiness, no less than their duty, to strive after each.

This particular attainment is, in a marked manner, its own reward. Once let another's happiness, another's honour, another's enjoyment, become really ours by a sincere and hearty sympathy, and it is quite evident that the happiness of our own life must be, not doubled, but multiplied a thousand-fold. The chances of marked joy, if I might so express it, are perhaps, for any one given person, less than one to a million; but the chances of some one whom we know thus rejoicing are infinitely greater; and, if it once matters not to us whether the cause of rejoicing be in another's lot or in our own, then, from some source or other, we are quite sure of joy: he who can *rejoice with* them that rejoice must be a happy man: the waves of personal accident beat upon the rocks far below him: he himself dwells in the region above, where eternal sunshine settles and gladdens. *He that hath the bride is the bridegroom: but the friend of the bridegroom, which standeth and heareth him, rejoiceth greatly because of the bridegroom's voice: this my joy therefore is fulfilled* (John iii. 9).

And weep with them that weep. Said we that this was an easier rule? Look into it, and we shall find that it also has its difficulties.

Many persons in this generation—and we may well thank God for it—exert themselves in ministering to human suffering. It is a first Christian duty. It is made the very test of Christian discipleship. *Inasmuch as ye have done it*—ministered, that is, to the sick, the hungry, the prisoner—*unto one of the least of these my brethren, ye have done it unto me* (Matt. xxv. 40).

And, amongst equals in social position, we count any one heartless who does not in some way, by word or act, show sympathy with sorrow. But again, even here, I would say that it is far easier to do these things than really to know anything of *fellow-sorrow*, of community in sorrowing, of weeping with them that weep.

Much of what passes for ministration to the poor fails in this point, on this account. A Christian minister, or a Christian visitor, sits by the bedside of the sick, or enters the home of poverty or bereavement. It is well. He discharges a duty in so doing. But how? in what spirit? Has he left self behind him in that visit? Does he forget himself as he sits there? Does he throw his whole mind into the mind of him to whom he is ministering? Or does he utter the commonplaces of Christian consolation, with a mere official propriety, with a self-centred, unsympathizing, unsorrowing heart? You will wonder at the question: the act itself, you say, shows sympathy with sorrow: why is he there if he does not feel for the sufferer? Yes, he may feel for him, but does he —for that is the question—does he feel with him? Some persons visit the afflicted as if for the purpose of inverting the Apostle's direction, and rejoicing with them that weep; as if the duty of the comforter were to ignore the suffering which he is to console; as if he were sent to disparage the woe which summoned him, and to deny the wounds which he came to heal. The first requisite in all human consolation—might I not say, the Scriptures being my guide, in all Divine consolation also—is sympathy, fellow-feeling, the appreciation of the calamity, whatever it be, in its breadth and in its depth. Do not obtrude upon me, exclaims the stricken spirit, considerations of which you yourself feel not the appropriateness. You say that God's chastisements all work for good: I hope it, I know it, He has said so: but do not you repeat such assurances to me unless you understand first what the chastisement is. Show me, by voice or sign, that you measure my woe, and then I can listen to you: then I can take you to my heart, and let your words in.

O there is a depth of meaning in the rule, *Weep with them that weep*, which they in this congregation who have ever truly mourned can well and truly estimate. To whom do we turn in sorrow? Is it to the most voluble talker? Is it to the best-read divine? Is it, alas! always, to the most advanced Christian—measuring advancement by any usual standard? Is it not to the most loving heart? Is it not to the person who, we know, has himself sorrowed? Is it not to the tenderest, the gentlest, the most soothing voice that we know, even if it be that of an inferior, of a servant, of one more ignorant than ourselves, if only we be assured that in that heart our sorrow is its own?

Here then, as in the former half of the rule, I would say, we must practise this healing art; practise it as a difficult art; practise it, as we would any other difficult attainment, by care, by pains, by prayer, by studying our Saviour's example, by watchful self-forgetfulness; practise it, not as a thing to be assumed —sorrow is quick-sighted, and will soon find out the pretence of sympathy—but rather as a thing to be inspired into us by the Holy Spirit of God, who can, by His mighty working, turn the stoniest, the most selfish heart into a very fountain of sympathy and of tenderness. Of all the designations which a human being, under Christ's teaching, can acquire, none is so valuable, in the estimate of a truly Christian ambition, as this, *a son of consolation* (Acts iv. 36).

2. I pass to my latest topic of remark for this morning. *Mind not high things, but condescend to men of low estate.* I think it probable that the more correct rendering of the words would be, *Condescend to those things which are lowly.* We see a reference here to the words of the Psalmist, *Lord, I am not highminded: I have no proud looks. I do not exercise myself in great matters, which are too high for me. But I refrain my soul, and keep it low, like as a child that is weaned from his mother* (Psalm cxxxi).

I am quite sure that, thus understood, or understood indeed in either sense, it is a rule of the utmost importance, everywhere, and not least in a congregation like this. There are many whose Christian life is ruined by neglecting it.

Is it not just the neglect of this rule, which makes the chief evil of what is called society? Not even frivolity, not even waste of time, not even dissipation of thought, not even disregard of duty, is a more serious charge against a professedly Christian world in its mode of social intercourse, than this; that it will set its heart on high things, and will not condescend either to persons or to things of low degree. It is a constant pursuit of high things; a struggle to rise one step higher, and then one yet higher, on the ladder of ambition, whatever its particular ambition be; it may be of rank, it may be of fame, it may be of fashion, it may be of excitement generally; most often it is, in some shape or other, the ambition of distinction; but, whatever the particular aim, it is briefly to be described as *a minding of high things*, and the proper remedy for it is that here prescribed by St Paul, *Condescend to things that are lowly*.

How great a work might true charity do in this respect, in relation to society! Even in its choice of associates: why call only to thy feasts the rich, the great, the intellectual? why not remember sometimes those to whom to visit would be a pleasure received rather than given; to whom the sight of a new face, the hearing of a new voice, would be of itself a luxury and a progress? And how good would it be for all who are much, of necessity or by choice, in what we call briefly the world, to force themselves sometimes into a totally opposite scene: let them learn by their own observation what human life is to a different and far larger part of their race: let them look in upon the abodes of poverty, of privation, of sickness, of unhappiness, which surround here on every side the dwellings of luxury and of abundance: let them listen sometimes to the history of such a life; its tale of gradual deterioration or of sudden sin, of early neglect, of vicious example, of total disregard on the part of those who ought to have instructed and remonstrated and warned, at last of utter hopelessness, of despair for both worlds: let them hear and ponder these things, condescending, with humility, and surely with thankfulness to Him who has made them to differ, to persons and things of low degree; and assuredly they will return into their own circle of life wiser if sadder men; set upon redeeming the time; set upon remembering God and their brethren; set upon raising the tone, both in point of religion and of charity, of those with whom they associate; set upon doing good, while they live, with the talents, material, mental, and spiritual, with which God has so largely, so distinctively, endowed them.

And, for us all, whether in the world (so called) or out of it; for persons, more especially, who live much alone; above all, for deep thinkers and large readers, for persons who enter into abstruse doctrines whether of science, philosophy, or religion; how wise a rule is that which bids them not always to be minding high things, but to take care that they condescend also to things as well as to persons of low degree. There is a narrowing effect, as well as a widening, in the pursuit of knowledge, yes, even of Divine knowledge, if that knowledge be chiefly intellectual. A man who lives much in study must be to a great degree a solitary man; and a solitary man must be, in some most important respects, a narrow man.

His charities become contracted; the ties of sympathy with his fellows, except a few chosen associates, become weaker; and, where these things are feeble, the minding of high things is at once perilous; perilous even to the search for truth; perilous, yet more surely, to the growth of grace. How many a man, with every desire to be right, with the most patient and earnest pursuit of the highest truth, has ended his course a doubter or a disbeliever, mainly, we may well believe, for this reason, that he never forced himself to condescend to the humble, never sought in the poor man's cottage a deeper wisdom than was dreamed of in his philosophy, never communed with the suffering and the unhappy, never saw for himself what truth is alone applicable to the sick-chamber and the dying-bed, never discovered that the true way to knowledge is through love; that, *if any man love God, the same is known of Him* (1 Cor. viii. 3); and therefore, taking a wrong turning in his journey, never reached its end, but lived ignorant of a Saviour, and died doubtful of a heaven. If he had learned betimes to condescend to things lowly, he would have entered at length, with a true insight, into the things which transcend knowledge.

My brethren, if we have been humbled, as we surely must have been, by the teaching of this day's Epistle, let us not depart without a thankful acknowledgment of the truth and value of that teaching, and an earnest prayer that He who alone can, will be pleased to write it on our hearts. *The word that I have spoken,* our Lord said, *the same shall judge him in the last day* (John xii. 48). Let us not form the habit of putting that word from us now, to meet it again at the great day as our accuser and our judge. Let us begin by putting into practice its wise yet simple lessons, as we learn them from Sunday to Sunday. Let us gather now around Christ's Table, to seal our allegiance to Him as our Divine Teacher as well as our Almighty and most merciful Saviour. Let this coming week see in all of us some fruit of God's instruction to-day. And let us come together, week by week, as persons who need and expect that instruction; as persons *desiring*, to use St Peter's expression, *the sincere milk of the word, that we may grow thereby* (1 Pet. ii. 2).

SERMON III.

THE DOCTRINE OF OBEDIENCE.

EPISTLE FOR THE FOURTH SUNDAY AFTER THE EPIPHANY.

ROMANS XIII. 1—7.

1 *Let every soul submit to superior authorities: for there is no authority but from God, and those that are have been*
2 *appointed by God; so that he who resists the authority withstands the arrangement of God; and they that withstand*
3 *shall receive for themselves judgment. For rulers are not a terror to the good work, but to the evil. And wouldest thou not fear the authority? do that which is good, and thou*
4 *shalt have praise from it: for it is a minister of God to thee for that which is good. But, if thou do that which is evil, fear it: for not in vain it bears the sword: for it is a minister of God, an avenger for wrath to him that doeth that*
5 *which is evil. Wherefore there is a necessity to submit, not only on account of the wrath, but also for the sake of the*
6 *conscience. For for this cause ye pay tribute also: for they are officers of God, constantly engaged upon this very thing.*
7 *Render to all their dues: to him to whom you owe tribute, tribute; to whom custom, custom; to whom fear, fear; to whom honour, honour.*

SERMON III.[1]

THE DOCTRINE OF OBEDIENCE.

ROMANS XIII. 7.

Render therefore to all their dues: tribute to whom tribute is due; custom to whom custom; fear to whom fear; honour to whom honour.

THE various precepts of the twelfth chapter are ended. The principle has been laid down: we are to present ourselves to God as a living sacrifice. We are to live as persons belonging to a different world from this in which we live; belonging to eternity, not to time. In carrying out this principle, we are, first of all, to be humble; meaning by humility not *voluntary humility* (Col. ii. 18), not condescension, of our own free will, to a place lower than that which we, all along, feel to belong to us; but a sober and therefore a low estimate of our own powers, our own merits, and our own rights. In the next place, we are to recognize our membership in a body; we are to think of ourselves as parts, as items, not as totals; we are to do that which we are set to do, and qualified to do, with the same undivided

[1] A collection was made after this Sermon for the Pimlico Dispensary.

attention, and the same simplicity of duty, with which an eye or a hand does its part in a human body, neither priding itself upon its own work, nor intruding into another's. In the next place, amongst a multitude of separate duties, we are never to lose sight of love as the great and comprehensive office of every one; love, showing itself in kindness; love, showing itself in sympathy; love, showing itself in forbearance; love, showing itself in returning good for evil, and in conquering evil by good.

To-day we reach a further rule of Christian duty; that of obedience to constituted authority. *Let every soul,* every living person, *submit to superior authorities: for there is no authority but from God: and those that are in existence have been appointed by God. So that he who resists the authority,* the particular authority under which he is placed in any respect, *withstands the arrangement,* the ordinance or appointment, *of God; and they that so withstand shall receive for themselves judgment;* punishment here, and God's disapprobation and displeasure with it. *For rulers are not a terror to the good work,* to the welldoer, *but to the evil. And wouldest thou not fear the authority,* have no cause to dread the power of the human ruler? *do that which is good, and,* instead of punishment, *thou shalt have praise from it: for it is a minister of God to thee for that which is good;* to bring thee safety, honour, and peace. *But, if thou do that which is evil, fear it;* thou hast cause to do so; *for not in vain it bears the sword;* that sword which is

The Doctrine of Obedience. 39

the emblem of the power to punish; *for it*, the authority of the human ruler, *is*, in this case also, *a minister of God;* and charged with a very different office from that which it exercises towards the good; namely, that of *an avenger for wrath*, to assign punishment, *to him that doeth that which is evil. Wherefore there is a necessity to submit*, to be submissive and obedient, *not only on account of the wrath*, that wrath of which the foregoing verse spoke, *but also for the sake of the conscience*, to keep it clear and without offence in the sight of God. *For for this cause ye pay tribute also:* it is this consideration which justifies the imposition of pecuniary burdens upon the subject: namely, *because they*, human rulers, *are officers of God, constantly engaged upon this very thing;* upon God's work in one of its definite departments. *Render* therefore, give back—it is an act of simple restitution; not of merit, but of honesty and equity—*to all their dues;* whatever it be to which they are entitled at your hands: *to him to whom you owe tribute, tribute; to whom custom, custom;* the former word probably denoting all payments levied upon persons, whether by a foreign power, or in the form of direct taxation at home; and the latter, *custom*, all duties upon things, whether in the form of toll, custom, or duty; *to whom fear, fear; to whom honour, honour.*

And now, my brethren, having read to you once again this important, though often neglected and sometimes misapplied, passage of the Holy Word of

God, I would ask you to go on with me into one or two considerations, first upon the passage itself as a whole, and then in reference to our own conduct and circumstances. We shall find, in so doing, that the special practical request with which my sermon is to conclude has not been lost sight of nor put aside.

1. First, then, I would notice, as suggested by the passage generally, *the breadth and largeness of the Gospel precepts.*

The Bible contains nothing of what is commonly called casuistry. It does not deal in cases of conscience. It supposes the minds of its readers to be capable of treating it rationally; of exercising good sense and sound judgment in its adaptation to varying and sometimes trying conjunctures.

People say, on reading this passage, St Paul makes no exceptions here. He lays down a principle too broad for literal obedience. He says nothing here, for example, of bad rulers. He does not introduce, after the charge to obey human authorities, the words, "So far as their own character is decently good, or their commands not clearly opposed to the law of justice and right." He does not say, "When conscience clashes with authority, then you must obey God rather than men." No, he does not say this. And why? Because he is writing to Christian men, who know this well enough already. He is writing to those who showed by their lives, by their constancy (in many cases) even unto death, that they were well aware that, if the emergency should arise, they must

The Doctrine of Obedience. 41

be prepared to make any sacrifice, even that of life itself, rather than obey the command of a human ruler to dishonour or deny their Saviour.

Nor does St Paul enter here into the case which has sometimes proved so perplexing, that of persons living in disturbed times, and called to witness, or even to take part in, a transfer of power, a change of dynasty, a period of revolution, or of usurpation. He has laid down no rule as to the precise point at which authority becomes established; at which adhesion to the old becomes a senseless fanaticism, and allegiance to the new a rational and therefore also a Christian duty. These things have been found by experience to be not merely matters of anxiety and of peril, but questions too of right and wrong, upon which it was easy to err, and in which error was of no trivial import. But here also the precept must be broadly stated, and the application of it to circumstances left to the individual judgment. St Paul knew that the Bible is not God's only gift to man. There is the gift of conscience too. There is the gift of intelligence and of practical wisdom. There is the gift, above all, of His Holy Spirit, whose bright shining within, in the hearts of those who believe, is a guide not less amidst the difficulties of God's Word than in the intricacies of human life and circumstance.

Nor does St Paul in this passage enter into any of those distinctions, which sometimes have to be made, between the Christian's duty to particular rulers, and his duty to those higher laws by which they rule. No particular authority stands entirely isolated. *By me kings reign* (Prov. viii. 15). The power of every sovereign is limited by some law; if not by constitutional law, yet at least by human and by Divine law; by those restrictions of common humanity and of religious responsibility, which are in one point of view checks upon the ruler, and in another point of view rights of the subject. St Paul himself did not consider that he was precluded from urging his rights as a citizen in bar of inhumanity and injustice. *As they bound him with thongs, Paul said unto the centurion that stood by, Is it lawful for you to scourge a man that is a Roman, and uncondemned?* (Acts xxii. 25). He was not one of those who court martyrdom, though he met it bravely when it came to him. The preservation of life is a duty in its place. The maintenance of rights is a duty in its place. It is an act of suicide to disregard the one, and it is an act of treason to be indifferent to the other. When St Paul speaks here of constituted authorities, he includes those higher laws under which all human rulers act, as well as the special and lower laws made under them. It is one of the most anxious questions for a Christian in certain times, how far he is justified in waiving rights which are a national birthright, in deference to edicts which derive their binding force from the very constitution which they violate. And nothing, assuredly, contained in this chapter, calls upon any man to forego the exercise of powers conferred upon him by his own citizenship, and which as truly come under the description of *powers that be*, of *authorities ordained of God*, as the prerogatives of princes or the majesty of a throne.

But the remark at present made is upon the absence of any such express exceptions and limitations with reference to the precept here enforced. The broad principle is stated; obedience to lawful power. The application of it is left to reason, to conscience, to the inward guidance of the Holy Spirit. And which of us may not thankfully acknowledge that for us, at all events, the absence of exceptions makes the passage only the more suitable? We live in times which need no such limitations. Our duty is clear and plain. There is no conflict, for us, between authority and conscience. There is no question, for us, of disputed or divided allegiance. There is no restriction attempted, for us, upon the rights of the subject, the freedom of thought or the freedom of discussion. In the same degree we recognize here the adaptation of the Bible to all times, arising, in great part, out of the breadth of its precepts and the largeness of its principles.

2. I would notice briefly, in the second place, what I may describe as *the wholesomeness of the Gospel teaching*.

There is nothing morbid in the Bible. It is written, in one sense, for the diseased; but, if so, it is written to bring them to health. It is written for the sinful, for the weak, for the tempted, for the often troubled and distressed: but it is not written for the perverse, for the crooked-minded, for the ingenious self-tormentor, or the sophistical speculator.

Take an example from this day's Epistle. What a sound, healthy, profitable principle is here laid down! If you are a Christian, remember, you are not of this world. In it you are; of it you are not. Christ's *kingdom is not of this world* (John xviii. 36). What then? Does the being a Christian set you loose from the restraints of human society? Does it give you licence to say, I am above these things; I can look down upon them; I can judge for myself how far they are for me, and, as I judge, I shall either obey or rebel? No; the Christian's being above all these things is only a reason why it should be easier to him to acquiesce in them: if he knows that this world is but a shadow, its restrictions, as well as its vexations, ought to be the lighter and more tolerable: if he has a Master, a Lord, a King, above, he must show it by being the most orderly, the most loyal, the most respectful, the most reverent, of all the subjects of that throne on earth which derives its authority over him from the throne in heaven. Every one of Christ's precepts—this one first of all—tends to make earth a scene of order and tranquillity in the very same degree in which it teaches men to regard earth as a small and insignificant portion of the whole of their space and the whole of their time.

3. But now I must pass, in the third place, to a few practical suggestions upon the principle here laid down.

i. Amongst these I must place foremost the charge to carry it out consistently in all departments of life.

The Doctrine of Obedience. 45

Do not imagine that you have obeyed this inspired rule when you have refrained from disobedience or disloyalty towards the throne. Which of us is tempted to such acts? But observe how wide the charge is. *Let every soul be subject to superior authorities: for there is no authority save from God: the authorities that exist are all ordained of God.* Is not parental authority included here? Is not the authority of the master of a family recognized here? Is not the authority of every person towards whom we stand in a position of dependence or subordination asserted here? Does not the Clergyman read here the Divine warrant for the authority of his Bishop in all things indifferent and in all things lawful? Does not every Englishman read here the Divine warrant for the authority of Parliament; none the less because he himself may possess in the expression of that authority either a suggesting or at least a controlling voice? St Paul wrote under a despotic government: he asserts for a Nero the Divine right to rule: would he not have claimed at least the same amount of Christian loyalty for a constitutional throne, and would he not have included in that claim (in due place and degree) every one of the adjuncts and complements of the royal power, whether in the form of administration or of legislation, whether exercised through the State, the Church, or the family?

ii. Again, let us remember—in a congregation like this well may we be reminded of it—that every relative duty has its correlative: if it is the duty of one to obey reverently, it must be the duty of another to rule well. Whatever be our position, however humble it may be in some aspects, yet, so far as it is one of authority, if it be but over a few servants, each one of us is, in the sense here designed, a minister of God, an officer of God. There is nothing presumptuous in taking that title. We do a great injury to ourselves when we restrict that title to one particular calling; to those who officiate in the Church as pastors and teachers. Every head of a family is a minister of God. Every parent is a minister of God. Every employer of workmen, every instructor of the young, every superintendent of an office, is a minister of God. In a yet higher sense is every one who holds office in the State, every one who presides over a department, every one who has a place in the Legislature, a minister of God. It is not that we overestimate our positions: that is not the danger against which we need to be warned: it is rather that we undervalue them; we think it a part of humility to do so: in reality it is often a cloke for worldliness, an excuse for shirking responsibility and avoiding those serious thoughts which a sense of responsibility brings after it. Of ourselves we cannot think too meanly; but we have the example and authority of St Paul himself for *magnifying our office* (Rom. xi. 13).

iii. Again, we must act upon the charge before us in small details. I will mention two of these.

Cheerfulness in bearing the burdens imposed upon us for the State-service. The laws of the country, in theory at least, give to the people a veto upon tax-

The Doctrine of Obedience. 47

ation. There is nothing wrong therefore in the constitutional and orderly exercise of that controlling power. But, when discussion is ended, and the judgment of the Legislature has decided upon a particular amount and form of impost, then there ought to be, on the part of all Christian subjects, a cheerfulness in paying. We ought to regard the burden as definitely and directly occasioned by God's gift to us of a constitutional government.

The other point I would mention is, respectful language at all times about those in authority. A general loyalty of feeling is often made compatible with a great want of respect, in private conversation, towards the royal house, if not towards the royal person. This is much to be regretted. As Christians, we ought not to allow this in ourselves. The habit of retailing disrespectful and disparaging anecdotes, still more of imputing unworthy intentions and motives, as it is at all times a breach of the law of charity, so, in this particular application of it, is a breach also of the rule of loyalty.

iv. Once more, we are bound at all times to cherish, and from time to time more earnestly to express, a spirit of thankfulness to God Himself for what I have just called His gift to us of government. Any government is better than none. Any evils in government are less than the least of those evils from which the worst of governments releases us. No tyranny can be comparable in wretchedness to anarchy. St Paul taught Christians to be thankful for the rule of a licentious, a cruel, and a heathen Emperor. What would he have prescribed to us as the due measure of gratitude for a constitutional and a free government? for a throne of spotless purity in example, and of deep and lively sympathy with the people's joys and woes? for laws which recognize religion, maintain order, secure liberty, and coerce where they cannot extirpate crime? To give thanks to God for these things is the duty of every heart which is not most ungrateful.

v. I add one concluding word of exhortation. And this is, that we take a more lively interest than is, I fear, common amongst us, in those parts of our Public Worship which have a direct reference to the persons of our rulers and to the deliberations of our Legislature. We are all apt to slur over these portions of the service, these (as they are sometimes unhappily designated) State-prayers. Some persons complain of them as too long, too frequent. How cold is often the *Amen* which closes the Prayer for the Queen, the Prayer for the Royal Family, the Prayer for the Houses of Parliament! These things, my brethren, ought not so to be. St Paul, if he were amongst us, would reprove such indifference. The Holy Spirit, who is still amongst us, has caused the admonition to come home, I doubt not, to some hearts. No blessing, depend upon it, is more certain than that which attends what may be truly called disinterested petitions; prayers for others; prayers which really do forget ourselves, and take a wider and less selfish range. But the prayers of which I now speak, if in one sense disinter-

The Doctrine of Obedience. 49

ested, can scarcely be so described in every sense. We are deeply concerned in them. In the example set by our rulers—most of all, I say it deliberately, in the example set by our Court—we are all directly and personally concerned. We know not what we owe to it, in the length and breadth of our land, in the privacy of our humblest homes as well as in our influence upon surrounding nations. In the administration of our rulers, in the legislation of our Parliament, I need not stay to show that we are most distinctly interested. But on all accounts, whether for our own sake, or not for our own sake at all, we are bound to pray these prayers with all our hearts. *I exhort therefore*, wrote the same inspired Apostle to his beloved disciple whom he had left in charge of the Ephesian congregations, *that, first of all, supplications, prayers, intercessions, and giving of thanks, be made for all men; for kings, and for all that are in authority; that we may lead a quiet and peaceable life in all godliness and honesty: for this is good and acceptable in the sight of God our Saviour* (1 Tim. ii. 1).

4. And now, finally, I have to give a yet wider scope to the words of the text, *Render therefore to all their dues*. I have to remind you that, besides the dues of princes, there are also dues of the humble.

Honour all men, St Peter says (1 Pet. ii. 17): and therefore the words of the text, *honour to whom honour*, may be made to embrace even the poor. But you will not ask me for a text to justify that act of kindness to which you are invited to-day. You feel in your hearts, as well as know in your understandings, that they to whom God has been so bountiful in His outward gifts as He has been to us, do owe some acknowledgment of this undeserved difference to those who have been less favoured. And of all the ways in which this can be done, there is none more plainly useful than the supply of help, skilful help, in time of sickness. Sickness is a serious thing to the rich: what must it be to the poor! Those who have no access of their own to the physician, and no means of paying for medicine even if they could obtain advice, must become, at such times, helpless and hopeless indeed. It is to meet such distress, that sort of distress which makes the most marked, and one of the most real, of all the differences between the rich man and the poor, that the present call is addressed to you. The words of the preacher on such an occasion are not needed. Nothing, on such a topic, can be so eloquent as facts. I may briefly state to you that, whereas upwards of seven thousand cases of accident or disease were ministered to by this charity during the past year, being an increase of one thousand cases upon the year preceding, the expenses during the same period exceeded the income by almost seventy pounds. I am sure it is only needful to state this fact in order to secure your ready and hearty interposition. You will take care that this debt is forthwith discharged. But I have to add that help of a larger and more expensive kind is also urgently needed. The premises of this Dispensary are small and unhealthy. During the hours of daily application, the rooms in which the poor patients await their turn of ministration are crowded to overflowing, and the hot air, charged with disease, is working new mischief in those who are seeking relief from former ills. If the charity is not to defeat its own aim, there must be a large and a prompt addition to the buildings themselves. I say once again that, when you know these things, you will, I am quite sure, be prompt in meeting them. You will recognize here a want which it is in your power, as I know that it is in your will, to supply. You will secure for yourselves the happiness of feeling that your enjoyment of life is not selfish, not uncharitable, not unblessed; but rather that of those who consider the poor and needy, and know, that in ministering to them, it is their privilege and their happiness to minister to Christ.

Yes, to minister to Christ. In rendering other dues, readily and cheerfully, we must not forget the highest of all. *Render therefore unto Cæsar the things which are Cæsar's, and unto God the things that are God's* (Matt. xxii. 21). The claim of God upon us is one which we can never discharge. Yet the thankful heart "by owing owes not, but still pays, at once indebted and discharged." Thankfulness, by God's grace, we can give Him. Let it not be withheld. And thankfulness to God will ever show itself in charity to man. *We love Him, because He first loved us. And this commandment have we from Him, That he who loveth God love his brother also* (1 John iv. 19, 21).

SERMON IV.

VAGUE RUNNING AND INEFFECTIVE FIGHTING.

EPISTLE FOR SEPTUAGESIMA SUNDAY.

1 CORINTHIANS IX. 24—27.

24 *KNOW ye not that they who run in a course all run, but one receiveth the prize? So run, that ye may obtain.*
25 *And every one who contends for a prize controls himself in all things: they then, that they may receive a perishable*
26 *wreath; but we, an imperishable. I therefore so run, as*
27 *not vaguely; so combat, as not beating air: but I buffet my body, and bring it into servitude; lest by any means, after making proclamation to others, I myself should prove rejected.*

SERMON IV.

VAGUE RUNNING AND INEFFECTIVE FIGHTING.

1 CORINTHIANS IX. 26.

I therefore so run, not as uncertainly: so fight I, not as one that beateth the air.

THE general subject of this chapter is St Paul's voluntary cession of certain rights which belonged to him as an Apostle. He might have claimed an entire exemption from all labours for his own support. He might have urged in his own behalf the universal right of all teachers of the Gospel, to *live of the Gospel;* to receive a maintenance from the congregations to which they minister. But he had not done so. He blames no one for accepting such a maintenance: but it was a sort of pride with him, what he calls a matter of *glorying*, not to accept a maintenance himself. He hoped to make his Gospel more acceptable by removing out of its way the suspicion, however unfounded, however unreasonable, that it was either idleness or covetousness which prompted him to proclaim it. In short, in this, as in all things, he kept his eye steadily fixed on an object; and that object was, to "gain" all men. *I seek not yours but you* (2 Cor. xii. 14), was the motto of his ministry. Gain, with him, was success in winning souls. And he thought no sacrifice too great, and no skill and ingenuity misplaced, in effecting this work. He sought to adapt himself to every variety of natural character and of religious circumstance, that he might succeed in bringing Christ home to each, and in rescuing and saving souls for Him.

O that this, my brethren, were still the one sole object of all who undertake, in our days, the like office! What trifles should we then esteem all the little ornaments and appendages of religion on which some of us, as it is, spend so much thought and argument! How dreadful should we then think it, to be putting stumbling-blocks in the way of our own ministry, by appearing to give importance to things at best indifferent, whether in the way of ceremonial or of doctrine!

And this I do, he proceeds to say, *for the Gospel's sake, that I might be partaker thereof with you.* This is the starting-point of the Epistle for this day. *I seek you, but I must not forget myself.* It would be a poor thing for me to have seen *spirits subject* to me, if at last it should be found that my own name was never *written in heaven* (Luke x. 20). It would be a heartless and a hollow service, if, while carrying the Gospel to you, I were not myself to be a partaker of it. In short, we all, you and I alike, are engaged in a life-long contest, which has a very precise aim, and which demands a very severe and continued exertion.

Know ye not that they who run in a course all run, but one receiveth the prize? Ye inhabitants of Corinth, who have so often flocked together from your city to your far-famed Stadium, to witness, in company with all Greece, your own Isthmian games; have you never noticed, have you never read the meaning of, that intense, that concentrated energy, with which the runners in the foot-race strain every nerve to be the first to reach the goal? All run, though but one can attain. Each runs in the hope of being that one. The slightest relaxation of the tension of one muscle, a momentary failure of the very utmost speed, would be fatal to the chance of one of those eager runners. *So*, even so, even with that intense eagerness, even with that vigorous determination, even so *run ye, in order that ye may obtain.* Such be your zeal, such your earnestness, such your sustained constancy, in order that you may obtain that prize which is the object of the Christian runner.

But remember one other thing. *Every one who contends for a prize*—not the runner only, but every one who takes part in any of these athletic contests which are the pride of Greece, which form so large a part in the education of every citizen—*controls himself*, practises self-restraint, *in all things;* has to submit, for many months beforehand, to a system of the most rigid training: every habit of life, every function of the body, is subjected to rule and discipline of a severe and irksome strictness, to give him the slightest chance of success in the competition to which he is looking forward: remember this, ye Christian combatants, and remember also the disparity, as well as the resemblance, between you and them: *they then* submit to their discipline *that they may receive a corruptible crown*, a perishable garland, like that which was the prize in the games of Greece, of a few leaves of bay or olive, of pine or parsley; *but we an incorruptible*, an imperishable, a heavenly prize.

I therefore—for in this I am one of you; I have no exemption from the personal anxieties, as well as the personal responsibilities, of the Christian conflict; rather would I be your example in bearing and in facing all; *I therefore so run, as not uncertainly; not vaguely*, is the exact sense: *so fight I*—but the figure thus expressed is derived, in the original, from one particular department of the Grecian games, the encounter of the pugilists—*so fight I, as not beating air;* as one who does not allow his blows to fall short of his antagonist, but who takes care that each one shall tell, and tell heavily: *but I buffet my body*—the metaphor is still from the same subject: the word is properly, *I cover my body with bruises:* my own body, with its appetites, desires, and slothfulnesses, is my chief antagonist in this daily contest: through it, if not from it, come all the perils and all the conflicts of this mortal life: its infirmities make us sluggish, its lusts tempt, its wants enchain us to earth, its vanities puff us up, its selfishnesses make us quarrelsome: it is, as elsewhere expressed, *the flesh with its affections and lusts* which *they that are Christ's* have to *crucify* (Gal. v. 24): *I buffet* therefore *my body, and bring it into servitude;* I make it my slave, instead of being, as it expects and claims to be, my master; *lest by any means, after making proclamation to others,* after *playing the herald* to others—a figure still from the games, where it was the office of the herald both to give out the rules of the contest, and to announce their commencement, and to proclaim their result—*lest,* then, *after heralding for others*—after making to them the proclamation of Christ's Gospel, with its promises and its hopes, its terms and its duties—*I myself should prove rejected,* should find myself refused and outcast in the day of the manifestation of the sons of God, as one who had himself run negligently, or unfairly, or presumptuously, and who therefore must expect only shame and discomfiture when he would come forward to take his crown.

My brethren, if I were addressing an assembly of Christian ministers, these last words would furnish the most suitable as well as the most striking subject. And I hope that no clergyman ever reads them in the congregation without serious and even anxious self-application. It is possible, or St Paul, under the inspiration of God, would not thus have expressed himself, for a minister of the Gospel to be even diligent and respected and successful, and yet, all the time, unsound at heart, and yet therefore, in the end, rejected and cast away. It is possible too, or St

Paul, under the inspiration of God, would not thus have expressed himself, for a Christian minister or a Christian man to fall away from grace once given; possible, as it is written in another place, for *those who were once enlightened, and have tasted of the heavenly gift, to fall away* (Heb. vi. 4), and that beyond repentance. Let us lay these things to heart, for our quickening, and for our humbling, and for our sobering; for the extirpation of all self-confidence, and for the awakening in us of a godly fear.

But it is in the verse read as the text of my sermon that I desire to seek a few words of advice and of admonition, as the special lesson of this morning.

I therefore so run, as not uncertainly: so fight I, as not beating the air. We have here two topics: first, the danger of running vaguely; and secondly, the danger of fighting ineffectively.

1. *I so run*, St Paul says, *as not vaguely*. There is a danger, then, of doing that; of running vaguely. And I will mention two modes of this error.

i. We may fail to keep the goal in view.

My brethren, the Christian life is a precarious thing, humanly speaking—and, indeed, more than humanly speaking—in each one of us. Precarious on many accounts: but on no account more precarious, than because we are so apt to lose sight of our goal; and, if we do this, we must run at hazard, or go wrong.

I greatly fear that many of us have no definite goal at all. Every one, when asked, hopes to reach heaven. But what is heaven? and what is reaching it? I am sure we many of us have no real, certainly no adequate, notion of heaven. A safe place; a place of rest after earth; a place of meeting lost friends; a place of calm and tranquillity; a place where our sins will give us no trouble; a place where sorrow, and crying, and pain, and change, will be no more. These are our more thoughtful ideas of heaven. I hope and believe that they are all true. But I am quite sure they are not the whole of heaven. I am quite sure they do not altogether make up, they scarcely touch, St Paul's idea of heaven. I am quite sure that, if heaven at all, they are heaven without its foundation, and heaven without its sun. St Paul's heaven was very briefly defined; where Christ is. *I have a desire to depart, and to be with Christ* (Phil. i. 23).

It is impossible that we should desire this sort of heaven, or have it for our goal, unless we know something of Christ, unless we know much of Christ, here below. This is obviously a first requisite. Many of us do without Christ here; yes, I say it very seriously, many of us dispense with Christ, set Him aside, in our daily life below. They cannot, except in a very figurative and feeble sense, have the place, or the world, or the eternity—call it which you will—where Christ is, for their aim, their desire, their goal.

But even those who know something of Christ may yet run vaguely in the same sense. They often lose sight of their goal. Which of us keeps the goal always in view? Be not hasty to answer that question. Think what it implies. It implies that, in all we do, in all that we busy ourselves in, in all our chief plans and desires and judgments, we regard everything as conducive, or the contrary, to our reaching heaven, to our at last departing and being with Christ. Think what that means. Think how unworldly, think how heavenly-minded, think how charitable and unselfish and pure, that man must be, who is, in the sense thus explained, running as not vaguely; running, that is, first of all, with his goal full in view, and that goal the right one.

ii. But, again, we may run vaguely, by failing to keep within the course.

There were very strict rules on this point in the games of Greece. Every part of the course was rigidly marked out. There was no surreptitious way of reaching the goal. There was no short cut to the goal. The course must be all fairly traversed. In some of these competitions it was a double race; to the goal and back again: or rather, the goal was on the starting-line, and the safe return was everything. In this case there were many perils attending the turning-point. An unskilful charioteer was either thrown out of the competition by a too circuitous turning, or by too abrupt a turning wrecked upon the limit-post.

Now in that to which St Paul here applies this earthly comparison, all these dangers have their counterpart. A Christian has not only to keep the goal in view, but he has also all along to keep within the course. What does this mean? My brethren, it denotes something very important, and something which can by no means be assumed. It means that we must live exactly by Christ's rules throughout our life on earth. And what are Christ's rules? They are something different, remember, from inclination; more often than not, they are even contrary to it. They are something different from the customs and principles of the world; very often, they are contrary to them: but at all events, and at all times, they spring from a different motive, and have a totally different aim. When a Christian gives way to worldly ambition, then he is running vaguely, because he is straying out of the course. When a Christian speaks uncharitably, when he judges harshly, when he in any way (as we express it by a most significant phrase) forgets himself, then he is running vaguely, because he is straying out of the course. He is forgetting his Master's rules: he is breaking the rule of charity, or the rule of humility, or the rule of unworldliness, or the rule of reverence. And if this goes on, if it is not repented of, if it is not remedied, if it is not by the appointed means rectified, such a person must take heed lest, having made perhaps great professions, and led, in some respects, a religious life, he should find himself in the end declared and treated as a castaway.

2. But I must turn, for a very few moments, to the second danger; that of fighting ineffectively. *So fight I, as not beating the air.* That was an expression applied by the ancient writers to strokes that fell

short of the adversary, whether by misdirection on the one side, or by skilful evasion on the other.

Now we may beat the air, in a similar sense, that is, fight ineffectively, in either of two ways.

i. We may mistake our real enemy. We may direct our attacks upon a wrong point. We may assail the wrong person. We have an enemy, but we do not always know who that enemy is.

For example—and indeed every word here is most directly practical—there are those amongst us who are spending much of their strength upon what they deem errors of opinion.

Do not suppose that I am indifferent to truth, or even to the most exact expression of Christian doctrine, if I say that a great part of such exertion is a waste of strength. It is the duty, no doubt, of Christian teachers to see that they use as correct a form of language in the exposition of the truths of Revelation as human infirmity will allow. And it is more especially the duty of writers upon such topics, and, most of all, of writers upon the doctrines of the Gospel, to be anxiously careful in their choice of words, lest they either mar the beauty of the faith as once delivered to the saints, or cause difficulty and distress to the minds of those who may turn to them for instruction. But how different is all this from the practice of our own day in a Christian world! How are men made offenders for a word! How do hearers sit in judgment upon their teachers! How do reviewers fasten upon slips of expression, arising oftentimes out of candour, or else out of fervour; out of an earnestness to keep within the bounds of individual conviction, or else an earnestness to express forcibly to others some portion of the truth which is deeply felt within! With how many persons, even in private life, even in that sex which might well be suffered to stand altogether aloof from controversy, is religion itself made to consist of two parts only; a profitless repetition of a few formulas of doctrine, and an uncharitable inquisition into the conformity of others, on these few points, to their own opinions! This is a mistaking of our adversary. Opinion is an important thing, and expression is an important thing, each in its place; but one whose chief conflict on earth is with errors of opinion must either be a person whose great enemy has been unusually early vanquished, so as to give him leisure for the very fancy-work of religion, or else a person who has turned aside from his own conflict to watch the conflicts of others, or, let me rather say, with all reluctance and regret, to impede those conflicts themselves by his own uncharitable intrusiveness.

But, again, we may mistake our adversary by a very common want of self-knowledge.

We all take it for granted that we know our own faults. We suppose it to be a matter of course that conscience reveals to us our chief deficiencies as Christians, and our chief inconsistencies, infirmities, and sins. And, where there is one very strong besetting sin in any of us, no doubt this is so. A man whose passions are strong, and who has suffered those passions to remain unchecked, can have no uncertainty as to the direction in which the power of evil points most strongly within. Where, on the other hand, the character has been either less distinctly marked or more carefully watched and regulated, where the life has been kept pure from actual stain, and the supremacy of conscience from early days acknowledged and obeyed, it often happens that there is an almost entire ignorance of faults, patent to others, in the spirit and temper, and consequently an almost total misdirection of the efforts against evil which yet may be made, and made with some regularity and some earnestness. How often has some particular virtue been magnified, in such minds, into the whole of duty; the virtue, for example, of temperance, or of devotion, or of purity! How many seeds of most unchristian faults have been suffered to germinate and spread and grow within—worldliness, vanity, perverseness, unreasonableness, ill-temper, deceit, uncharitableness—while the Christian combatant, as he still thought himself, and as perhaps in some sense he still was, was exhausting his strength against some far less real antagonist, beating the air with vehement and self-enfeebling blows, every one of which, in reference to the all-important issue of life, fell short and failed and came to nothing!

Thus, my brethren, and not thus only, we may fight ineffectively by missing our real enemy.

ii. But, yet once more, and finally, we may "beat

Ineffective Fighting.

the air" in fighting, not by fighting with the wrong foe, but by fighting with the real foe wrongly.

Which of us has not done this? I bring the matter now closely home to each one who is here present, and ask, which of us has not often combated ineffectually within? Which of us, that is, has not often been foiled in encountering his known, his real fault, his besetting sin? Which of us has not regretted, and resolved, and determined, yes, and prayed, against his chief sin, and yet fallen again before it as soon as it assailed him? This is sad, and wrong, and deeply discouraging: we ought to have strength, considering what a motive Christ has given us in His own death, considering what an Almighty helper Christ has promised to us in His Holy Spirit. It is for want of faith; for want of simply accepting what is simply offered; for want of really believing that there is a Holy Spirit given to all men for the asking: for want of believing this; because, if we did believe, we should certainly use it: it is for want of this that we thus fall, even when experience of sin, and sorrow for sin, and resolution against sin, and even prayer for victory over sin, has not been wholly wanting.

But, if this be so, even with regret, even with resolution, even with prayer, what can be expected where all these things are in great part wanting? where there is an utter want of earnestness, of appreciation of holiness, of desire after heaven? where a person goes to the very edge of temptation, and only just hopes that he may not pass the bounds? where the means of grace are slightly used and little valued? where the conscience only wakes to punish, never to forewarn, never to forearm? Can we call such Christians combatants at all? Who shall call that fighting, in which every single blow beats the air?

Yet was every brow in this congregation once signed with the sign of the cross, in token that hereafter that soul should not be ashamed to fight under Christ's banner against all evil, and to continue His faithful soldier to the very end of the life then just begun. Where is that mark now? Will this day see that vow kept? Will every such soldier come forth now to renew his "sacrament," his oath of service, to the living Captain of his salvation? And, of those who renew that "sacrament," how many will, but for one day, keep it? God is faithful, Christ is faithful, the Holy Spirit is faithful, to us: why are not we faithful to Him? Let us, as St Paul says, obtain mercy of Christ to be so. *I give my judgment*, he says, *as one that hath obtained mercy of the Lord to be faithful* (1 Cor. vii. 25).

SERMON V.

GLORYING IN INFIRMITIES.

EPISTLE FOR SEXAGESIMA SUNDAY.

2 Corinthians XI. 19—31.

19, 20 GLADLY *ye bear with the foolish, being wise. For ye bear with it, if any one enslaves, if any one devours, if any one entraps you, if any one exalts himself, if any one*
21 *strikes you on the face. I speak in the way of dishonour*[1], *as if that we were weak: but in whatsoever any one is confident—in foolishness I speak—confident also am I.*
22 *Hebrews are they? I also. Israelites are they? I also.*
23 *Seed of Abraham are they? I also. Ministers of Christ are they? beside myself I say it*[2], *yet more so am I; in toils more abundantly so*[3], *in stripes surpassingly, in im-*
24 *prisonments more abundantly, in deaths oftentimes*[4]: *at the hands of Jews five times received I forty stripes*
25 *save one; thrice was I beaten with rods; once was I stoned; thrice I suffered shipwreck; a night and a day*
26 *have I spent on the deep*[5]: *by journeyings often*[6], *by perils of rivers, by perils of robbers, by perils from countrymen,*

---

[1] *In assigning so powerful a position to your new teachers, I am using a disparaging, a needlessly disparaging, language with regard to myself.*

[2] *In thus boasting, I know that I speak not foolishly only, but even as it were insanely.*

[3] *In point of labours endured for His sake, I am a minister of Christ in a sense beyond that in which others are so.*

[4] *In imminent risks of life I have often been proved a minister of Christ above others.*

[5] While escaping, perhaps, in an open boat from shipwreck.

[6] Understand again, *I have been proved a minister of Christ.*

Epistle for Sexagesima Sunday.

by perils from Gentiles, by perils in city, by perils in desert, by perils on sea, by perils among false brethren, by toil and labour, in watchings often, in hunger and thirst, in fastings often, in cold and nakedness. Apart from the things besides[1], there is the daily crowding upon me[2], the anxiety of all the congregations. Who is weak, and I am not weak? who is caused to stumble, and I am not on fire? If I must vaunt, I will vaunt the things of my weakness. The God and Father of our Lord Jesus, He who is blessed for ever, knows that I lie not. 27 28 29 30 31

[1] *Besides other things which I omit.*
[2] *That which crowds upon me daily, namely, the anxiety occasioned by the charge of all the Christian congregations.*

SERMON V.

GLORYING IN INFIRMITIES.

2 CORINTHIANS XI. 30.

If I must needs glory, I will glory of the things which concern mine infirmities.

ST PAUL, with all his gifts and all his triumphs as an Apostle of Christ, led a life of constant trial. *I die daily* (1 Cor. xv. 31), was his own brief description of it. There was one very peculiar trial to which he was subjected; that of constant disparagement. Scarcely had he planted the Church at Corinth, than another came after him to mar and deface his work. What made it worse was, that this enemy did not come avowedly as an enemy. He professed, like St Paul, to teach and to preach Jesus Christ. He professed to have a better and a purer Gospel of Christ than St Paul had brought with him. And no art of misrepresentation or calumny was wanting, to bring that devoted man into disrepute with those very persons and those very congregations which owed to him, not merely knowledge and happiness, but (to use his own expression to Philemon), *their own selves besides.*

These few words of necessary preface may serve to introduce us into the subject and connection of the Epistle for this day. It is full of topics. It might suggest matter for many sermons. The briefest glance at its contents must suffice us to-day; and then we will turn our thoughts more closely to the one verse which has been selected from the whole passage for special comment and special application.

The passage before us, extending from the 19th to the 31st verse, is a very remarkable one on many accounts. It is extremely difficult to express in a form readily intelligible to ordinary readers. And this, for reasons which will be incidentally mentioned at a later point. But perhaps the general sense of it may be given thus.

Ye Corinthians, so lately my attached friends and converts, have unhappily listened, since my departure, to a very different teaching. You have been flattered into a very high conceit of your own enlightenment, gifts, and graces. Wise in your own eyes, you have been taught to look down upon me, your original teacher, as on a far lower level, in all these respects, than your new instructors and even than yourselves. In your present estimate of me, I am a feeble man, a but half enlightened man, one who uses strong expressions in writing, but in bodily presence is weak, and in speech contemptible. Be it so. I accept your judgment. You are wise men, and I am a fool. I will speak as such. I will take the privilege of the foolish, and boast. There is no one else to sing my praises: I must do it myself. And you, I am quite sure, from the elevation of your supposed superior wisdom, can afford to bear for a moment with the weakness which you despise. You bear with worse things than folly in your new teachers. You bear with oppression, you bear with rapacity, you bear with deception, you bear with assumption, you bear with injury and with insult. Compared with these things the innocent weakness of a little boasting must be a small matter to you. And let me tell you that, though I use the language of self-depreciation and of self-disparagement, I have no need to shrink from the comparison with even the boldest and most confident of my rivals. Whatever they may be in the boasted purity of their descent from Israel or from Abraham, that am I also. And, whatever they may be in zeal or devotion as ministers of Christ, that, assuredly, am I, not equally, but above them all: in labours more abundant, in stripes above measure, in prisons more frequent, in deaths oft. Of the Jews five times received I the forty stripes save one. Thrice was I beaten with the Roman rods, once was I stoned, thrice I suffered shipwreck, a night and a day have I spent on the open sea: in journeyings often, in perils of rivers, in perils of robbers, in perils from Jews, in perils from Gentiles, in perils in city, in perils in desert, in perils by sea, in perils among false brethren; by toil and hardship, in watchings often, in hunger and thirst, in fastings often, *in cold and nakedness. And, beside other things, of which I omit many in my enumeration, there is that which crowds upon me daily, the anxiety of all the congregations. Who is weak in faith, and I am not weak with him by a deep sympathy? who is made to stumble in his Christian course, and I am not fired with a holy indignation? If I must boast, if in self-defence I am driven into the unwonted language of self-assertion and of glorying, it shall be rather of my weakness than of my strength that I thus glory; not so much of gifts given to me, or of service rendered by me in return, but rather of infirmities under which I have been supported, of a daily burden borne in Christ's strength, of a daily dying which has shown forth the life of Jesus. And, in thus speaking, in thus detailing the story of my life of suffering, I can appeal to One above for the confirmation of every single fact. The God and Father of our Lord Jesus, He who is blessed for evermore, knoweth that I lie not.*

One or two obvious remarks will have suggested themselves already upon this passage.

1. And one is as to the character of the Scriptures generally, in reference to their details of facts.

It has been often noticed that, if any one compares this enumeration with the record of St Paul's life in the Acts of the Apostles, he will find himself directly at fault. Of all the particular sufferings here detailed, imprisonments, scourgings Jewish and Roman, stonings, shipwrecks, scarcely one or two are described in the Acts prior to the twentieth chapter of that Book, with which the writing of this Epistle corresponds. There is no contradiction between the two records; that is carefully to be noticed. The Epistle does not say, *Once was I stoned*, and the history give the narrative of two such punishments prior to the time at which the Epistle was written. No contradiction: yet the list given in the Epistle is incomparably the fuller of the two. Learn then to read the Scriptures with intelligence. Admire the simplicity, appreciate the aim, with which they were written. All the books of Scriptures are of what is called incidental character. The Gospels were not written to give a complete life of Jesus. One supplies what another omits; and, after all, an Evangelist himself says, that *there were also many other things which Jesus did, the which if they should be written every one, even the world itself could not contain the books that should be written* (John xxi. 25). And in like manner the history in the Acts was not written to give a complete life of each of the Apostles; not even of the two Apostles principally spoken of, St Paul and St Peter. In each case specimens of the life are given; enough to exemplify the character and the history of the first disciples; enough to furnish models for later imitation, by illustrating the principles on which a Christian should act, and the sort of help and support from above which he may look for in so acting. Thus too the Epistles do not profess to give a systematic account of all Christian doctrine: there is nothing in any one of them like the formality of a Creed, or of a table of Articles of Religion: each one illustrates some new particular of doctrine and practice, but still in a thoroughly easy, occasional, and incidental manner, with reference to some particular want or circumstance of him or of those to whom each is addressed. The observation of these things gives a double interest to the study of the Bible, and guards us against some serious misapprehensions and misapplications of its teaching. It increases our thankfulness to God, not only for the gift of His Revelation, but for the particular form and shape into which He has thrown it; so attractive, so natural, so well adapted to use, so consistent in all its parts yet so various, so plainly designed not to supersede all other teaching but to furnish a guide at once and a check to it, to give material for all Christian instruction, and still to demand care, skill, and patience on the part of all who would elucidate or interpret it.

2. Another remark, not wholly unconnected with this, is as to the style and general character of this particular passage and its context.

Ye suffer fools gladly, seeing ye yourselves are wise. It is what we call ironical language. And there is very much of this tone in these chapters. I am not going to dwell upon the remark: but I will beg you to notice what a very natural person St Paul was; how he expressed strongly what he strongly felt; how he did not disdain even what are commonly called the arts of rhetoric in enforcing upon his hearers or readers matters which he knew to be important; how he did not allow a misplaced or morbid charity to keep him from exposing, as any human writer would seek to do, the fraudulent designs and underhand practices of those whose influence over a congregation he saw to be full of danger; how, like all those who have been set to do God's great work in days of unsettlement, and more especially of religious transition, he was in the habit of calling things by their real names, and of subverting error or unmasking hypocrisy by the most effective weapons which natural or acquired ability, under the control of Christian truth and love, could furnish for the purpose. I would bid you admire the natural man, while you listen to the inspired man. I would bid you recognize the wisdom of God's choice of instruments, as that wisdom is here exemplified; and never forget, in reading the words of an inspired writer, that he was a man like other men in all natural dispositions, feelings and passions, all the time that he was a man raised for certain purposes above other men by the predominating agency and constant presence of the informing and transforming Spirit of God Himself within.

3. But I must draw my third remark from the text itself, and thus prepare the way for its brief concluding enforcement.

St Paul says, *If I must needs glory, I will glory in the things which concern mine infirmities.*

I fear these words have been sometimes much misapplied. People have spoken of glorying in their infirmities, as though they were using St Paul's language, when they really meant something most opposite. They have applied the words, all but avowedly, to infirmities of temper and of character, as though the consciousness of sin were a thing to be proud of; as though it gave them some claim to the estimation of Christians, to be aware of their own liability to sudden outbreaks or habitual unsoundnesses of prevailing evil within. But now observe the three things to which St Paul here applies the term infirmity or weakness.

i. The first of these is suffering. Suffering for Christ's sake. Suffering of a most painful kind and a most frequent repetition. Bodily discomfort, bodily privation, bodily pain. Such was one part of his *infirmity*. Suffering reminded him of his human nature; of his material frame, not yet redeemed by resurrection; of his sojourn in a tabernacle, the dissolution of which was ever going on, but which was not yet exchanged for that *building of God, that house not made with hands, eternal in the heavens* (2 Cor. v. 1), in other words, for that resurrection body, for the gift of which he was ever waiting and watching.

ii. The second kind of infirmity is denoted in the words, *that which crowds upon me daily, the anxiety of all the congregations*. A keen sense of responsibility is his second weakness. The thought of his Churches; of those communities of living men, women, and children, which he had been the means of gathering from among the surrounding Jews or idolaters to bear the name of Christ and to be His witnesses in the midst of an ungodly world; the thought of these communities pressed upon him every day with an importunate and almost overwhelming power. Anxiety about their welfare was always at his heart. He knew so much in himself, he had seen so much in others, of the malice and skill of the tempter, that, when he was absent from a congregation, and more especially from a young congregation, busy in the formation or in the charge of distant churches, he was distracted with painful care, and even faith itself was not enough sometimes to soothe and to reassure him. He called this anxiety an infirmity. Perhaps, in the very highest view of all, it was so. Perhaps he ought to have been able (as some ministers are but too ready to do) to trust his congregation in God's hands in his absence. He called it an infirmity. But sure I am that it was a weakness for which we may well love him; a weakness with which we ourselves, in behalf of those committed to us, might well desire and pray to be oftener and more justly chargeable.

iii. There was a third weakness, growing out of the last-named. And that was the weakness of a most acute sympathy. *Who is weak, and I am not weak? who is offended, and I burn not?* That is, Whenever I notice or hear of a weakness in the faith of any one, such a weakness as exposes him to the risk of fainting or failing in his Christian course, I have a sense of interest and concern in that case such as makes me a very partaker in its anxieties. I cannot get rid of it by putting it from me. I feel that weakness of

Glorying in Infirmities. 81

character as my weakness. I feel that weakness of resistance as my weakness. I feel that weakness of faith as my weakness. That is one half of my sympathy. But there is, along with this, another feeling. *Who is offended*, who is caused to stumble, who is tempted to sin, who is misled, or daunted, or persecuted, so as to be in danger of making utter shipwreck of his Christian hope, *and I am not on fire* with righteous indignation against the wickedness which is doing this work upon him. Sympathy with the tempted is also indignation against the tempter. They are not two things, they are one. Sympathy has two offices: towards the offended it is fellow-weakness; towards the offender it is indignant strength. But in its two parts combined, he calls the disposition thus described—calls it, perhaps, with something of that irony of which I have spoken, and which runs through the whole passage—an infirmity; one of the things which concern his infirmities; and on that account, just because it is not so much a strength as a weakness, one of those things of which he may be permitted, without offence to modesty, to make a boast.

These were the three parts then of St Paul's *infirmity:* constant suffering for Christ's sake; a constant sense of responsibility; a constant sympathy with the weak, the erring, the tempted. I have dwelt upon these things for the sake of putting very seriously before you and before myself the contrast between St Paul's weaknesses and our own. Our own infirmities are of a kind which a severer judge than

G

we are of ourselves would certainly designate by the plainer names of defects, faults, and sins. Indolence, carelessness, vanity, a desire for applause, a sensitiveness to other men's opinion of us, a shrinking from that faithful acting and plain speaking which might give us trouble or cause wholesome pain, a selfishness which makes us resent interruption or contradiction as a wrong, a willingness to forego any duty at the call of pleasure, a frequent misplacing of the very name of duty so as to make it perforce almost the echo of inclination, these are the things which most of us would call infirmities in ourselves, by whatever title we might describe them in another. Compared with such things, how withering to our self-love must be St Paul's (so called) weaknesses! The very least of them is a virtue beyond our highest attainments. Which of us ever suffered anything in Christ's behalf? To talk of bonds and imprisonment, of watchings and fastings, of stripes and shipwrecks, voluntarily borne for the sake of Him who died for us, would be a mere mockery in this land and age: but which of us ever made an exertion, which of us ever denied himself anything, which of us ever did anything or refused anything, simply because Christ was his Saviour, simply because he loved Christ, and would not dishonour or displease Him for the world? When we examine ourselves closely, my brethren, on such a subject, we shall be surprised to see how little there is really in us of an earnest Christianity. We shall be surprised: God grant that we be humbled and aroused also! But pass on to the other two questions. Where is our sense of responsibility? our anxiety about those committed to us? Where, in us, is that feeling which expressed itself in St Paul, not in prayers and tears only, but in such irrepressible desires to be assured of the spiritual well-being of others as led him, on one occasion well known to the readers of his Epistles, to choose to be left absolutely alone in a strange and unfriendly city, that he might send back his one companion to bring him tidings of a Church which he had but lately seen himself? (1 Thess. iii. 1, 2). Such ought to be—but is it? our feeling with respect to the highest welfare of each one of our family, our household, our kindred, our friends, even if we have no more definite trust committed to us in the form of direct dependents, of a school, a parish, or a congregation. Yes, and however wide may be the circle of our connections, our interests, or our responsibilities, with regard to each individual within that circle ours ought to be the feeling here expressed by St Paul, *Who is weak, and I am not weak? who is offended, and I burn not?* The danger of each one is felt as my own: the fall of any one is felt and mourned over as my own.

4. Finally, I would give a wider scope to the language of the text, and urge upon each one who hears me the duty and the happiness of saying to himself in the words of St Paul, *If I must needs glory, I will glory in those things which concern,* not my strength, but *my weakness.* The things on which we commonly pride ourselves are our advantages, less or greater; our

talents, our gifts, our powers of mind or body, our estimation with others, our position in society, the pleasures we can command, or the wealth we have accumulated. But these things, by their very nature, are the possession of the few. Many can assert no claim at all to such grounds of glorying: all must lose it one day. St Paul tells us how we may glory safely; how we may all glory; how we may glory to the very end. Glory, he says, not in your strength, but in your weakness.

Has God denied to you, or has God taken away from you, His gift of health? Has He seen fit by His Providence to impair any of your bodily organs, your sight, your hearing, your enjoyment of taste or your power of motion? Or, has He, in the original allotment of His bounties, made you less beautiful, or less pleasing, less clever, or less attractive, than some others; some others, perhaps, in your own family and home? Or have you been treated with neglect and coldness by some one to whom you had felt and shown only kindness? Has the poison of disappointment entered your heart, and made earth itself dull and distasteful to you for ever? Or are you destined (as men speak) to a lot of obscurity, if not of poverty; unable to rise as others rise; obliged to stand by and look on, while others do the work and reap the honour which once perhaps you hoped might be your own? Or are you, yet once more, at this time mourning under one of God's afflictive appointments, bereaved and crushed, scarcely able to look either above or beyond the present, so dark does all seem to you, so blank, so naked?

My brethren, it is just in these very things, or in any one of them, that St Paul would have you glory. For God's gifts to us we may be thankful: but it is in His deprivations alone that we may glory. And St Paul tells us why we may thus glory in our disadvantages, in our postponements, in our losses, in our bereavements. He says in another passage of this same Epistle, *Most gladly therefore will I rather glory in my infirmities, that the power of Christ may rest (tabernacle) upon me* (2 Cor. xii. 9). And he speaks, yet again, in the same spirit, *of bearing about in the body the dying of the Lord Jesus*, being made like Him, that is, in His humiliation and in His death for us, *that the life also of Jesus*, His living power as it is now put forth in His servants, *might be made manifest in our body* (2 Cor. iv. 10). It is the dark side of life which brings us most closely, most consciously, into connection with the supporting and comforting help of Christ within. Everything that lowers the exuberance of animal spirits, everything that tends to depress and humble us as merely human and earthly beings, tends also, if it be but meekly and faithfully borne, to show in us and to us how near Christ is, how loving, how real, how powerful. *When I am weak, then am I strong* (2 Cor. xii. 10). Regard every painful point in your position or in your circumstances as an indication of Divine love; of a love as farsighted as it is tender; and be assured that it is so.

Regard everything which you naturally dislike and fret under, as a new motive for calling in Christ's help to bear it; and you will find it a stepping-stone between you and Him. He will cause His power to rest upon you, and by degrees you will be conscious of it. He will guide you with His counsel; He will uphold you with His arm; and at last receive you to glory.

SERMON VI.

PRESENT KNOWLEDGE AND FUTURE.

EPISTLE FOR QUINQUAGESIMA SUNDAY.

1 Corinthians XIII. 1—13.

1 *If I speak with the tongues of men and of angels, and have not charity, I am become but sounding brass or a clanging*
2 *cymbal. And if I have prophecy, and know all mysteries and all knowledge, and if I have all faith so as to remove*
3 *mountains, and have not charity, I am nothing. And if I feed others with all my substance, and if I surrender my body that I may be burned, and have not charity, I am*
4 *nothing profited. Charity is longsuffering, and kind; charity envieth not; charity vaunteth not herself; is not*
5 *puffed up; is not unmannerly; seeketh not her own; is not*
6 *provoked; reckoneth not evil; rejoiceth not at iniquity, but*
7 *rejoiceth with the truth; covereth all things, believeth all*
8 *things, hopeth all things, endureth all things. Charity never faileth: but, whether it be prophesyings, they will be abolished; or tongues, they will cease; or knowledge, it*
9 *will be abolished. For in part we know, and in part we*
10 *prophesy; and, whenever the perfect has come, that which*
11 *is in part will be abolished. When I was a child, I talked as a child, I felt*[1] *as a child, I reasoned as a child: when I have become a man, I have abolished the things of the*
12 *child. For we see now by a mirror, in riddle; but then face to face: now I know in part; but then I shall know*
13 *fully, even as also I was fully known. But at present there remaineth faith, hope, charity, these three things; and the greatest of these is charity.*

[1] Literally, *I was minded as a child;* that is, *my sentiments* (*thoughts and feelings*) *were those of a child.*

SERMON VI.

PRESENT KNOWLEDGE AND FUTURE.

1 CORINTHIANS XIII. 12.

For now we see through a glass, darkly: but then face to face; now I know in part; but then shall I know even as also I am known.

WE reach to-day what may be called, without disparagement to others, the most beautiful of all the Sunday Epistles. That short chapter which records the workings and celebrates the praises of charity or Christian love, has been familiar to all of us from childhood. If it had been always made, as it ought to have been, the touchstone of Christianity in communities and in individuals; if the confession of a true faith had been made to consist less in the correct enunciation of abstruse doctrine, and more in the watchful maintenance of a spirit of love, it would have been well for the cause of Christ on earth, and well for the souls of His people both in this world and in that which is to come. Let us pray for a special blessing on the brief consideration of this glorious passage to-day.

This chapter forms what a human critic might call an episode in the Epistle. But not on that account is it without its link before and after. St Paul is speaking of those spiritual gifts, on the possession of which the congregation at Corinth was so much priding itself; priding itself with little appreciation either of the aim of all gifts—the spiritual good of others—or of the relative value of the various gifts as measured by this standard. *Covet earnestly*, he says in the last verse of the preceding chapter, *the greater gifts;* that is, the higher and the better because the more practical and profitable gifts; *and yet show I unto you a more excellent way:* there is something higher and greater yet than any gift: take heed that ye miss not that one straight unerring road to life, from which there are so many paths diverging, which end not in life but in death.

Now follow the train of thought thus introduced.

There is a very showy and a very marvellous gift, by which a man, under the influence of the Almighty Spirit, may speak to a congregation gathered from all parts of the earth in the very tongue wherein each was born. And yet he might speak thus every language and every dialect both of heaven and earth, and, lacking withal the spirit of a living love, be found, for any practical purpose, the utterer of unmeaning sounds, like those of the echoing brass or the clanging cymbal. And there is another gift, higher than the former, even that power of prophesying, which is the intelligent utterance, under Divine direction, of the revealed secrets of the

Gospel: and there is, yet beyond this, that supernatural gift of faith by which a man, in his Master's service, may bid the very mountain, which opposes his progress, to be removed and cast into the sea: and yet, in either case, the possessor of these mighty powers may be destitute of a gentler influence, the voice of love within; and, if so, if he be indeed so, all his prodigies of speech and action will have been, for himself, in vain: he is nothing; nothing in the sight of God, nothing in the awards of eternity. And there is yet a quality which approaches very closely indeed in form and feature to the blessed principle of charity; so closely that in the later days of the Church it shall even take its name and reap its honour; there is a liberality of almsgiving, which may go to great lengths of self-denial, even to the bestowal of all that a man has upon the relief, in soul or body, of the destitute; and there is a zeal too of devotion, which may carry a man to martyrdom in defence of what he deems, and perhaps justly deems, to be the cause of truth and right: and yet neither the one nor the other of these is charity; both the one and the other may be wholly dissevered from charity: and, if it be so, if it be indeed so, then shall it profit a man nothing to have possessed and displayed either this or that, in the day when God looks for one thing, and can accept in its stead no substitute and no counterfeit.

And what then is that great grace, on the possession of which all depends? How shall I trace its features, so that you may hold up the mirror to yourselves, and see whether they are your likeness or no?

Charity suffereth long, and is kind: charity envieth not: charity vaunteth not herself; makes no display: *is not puffed up;* is not vain, is not conceited: *doth not behave herself unseemly;* is not rude, arrogant, or unmannerly: *seeketh not her own;* is not selfish, is no self-seeker: *is not provoked*[1]*: reckoneth not evil;* does not put down a wrong in her account, as though it needed to be paid off by retaliation: *rejoiceth not at iniquity,* has no pleasure in reading or hearing of another's ill-doing, another's crime or folly, *but,* on the contrary, *rejoiceth with the truth,* shares, as it were, in the joy of the truth, of righteousness and of good, when a triumph is vouchsafed to it in the world of human conflict: *covereth all things* by a merciful reticence, *believeth all things* by a refusal to mistrust, *hopeth all things* where she cannot approve, *endureth all things* where she is herself oppressed and overborne. As it has been beautifully expressed in a brief paraphrase of the original, *Charity hides the evil, believes the good, hopes the best, bears the worst*[2].

Charity never faileth: but, whether it be prophesyings, they will be abolished; or tongues, they will cease; or knowledge, it will be abolished. For our knowledge is partial, and our prophesyings are partial; and, whenever the perfect has come, the partial will

---

[1] The word *easily* in the Authorized Version comes I know not whence.

[2] Dean Stanley's *Epistles of St Paul to the Corinthians*, Vol. I. p. 280, 1st Edition. He prefers, however, the other rendering of the first clause; *bears all things.*

be abolished. It is with these greater matters, as it is with the progress of a human life from childhood to maturity: *when I was a child, I talked as a child; I felt as a child,* my sentiments were those of a child; *I reasoned as a child; when I have become a man, I have abolished the things of the child:* the arrival at man's estate brings with it, as a matter of course, the abolition of all the circumstances of the child. Or take another similitude. *We see now,* in the present life, *by means of a mirror,* reflecting the images of heavenly things in a manner tempered to the infirmities of our sight; *darkly, in enigma* or *riddle,* in dark sayings rather than in plain and direct disclosures: *but then,* in that life which is beyond this for the Christian, we shall see *face to face: now,* in the present life, *I know in part,* my knowledge is partial; *but then I shall know fully, even as* in this life *I was fully known. But at present,* as matters now are, *there remaineth faith, hope, charity, these three things:* these, in this life, are the three sure bulwarks, the abiding characteristics, of the man in Christ: *and greater than these,* or, in our idiom, *the greatest of these, is charity;* greatest—we may draw this inference from the words above—because it alone of all graces, alone of all spiritual gifts, can pass unaltered into the eternal world, and, while faith has changed its very nature in becoming sight, and hope has changed its very nature in passing into fruition, remains essentially the same for ever, the same in kind towards God, the same in kind towards His children.

Such, most imperfectly expressed, is the general sense of the Epistle for this day as a whole. I have now to fix your thoughts upon one of its subordinate though most interesting and most instructive portions; that which contrasts our present with our future knowledge, and sets before us, in brief but forcible figures, the imperfection of the one and the perfection of the other. *At present we see by means of a mirror, in riddle...at present I know but in part:* this is our first topic. *But then face to face...but then I shall know fully, even as in this life I was fully known:* this is the second.

I. First then, the imperfection of our present knowledge of Divine things is here said to be twofold; an imperfection of kind, and an imperfection of degree.

1. An imperfection of kind. This again is illustrated by two comparisons.

i. *We see by means of a mirror.* What we see at present is a sort of reflection of truth, not the very truth itself. A mirror may be very useful; but it can never give the accurate idea of the very figure, the very person, presented in it. If its copy of the person be ever so accurate, still it is not defective only, it is also misleading: the right side has become the left, and the left hand in the picture is awkwardly performing the functions of the right hand in the original: thus the effect produced is different, however carefully represented the details and the particulars. A mirror, too, can hold but one image at a time: if it be preoccupied by one figure, it is unavailable for another. And if, in addition to these essential defects of accuracy and limitations of capacity, there be also the slightest flaw in the glass or cloud upon the surface, there is an end at once of all beauty and of all truth in the representation, and what was before only defective becomes now a distortion and a caricature. And how much more expressive would be the figure in the Apostle's days, when not glass but stone or metal was commonly used for the purpose spoken of; when the colouring therefore of every object must have been lost in the reflection, and nothing would remain but a meagre and blurred outline to carry to the eye the impression of face or figure or landscape!

By such a reflection as this, St Paul says, we at present behold the things of God. We: yes, even he; even the man who had actually seen Jesus Christ (1 Cor. ix. 1), and had been caught up in vision to the third heaven (2 Cor. xii. 2). Well may *we* speak thus; we, whose knowledge and whose faith must be at the very best immeasurably inferior. It is with us, and far more literally, as it was even with the great lawgiver of old who desired to see God's glory. *Thou canst not see my face; for there shall no man see me and live ...While my glory passeth by, I will put thee in a clift of the rock, and will cover thee with my hand while I pass by; and I will take away mine hand, and thou shalt see that which is behind of me*, the reflection left by me in the mirror as I pass by, *but my face shall not be seen* (Exod. xxxiii. 20—23). How inaccurate, doubtless, are our clearest conceptions at present of the realities of Christ and of God, of truth and heaven! It is indeed as if the right side and the left of each were interchanged; as if the functions of a right hand were usurped by a left hand, and as if the impression of the whole were confused if not inverted. How tame, how colourless, how lifeless, to our eye is the general view of things above, even when the outline may be correctly drawn! How often too is the face of the mirror preoccupied with other images, when we would hold it up to receive the rays of the Divine glory! How does the world, how does self, fill up already that surface which ought to be all free and open for the reception of that which is so far worthier and more satisfying! How often too is there some fatal blemish in the very glass itself, some vein of prejudice or passion or perverseness or guilty remembrance, running across the field of vision, and distorting every image that can fall upon it from the throne of God and of the Lamb!

ii. Again, *we see*, as it is here added, *darkly;* but, as the marginal reading gives it more correctly, *in a riddle*, or *enigma*, or *dark saying*. Our present knowledge is imperfect in kind for this second reason also, that it is all, when regarded in comparison with that knowledge which shall be, and with that reality of truth which already is, enigmatical and not literal. Our present knowledge comes to us through words. Revelation itself has to be framed for us into words. All the deep things of God, which we can entertain in our minds at all, have to be embodied for our contemplation, for our examination, for our use, in words. Now think for a moment what words are. An inestimable treasure, doubtless; the very currency of thought and reason: but surely, when applied to some subjects, a mere expedient, inadequate at once, and temporary. There is a perpetual tendency in us to confound words with things, the sign with the thing signified. Half our theological controversies are illustrations of this error. A little calm mutual explanation of the terms employed, often a very little time spent in careful definition, would have closed them peaceably. This is an ungrateful use of God's gifts. He gives us words, to make the best approach that we can at present make to some faint knowledge of Himself; and then we turn these words into weapons, into stumbling-blocks, into idols: we begin by fighting with them, and we end by fighting for them.

I am not counselling the disparagement of words: they are inestimably precious. But I am endeavouring to correct an abuse of them. I am showing that, when St Paul wrote, *we know at present only in riddle, only enigmatically*, he wrote with exact truth in reference to the defects, the necessary defects, of all human language. We know of Divine things at present through the medium of words. Will any one say that what he thus knows he knows with the accuracy of an exact science? Take for an example the nature of God. The very attributes of God are an enigma to us. What is infinity? What is omniscience? What is omnipresence? What is eternity? Each is a riddle. Take for an example the character of God. Is it not all shadowed forth to us in the Scriptures, in the Old Testament at all events, in dark sayings? *It repented the Lord that He had made man, and it grieved Him at His heart* (Gen. vi. 6). Take for an example the mode of our redemption. We firmly believe in the truth of an atonement made for sin by the sacrifice of our Lord Jesus Christ. But is not every word in that statement an enigma? Who can explain, unless he would *darken counsel by words without knowledge* (Job xxxviii. 2), the precise mode and principle of that work of Christ, which is yet a sinner's one hope? Take for an example the operation of the Holy Spirit. Who can tell us how the Holy Spirit works in the hearts of men? *Thou hearest the sound thereof, but canst not tell whence it cometh and whither it goeth: so is every one that is born of the Spirit* (John iii. 8). Take for an example the process of the future judgment. Who will say that a thousand objections which he cannot answer might not be urged by human ingenuity against each part of that doctrine? We know it; we know it: but it is *in a riddle;* it is as a dark saying. Or take, once more, for an example the whole conception of heaven, of the future life of the saved; and O, ten thousand times more, of the future life of the lost. The revelation is made to us, made on the authority of God, but made to us also in human words, and therefore also made *in an enigma*.

    2. But the time is short, and I must say a word

upon the imperfection of our present knowledge in degree also. *I know in part.* Our present knowledge is partial.

It is indeed but a brief hint which I can give at any part of the vast subject. And upon this point I will only call you to notice that our great difficulty at present in religion is how to combine. We know in part. We have several portions of Divine truth communicated to us, but in very many cases a connecting link is at present wanting. Everything in revelation is true; but our faith is exercised, and our humility is exercised, and our patience is exercised, in having so little light as to how this and that in revelation can both be true. Many examples will rise to every mind as I speak. The mercy of God, and the justice of God. The almighty power of God, and the obstinate resistance of that power by souls refusing to be saved. God's hatred of sin, and God's permission of the existence of evil. Man's free will, and God's free grace. The efficacy of prayer, and God's foreknowledge and unchangeable purpose. The perfect happiness of the blessed, and the coexistent misery of the finally condemned. Our knowledge, you observe, is in part. We know each of two things, but we cannot put them together. The real difficulty is in the combination. Meanwhile we do not doubt that God sees them all in one. And *what I do, thou knowest not now, but thou shalt know hereafter* (John xiii. 7). So that we reach the second and far more glorious part of our subject, and have to set in contrast with the present imperfection the future perfection of our knowledge.

II. And here also we have two illustrations.

1. *But then, face to face.* No doubt there is a verbal reference here to the words spoken of Moses. *If there be a prophet among you, I the Lord will make myself known unto him in a vision, and will speak unto him in a dream. My servant Moses is not so, who is faithful in all mine house. With him will I speak mouth to mouth, even apparently, and not in dark speeches; and the similitude of the Lord shall he behold* (Num. xii. 6—8). We have the same contrast here. *Now we see through a glass, in a dark speech . . . but then face to face.* We shall all have that sort of communication with God Himself, which, alone of all men, the mediator of the first dispensation was privileged to enjoy in his day.

I shall see *face to face.* Our knowledge of truth hereafter will be, first, direct; and secondly, personal.

i. It will not be any longer a process of reflection, but a process of intuition. There will be no imperfect, no inverted, no distorted, images of things then: no inadequate representation, and no defective reception, of truth then: it will be all viewed directly, immediately, with nothing interposed between us and it, either to temper its rays or to discipline our vision.

ii. And this direct knowledge will be a personal knowledge also. *Face to face* implies a person. We shall see *the very glory of God in the face of Jesus Christ*

(2 Cor. iv. 6). But our words here must be few and reverent, lest we seem to forget that the thing spoken of is itself at present seen but *in a glass darkly*.

2. Again, *then shall I know, even as also I was known.* Our knowledge of Divine things hereafter will be of the same character with that knowledge of us which God has had through this life. A very solemn word, my brethren; and greatly do we need it. We cannot hope, in eternity, to know God better than He, through this life, has known each of us. I will say two things of this knowledge. First, that it will be thorough; and secondly, that it will be comprehensive.

i. *Thorough.* A knowledge (for that is the meaning of the word) through and through. God is a heart-searching God. There is no secret so deeply buried in us but God sees it as in the light of day. Even such is the insight into His truth and character, into His word and works, into His ways and will, which is promised to those of us who shall be faithful unto death, in a world beyond the grave. It will be indeed a thorough knowledge.

ii. It will be also a *comprehensive* knowledge. *At present I know in part, but then shall I know even as I was known.* God has not only a minute insight; it is also a large insight. He not only sees particulars; He sees each one of us as a whole. You know how impossible that is for any one of us with regard to another. We see particular faults and particular virtues, but we are not able, in very many instances, nor ought we, to speak decisively of the character as a whole, whether for good or evil. But God sees this also. God could judge each one of us at this moment. He could say, Notwithstanding this fault, that man is my servant: notwithstanding that good quality, this man I never knew. Now it shall be thus with *our* knowledge hereafter. Not only shall we believe and understand this item and that item, separately, of God's truth, but we shall see it all in its connection, in its combination, in its reconciling harmony, in its perfect unity. There will no longer be any spaces and gaps in our knowledge. There will be no longer crevasses and chasms, to be vaulted over on a staff of faith. *The crooked will then have been made straight, and the rough places plain* (Isai. xl. 4); *and all flesh will see,* as in one view, *the salvation of God* (Luke iii. 6). Then will not only *wisdom* be, as she ever has been, *justified of her children* (Matt. xi. 19), but also *the ways of God* will be universally and finally *justified to men.*

I close with a word of caution, and with a word of encouragement.

1. The contrast between the present imperfection and the future perfection of a Christian's knowledge, must make no one idle in the pursuit of truth below. They who seek not here find not there. It is they who seize and treasure and count over and use the separate fragments here vouchsafed to them of eternal truth, who will alone be capable of apprehending hereafter the key which is to unlock the mysterious

treasury which contains it all. In this sense, as in many others, *whosoever hath, to him shall be given* (Matt. xiii. 12).

2. Finally, do not imagine that, because we speak of imperfections of present knowledge, imperfections of kind as well as imperfections of degree; and because we would raise your thoughts to a time yet future, when *the mystery of God shall be* not only *finished* (Rev. x. 7), but unfolded in a manner in which it has never yet been to the living; therefore we would imply that the very Person in whom all truth is centred may prove eventually something wholly different from that which He has been pictured to us, or that we may not recognize in the features of that Jesus who shall return, the lineaments of the Son of Man who first ascended (Acts i. 11). Dismiss every such fear. All that we now conceive of holiness, of truth, of tenderness, of love, will be verified then, beyond but never against our anticipations. Much that we have elaborated for ourselves out of formal and ponderous theologies may then, and probably will, be contradicted; but nothing that we have known of the living Saviour Himself, nothing that we have learned of Him by experience, nothing that we have seen of Him in prayer. If we would ever know the truth, we must begin by loving the Person. *If a man love God, the same* knoweth, or, let me rather say, *is known of Him* (1 Cor. viii. 3).

SERMON VII.

THE PROTECTIVE POWER OF CONSISTENT HOLINESS.

EPISTLE FOR THE FIRST SUNDAY IN LENT.

2 Corinthians VI. 1—10.

1 AND *working with Him we entreat also that ye receive*
2 *not in vain the grace of God: (for He saith, "At an acceptable season I hearkened to thee; and in a day of salvation I succoured thee:" behold, now is a season of favourable acceptance; behold, now is a day of salvation:)*
3 *taking heed not*[1] *to give in anything any cause of stum-*
4 *bling, lest the ministry*[2] *be blamed; but in every thing recommending ourselves, like*[3] *God's ministers, in much*
5 *patience, in afflictions, in sufferings, in distresses, in stripes, in imprisonments, in tumults, in toils, in watch-*
6 *ings, in fastings; in purity, in knowledge, in longsuffer-*
7 *ing, in kindness, in the Holy Spirit, in love unfeigned, in word of truth*[4], *in power of God, through the armour of*
8 *righteousness on the right hand and on the left; through renown and dishonour, through evil report and good*
9 *report; as deceivers, and true; as unknown, and well known; as dying, and, behold, we live; as chastened,*
10 *and not killed; as sorrowing, but ever rejoicing; as poor, but making many rich; as having nothing, and possessing all things.*

[1] This appears to be the force of the particular negative particle here used.

[2] See chap. v. 18: *the ministry of the reconciliation.*

[3] Literally, *as God's ministers (should do).*

[4] The omission of the article is accounted for by the form of the sentence, as a sort of catalogue or enumeration of heads of enquiry.

SERMON VII.[1]

THE PROTECTIVE POWER OF CONSISTENT HOLINESS.

2 CORINTHIANS VI. 7.

By the armour of righteousness on the right hand and on the left.

THE opening of this day's Epistle reminds us that the Epistle itself has a context. *We then, as workers together with Him, beseech you also that ye receive not the grace of God in vain.* We look back to the close of the foregoing chapter, and find in it one of the most glorious summaries anywhere to be found of the work of Christ's redemption (2 Cor. v. 14—21).

The love of Christ constraineth us; because we thus judged; because this is our decision formed once and for ever, *that, if one died for all, then did all die,* in Him, and with Him: *and that He died for all, that the living might no longer live unto themselves,* in relation to themselves, with a selfish, self-seeking, self-contained life, *but unto Him who for them died and was raised* from death. The next verse describes a consequence of this. I look upon myself

---

[1] A collection was made after this Sermon for the Discharged Prisoners' Society.

as having died when Christ died, as having risen when Christ rose. I have done therefore with *flesh*, with the life which is merely bodily and worldly, in all its bearings. Even towards Christ Himself I have ceased to have any such relation. I no longer dwell upon my national connection with Him, as one of the house of Israel, of the seed of Abraham. *A man in Christ is a new creation. Old things*, for him, *are gone by;* old aims, old boasts, old advantages, old views and judgments: *behold, all things are become new.* And those "*all things*" which have thus become new *are all*, for him, *given and originated by that God who reconciled us to Himself through Christ, and gave to us the ministry of the reconciliation.* And what is that? *How that God was* engaged in *reconciling in Christ a world*, a whole world, *to Himself, by not reckoning to them*, not charging to their account, *their trespasses, and by having set in us*, constituted and established in our persons as His messengers and Apostles, *the word of the reconciliation. In behalf of Christ, then, are we ambassadors, as though God were entreating through us: we pray you in behalf of Christ, be reconciled*—and the original word says, be reconciled *once for all*, as by a single act—*to God. One who knew not sin He made sin for us, that we might become a* very *righteousness of God in Him.* So entire was the union between Christ and the sin-ruined world, that it was as though He took our sin and gave us in exchange His righteousness. When were words more express ever employed, to denote the thoroughness of Christ's expiation, or the completeness of the transfer of guilt from the soul of the sinner, who with hearty repentance and true faith turns to Him?

You will not blame me for having devoted a few moments to a passage so transcendent in its importance, and so intimately connected with the subject which comes before us in its order to-day. That subject itself I can express with very little amplification. Follow me through a brief paraphrase of the opening of this sixth chapter, the Epistle for the day.

I have told you of a grace which is above all grace; a taking away of sin, and a giving, in its stead, of the very righteousness of God to man. I have told you that this is God's work. It is no matter of indifference to Him whether man accepts or trifles with this great salvation. He beseeches by us. And we, praised be His holy Name! are permitted to work and to beseech with Him. Receive His grace. It is not much to ask of you. We bid you not to search heaven and earth for a Saviour and for a redemption. Receive only, and both it and He are yours. But O then, receive not in vain; "unto emptiness;" so that, when you look into your hand, there shall be nothing there. It will be so, if you receive carelessly. It will be so, if you hold negligently. It will be so, if you afterwards walk carelessly, as though regardless of the treasure entrusted to your keeping. Remember the words of God by His Prophet of old, "In an acceptable season I heard thee; in a day of salvation I succoured thee." O let those words ring in your ears, reminding you that there is a season, that there is a day, of acceptance, which if you miss, it comes not again. Not yesterday; not to-morrow: not yesterday, lest any say, It is too late; not to-morrow, lest any say, There is yet room for delay: to-day is the accepted time; this day, that now is, is the day of salvation.

We work with God, and we beseech for God; but in so doing we are careful that we ourselves give no cause of hindrance to our own message, lest we frustrate the very grace of God committed to our stewardship. Rather do we in every thing approve ourselves to your judgment and conscience, as ministers of God ought to do; that you may never doubt what we are, or say that word and life are in us at variance. Nay, surely, "the signs of an Apostle" (2 Cor. xii. 12) *are evident in us in each particular. Is endurance, hardihood, constancy under suffering, such a sign? We can point to much patience; we can point to afflictions, to necessities, to distresses; we can point to stripes, to imprisonments, to tumults; we can point to daily toils, to nightly watchings, to great privations. Or is personal character, is Divine grace, is pure doctrine, such a sign? I have sought to approve myself in these things also: in pureness, in knowledge, in longsuffering, in kindness, in the Holy Spirit, in unfeigned love, in the word of truth, in the power of God, by the armour of righteousness on the right hand and on the left. Is a firm maintenance of principle and practice amidst calumny, misrepresentation, and scorn, any sign of right and of good?* I too have striven to stand approved in the sight of God and man, through honour and dishonour, through evil report and good report: called a deceiver, yet all the while true; taunted as unknown, obscure and ignoble, yet all the while known and well known to those in whom the truth dwells; dying daily, through the multitude of my trials, yet endued daily with life from Him in whom my life is hidden; ever chastened, and sometimes, perhaps, like my Master before me, esteemed by contemptuous men as "stricken, smitten of God, and afflicted" (Isai. liii. 4), yet never quite unto death; ever sorrowful, yet, amidst all, ever rejoicing too; destitute altogether of the wealth of this world, yet able to make many rich with that which is far more precious; destitute, even to the extremity of want, yet with a hold firmer than possession, not upon something only, but on all things. "Whether the world, or life, or death, or things present, or things to come, all are ours; and we are Christ's, and Christ is God's" (1 Cor. iii. 22).

From the whole passage thus read in its connection, I select one single clause for careful consideration. It will be found readily to adapt itself to the subject of that special appeal with which I am to close this Sermon.

By the armour of righteousness on the right hand and on the left.

I understand *righteousness* here in what may be called its most obvious sense. Sometimes, we know, the word is used in a very comprehensive form for the whole of God's great gift to sinners in Jesus Christ. *But now the righteousness of God without the law is manifested, being witnessed by the law and the prophets; even the righteousness of God which is by faith of Jesus Christ, unto all and upon all them that believe* (Rom. iii. 21, 22). Thus understood, *the armour of righteousness* might be made equivalent to *the whole armour of God* spoken of in the Epistle to the Ephesians. As, however, some portions of that *whole armour* are here separately enumerated, in distinction from the armour of righteousness; *the Holy Spirit,* for example, and *the word of truth;* we must rather look to that use of the word righteousness in which it denotes a blameless discharge of all the duties and relations of life, a general uprightness and excellence of conduct and deportment in the various circumstances of an earthly state and conflict. It is thus employed in various passages, for example, of the Epistle to the Ephesians. *That ye put on the new man, which after God is created in righteousness and true holiness. For the fruit of the Spirit is in all goodness and righteousness and truth. Stand therefore, having your loins girt about with truth, and having on the breastplate of righteousness* (Eph. iv. 24. v. 9. vi. 14).

Thus our subject, briefly described, will be, the protective power of consistent holiness.

My brethren, it has been the fashion with some persons to disparage the value of what is called a moral life. I know it will not save a man. In this sense, *there is none righteous, no, not one. In Thy sight shall no man living be justified* (Psalm xiv. 3. cxliii. 2). But some have gone much beyond this in their depreciation of morality. They have spoken as if it had in itself a necessary tendency towards self-righteousness. They have spoken of a moral man as if he were further from the kingdom of God than a profligate or profane person. And, of course, if the definition of a moral man is made to include the *trusting in himself that he is righteous, and despising others* (Luke xviii. 9), no language can express too strongly the estrangement of such a character from an evangelical hope. But in the same degree must we assert its estrangement from a rightly defined morality. Vanity is no part of morality. Contempt is no part of morality. Self-righteousness is no part of morality. Just in proportion as any one of these ingredients is found in it, in the same proportion does the character itself become (and it may be in a very high degree) not moral, but immoral.

I do not read that our Lord Jesus Christ, when He was upon earth, discountenanced men for being moral. I read of one instance in which He is expressly said to have *loved* a young man who had nothing to recommend him but his morality. *All these,* the commandments of the second table, *have I observed from my youth: then Jesus beholding him loved him, and said unto him, One thing thou lackest* (Mark x. 20). He might, humanly speaking, have had that one thing also without having been in the slightest degree less moral. It was not morality, but worldliness, the natural consequence of great wealth, which kept that young man from salvation.

Cases indeed may be pointed out, in which a life of early profligacy has been totally reversed by a hearty reception of the Gospel, and in which the sense of wasted time and abused talents has given a tenfold zeal and earnestness to the faith of the renewed and rescued man. But let us not forget, in thankfulness for these merciful and glorious exceptions, how many thousands have gone on to the end in the broad way leading to destruction, for one who was turned by God's grace out of it in time to save his soul alive. And let us not be so unthankful as to forget, on the other side, in how many cases a human life has been indeed *as the shining light that shineth more and more unto the perfect day* (Prov. iv. 18), cases in which an early training in Christian habits has been rewarded, by Him who gives to them that have, by a gradual growth within of all that is more distinctively spiritual, and the whole life, from childhood to the grave, has been of one constant tenour, each age marked by its own proper characteristics, and preserved from its own peculiar faults and vices. This, within the bosom of a Christian Church, ought to be the normal condition of human life: we may pray and strive that it be so more and more, while we thank God with all our hearts for giving us, of His own unbounded mercy, so many opportunities, even after less favourable beginnings, of escaping, just with our lives, from the wrath to come (1 Cor. iii. 15. Jude 23).

I have before me in this congregation two classes. There are those who *have lived in all good conscience before God* (Acts xxiii. 1), and there are those who have not so lived, from their youth up. To the one class, for the sake of preaching thankfulness, and for the sake of preaching watchfulness, and for the sake of preaching also *a yet more excellent way* (1 Cor. xii. 31); to the other class, for the sake of inculcating repentance, and humiliation, and earnestness, and yet hope also; would I address myself this day on the protective power of an early and consistent uprightness. May the strength of the Word and of the Spirit be at work amongst us, while we briefly speak and devoutly listen.

I might dwell upon this protective power in two aspects. I might speak of its aspect towards the world. What a safeguard is there in a really unblemished life, in its contact with other men! How brave it makes a man, how fearless, how undaunted in word and action, to have on the armour of righteousness! *He shall not be afraid of evil tidings: his heart is fixed, trusting in the Lord* (Psalm cxii. 7). He will not have to remind himself, when duty calls, I cannot say that, lest I open myself to such a retort. He will not have to consider with himself, when duty calls, how he can avoid provoking such or such a taunt, or rousing against himself such or such a recrimination. He can go on his way, bearing a manful and perhaps a powerful testimony for the right and against the wrong: he can lie down and rise up, he can walk abroad and take his rest, none making him afraid: above all, he, if he be also a Christian in his heart, can command for his Master's cause that tribute of silent (or not always silent) respect, which the world itself, in our land and age, has ever ready for the man whose consistency it has tested and not found wanting.

Some may hear me to-day, who are still young enough to maintain or to lose this first armour. Young men, boys, yes children, can understand this at which I am aiming. I charge it upon you, that you indulge in yourselves no vague peradventures that, after going a little way, or for a little while, wrong in moral matters, matters of deceitfulness and truth, of undutifulness or obedience, of debt or honesty, of vice or purity, you may recover yourselves, and be good men and good Christians in time to live or at least in time to die. Be quite sure of one thing, and remember it, God helping you, all your life long, that no person who has ever fallen into definite sin can be quite the same ever again; that his sin will most certainly *find him out* (Num. xxxii. 23); find him out in weakness, or find him out in suffering, or find him out in shame; so that he will regret it to the very end of his days, even if, by God's great grace, he does not perish in it for ever.

But the season on which we have entered points rather to the second aspect of the protective power of righteousness. Towards the tempter.

Here I must expand the sense a little. Do not

suppose that there is in fallen human nature any safeguard against the power of the great enemy. It is only when the One Person who is *stronger than he comes upon him and overcomes him* (Luke xi. 22), that he acknowledges any superior in the form of man. And though there is, no doubt, some help to be found in a mere ignorance of evil; and some help in the mere fact of not having before tasted evil, whatever the cause of that forbearance; yet, when we are speaking of the armour of righteousness, we cannot forget that, in its true and real sense, it is a Christian armour; it is furnished only from Christ's armoury, and can be worn only under Christ's banner. Therefore let me say at once, that the protective power of the armour in question againt the tempter, whatever it may be as against the world, lies almost wholly in the difference between uprightness and righteousness, between morality and Christianity, between innocence and holiness. Adam was innocent, Adam was upright, Adam was moral, when temptation first assailed him: yet he fell under it on the instant. It is only our Lord who could say, *The prince of this world cometh, and hath nothing in me* (John xiv. 30); findeth no material in me on which to fasten as capable of assimilation to evil, no ear ready to respond to his whisper, no train of human infirmity laid to receive the spark of sinful suggestion. And it is only they who are Christ's, by hearty faith and honest self-dedication, who can be said even thus far to partake of the characteristic which He claims for Himself, that they are armed, in any true sense, against the assaults of the spiritual tempter.

But, when thus armed, how great is the gain not to have sinned before! O what would they give, who have tasted of evil, to have not so tasted! O what an advantage does it give to the assailant, to have before conquered! How are his spirits raised, and those of the defender depressed, by the remembrance of former conflicts which have so ended! Nay, in how many of the Christian combats is memory not only the tempter but the sin!

And suffer me to remind you more carefully of the amplitude of the expression, *on the right hand and on the left*. To be worth anything, the coat of mail must be complete. There must be no open point in it. Viewed on the one side, how perfect sometimes is the Christian armour! viewed on the other side, sometimes how defective! Estimated in reference to some particulars of duty, how irreproachable, how blameless, is the character! estimated in reference to other particulars of duty, how weak, how inconsistent, how reprehensible! In point of truth, perhaps, how excellent! in point of charity, how deficient! In diligence, perhaps, how exemplary! in reverence, how faulty! in purity, how sinful! *And whosoever shall keep the whole law, and yet offend in one point, he is guilty of all* (James ii. 10). And therefore the armour of righteousness is not in that case Christian armour: for he is a Christian in whom the Spirit

of Consistent Holiness.

of Christ is; and, where the Spirit of Christ is, there is a regard, equal as well as practical, to every word alike that proceeded out of the mouth of Christ.

Let us remember then, before we pass on to the last and more special topic, the bearing of this grave subject on two classes of hearers already indicated.

Some of you may be in danger of priding yourselves upon your good conscience. None can find fault, you think, and perhaps think truly, with your conduct or your principles. You owe no man anything, and even towards God your conscience scarcely misgives you. You are inclined to be very severe upon the less perfect virtue of your neighbours. You can almost respond to the Divine challenge, *He that is without sin among you, let him first cast a stone at her* (John viii. 7). My brethren, I tremble for you. I do not dispute your blamelessness of life; but I much fear lest, instead of being thankful to God for it, you are priding yourselves upon it; I much fear lest for you Christ have died in vain; I much fear lest your righteousness be rather that of the Pharisee, who has yet to learn his first lesson in the school of Christ, than that of the humble Christian who receives it day by day from his Saviour through the Holy Spirit, and who, even when he *thinketh he standeth*, has learned of Christ to *take heed lest he fall* (1 Cor. x. 12).

And others are writing bitter things against themselves because they know that they are not righteous. My brethren, there is One who can still make you so. You are weak in yourselves; *be strong in the Lord and in the power of His might* (Eph. vi. 10). Cast yourselves upon His help; ask for His Spirit; live in Him; let Him lead, let Him guide, let Him uphold you; and you too shall know what the meaning of those words is, *the righteousness which is of God by faith* (Phil. iii. 9).

Finally, the text may remind us that, as there are those in whom the armour is defective, even defective in principle, and valueless, so there are also persons who have parted with it utterly, so that all the world may see their helplessness. Such is the forlorn state of those for whom I ask your aid to-day.

I have spoken of the protective power, in some sense, of an unblemished morality; in a far higher sense, of a religious, a Christian, a thorough righteousness. But the poor convict, whose case is now before us, has no such protection. Fallen in his neighbour's esteem, fallen in his own esteem, what has he left? No armour certainly. Nothing to help him in withstanding the next assault of evil. Nothing to help him in rising towards something better than he has yet known. Nothing to keep him from sinking lower and lower, till he falls again into crime, again into the consequences of crime, temporal, spiritual, and eternal.

He comes out from a perhaps long captivity, to find neither work nor home, neither love nor help. Seven years, or ten years, or fifteen years, have made great havoc of his few friends. Dead, or scattered, or impoverished, or, at best, ashamed of him, what can be expected of them? The Government, which, with a praiseworthy liberality, allows him on his liberation the wages of his enforced labour during the years of his servitude, yet cannot stay to find him work again now, and in some sense might almost be said by its very liberality to tempt to idleness. O my brethren, take the case into your consideration as fellow-men, as fellow-citizens, as fellow-Christians, and is it not a sad one? We know the danger of making the criminal's lot too interesting; of diverting into a means of encouragement to offenders supplies which ought rather to be directed towards the support of honest and deserving labour. But the Society for which I now ask your support is liable to no such imputation. Its chief aim is to turn to useful account, for the real good of the fallen, those sums which in any case the country, humanely and justly, has decided to bestow. It offers to husband resources which would otherwise be hastily squandered, and to turn them to the very best account in assisting the resumption of labour whether at home or abroad.

But into these details the preacher cannot enter. He can deal only with principles. He can but bid you to feel for those who have lost the armour, such as it is, even of a decent morality, and to show your pity, as you can to-day, by a real and substantial help towards the resumption of that lost armour. There are turning-points in every human life, at which the power of evil is for a moment intermitted, and the poor sin-bound soul has a chance, as it were, given it of emancipation. To minister, at such a moment, to that soul's escape, is one of the most heavenly offices to which a human being can be invited. You are invited to that office to-day. You are asked to interpose, as it were, at one of those pauses of temptation, to which may be reverently applied the words heard already at the close of this day's Gospel, *Then the devil leaveth Him, and, behold, Angels came and ministered unto Him* (Matt. iv. 11).

SERMON VIII.

CHRIST THE STRENGTH OF THE TEMPTED.

GOSPEL FOR THE FIRST SUNDAY IN LENT.

St Matthew iv. 1—11.

1 *THEN Jesus was led up into the wilderness by the Spirit,*
2 *to be tempted by the devil. And when He had fasted forty*
3 *days and forty nights, He afterwards hungered. And the tempter drew nigh, and said to Him, If Thou art the Son of*
4 *God, bid that these stones become loaves. But He answered and said, It is written, Not on bread alone shall man live, but in*[1] *every word going forth through the mouth of God.*
5 *Then the devil taketh Him to the holy city, and setteth Him*
6 *on the top of the temple, and saith to Him, If Thou art the Son of God, cast Thyself down; for it is written, He shall charge His angels concerning Thee, and on their hands they shall bear Thee, lest at any time Thou strike Thy foot*
7 *against a stone. Jesus said to him, It is written again,*
8 *Thou shalt not tempt*[2] *the Lord thy God. Again the devil taketh Him to a very high mountain, and showeth Him all*
9 *the kingdoms of the world, and the glory of them; and saith to Him, All these things will I give Thee, if Thou*
10 *fall down and worship me. Then saith Jesus to him, Get thee behind me, Satan; for it is written, The Lord thy God shalt thou worship, and Him only shalt thou serve.*
11 *Then the devil leaveth Him, and, behold, Angels drew nigh and began to minister to Him.*

[1] That is, *in the strength of any word, any command, which God may be pleased to give for the support of life.* See the context in Deut. viii. 3.

[2] Or, *make trial of;* that is, *try experiments upon the protecting care of God.*

SERMON VIII.

CHRIST THE STRENGTH OF THE TEMPTED.

ST MATTHEW IV. 1.

Then was Jesus led up of the Spirit into the wilderness, to be tempted of the devil.

HEBREWS II. 18.

For in that He Himself hath suffered being tempted, He is able to succour them that are tempted.

I HAVE selected for consideration this evening, in pursuance of an intention announced last Sunday, that topic which the two verses just read to you jointly embody; *Christ, through temptation, the strength of the tempted.*

Suitable to the season of Lent, which commemorates the forty days of our Lord's own temptation in the wilderness; suitable to the services of this Sunday in particular, on which the Gospel has brought before us the record of that strange and awful, yet, as we believe, most necessary, scene of His trial; is not the subject also seasonable in this further sense; that life itself is for each of us one protracted period of similar temptation, rising at certain times into a more definite and concentrated assault, but never wholly losing that character, however varied and however irregular the mode of its manifestation?

Now, my brethren, this is a subject on which we cannot speak too simply, or listen too earnestly. It is indeed, in every sense that we can give to the words, a practical subject. It is a subject at once of the most universal and of the most individual application. Gather all your thoughts together, and fix them, with me, upon the scene about to be disclosed; a scene of man and of human life; a scene of conflict and of suffering, relieved and illuminated by the revelation of One standing by, who is not a Spectator only, but Himself in our behalf a Combatant, and, unlike us, a Combatant of irresistible, of Divine strength.

Now we must look, first, at the human side by itself. *The tempted; them that are being tempted.* What is temptation? The original word is closely connected with one denoting *to pierce*, or *perforate*, so as to let the light in upon something heretofore closed and covered. Thus to tempt is to explore, to try, to examine and expose the nature and material of a character or a person. It is very instructive to understand this. It is the key at once to some apparent contrarieties in Scripture. It explains in a moment how, for example, it should be said in one place, as you have heard to-night, that *God did tempt Abraham* (Gen. xxii. 1), and in another place, *Let* no man say when he is tempted, I am tempted of God (James i. 13).

To tempt is to try the character of a person. That is the meaning of the word, and all else must be learned from the context and connection of each particular passage in which the word occurs. Its particular sense in each place will be ascertained by asking either of the two questions, Who tempts? or, with what purpose? In either case, the nature of the act is a process of probing, testing, examining, exploring: but the whole aspect of the transaction will be altered by considering whether it is God who tempts, in which case the object will certainly be, man's good; or the evil spirit, in which case the object will as certainly be, man's evil.

God did tempt Abraham. He put his character to the test. He proposed to him a very difficult act. He placed him in circumstances in which any but a perfectly obedient man would assuredly have disobeyed. It would not have been difficult to find many excuses—we might almost say, many good reasons—for disobeying. *He that had received the promises* was bidden to sacrifice the very son in whom all those promises centred (Heb. xi. 17). It was not a mere question of doing or refusing to do a very painful thing; of crucifying, or refusing to crucify, the strongest of natural affections at the call of God. There was more than this in it. Abraham was commanded to do something which it seemed improbable that God could intend; which contradicted not only humane feeling, but religious feeling also. He was commanded not only to take away an innocent life, but also to take away a life given by promise, and given to be the very repository of the promises of God to man.

I take this as an illustration, in the strongest possible form, of what temptation, or trial, may be in the hands of God.

My brethren, we all believe that God guides human life. We believe that His Providence ordereth all things both in heaven and earth. Now therefore I bid you notice how He is still carrying on, in the case of each one of us, a process of temptation, though it be a far less severe process than that which He applied to the father of the faithful. Yes, we are all being tempted of God every day. That is, not a day passes in which God Himself is not making trial of us, what manner of spirit we are of. He needs not to ascertain this, but we need it. He sees in the spring of motive, at the fountain-head of will, that which we can only see in the course of movement, in the stream of conduct. And it is quite necessary that we should be shown this; that we should be taught, each one for himself, what he is; how far he is really serving Christ and pleasing God and how far, amidst whatever professions, he is really serving himself and pleasing men.

Now this is the key to a great part of the mystery of life. God, for our own good, with a view to our conversion, or our correction, or, at any rate, our salvation, is so ordering the events which befall us as that they may be the means of unveiling to us our own hearts. Sometimes He does this by adversity. Sorrow comes, or pain, or separation, or loss: how do we bear that? are we patient? are we submissive? can we say, *It is the Lord: let Him do what seemeth Him good* (1 Sam. iii. 18)? Sometimes He seeks the same end by prosperity. Success comes, honour, wealth, happiness: how do we bear that? it is quite as difficult to bear as the other: are we thankful? are we humble? are we of a quiet spirit then? do we still feel for others? do we then, yes then more than ever, wait still upon God? These things, adversity and prosperity, are alike, though perhaps not equally—perhaps the latter more of the two—great revealers of character. He that is in earnest will see the trying process in each kind of circumstance, and will bless God if even by very painful disclosures He shows him to himself as he is.

But I need not say that there is another application, perhaps a commoner, certainly a yet more grave one, of the word temptation. God tempts, or tries, us for our good. Even the bitter truths which we learn from His tempting are salutary. But there is another power, yes, let me say, another person, at work upon us besides Him. *God cannot be tempted of evil, neither tempteth He any man: but every man is tempted, when he is drawn away of his own lust, and enticed: then, when lust hath conceived, it bringeth forth sin; and sin, when it is finished, bringeth forth death*

K

(James i. 13). This is the brief description of that other process of temptation, which is not from God, but from God's enemy, and which is not designed for wholesome discipline, but for injury, sin, and death.

Probably I address none to-night who have not, at some time or other, been consciously subject to this kind of temptation. I think I may venture to say that I address no one to-night who has not really been subject to this kind of temptation, and that many times over. Sometimes it comes in a very direct form. Some companion, some so-called friend, asks you to come with him somewhere where you know you ought not to go, to do with him something which you know you ought not to do. That person is for you at that moment the mouthpiece of the tempter. The tempter is exploring you, to see what you are made of, what your principles are worth, what your courage is worth, what your faith is worth. And this, not for your good, that you may see your own weakness, and flee for refuge to a better strength, but in the hope that you will yield to the solicitation, that you will say, I must do this one sin, if I die for it. Or, again, the process may be wholly internal, wholly mental. Your own sinful desire has started into energy, and would hurry you before it. Some sudden impulse, some unexpected thought, has seized you: a single spark, thrown you know not whence nor by whom, has fired a whole train of ungodly imagination, and it is as if a voice in your

Christ the Strength of the Tempted. 131

ear told you that this or that sinful act was essential to your happiness, and bade you risk your all upon the venture. This, again, is temptation. This is the case described by St James; a man *drawn away of his own lust, and enticed.* And sometimes the suggestion is so sudden, the impulse so unaccountable, yet the order to obey it so imperious, that we feel in our own experience a wonderful confirmation of the truth of the Scripture revelation, which tells of a living personal spirit having access to our souls for evil; of *Satan desiring to have men*, at certain times more especially, *that he may sift them as wheat* (Luke xxii. 31); may exercise upon them a process of separating and of discriminating, as if to see which of them, or how much in any of them, might prove to be good, and to turn to his account the far more probable discovery of infirmity, of corruption, of guile.

We must distinguish between ordinary and occasional processes of temptation. *Your adversary the devil*, St Peter says, *as a roaring lion, walketh about, seeking whom he may devour* (1 Pet. v. 8). There is a constant pursuit of us going on, day by day; an evil eye, as it were, ever upon us; a constant desire of our fall and of our ruin, and a constant succession of snares laid to draw us into it. But the real hope is, that we may be caught, at some particular moment, off our guard, and then the ordinary effort rises into the extraordinary, and that aggravated attack is made upon us by the ever watchful foe, against which we pray daily in the words of our all-wise Counsellor, *Lead us not into temptation;* suffer us not to fall into that aggravation of spiritual danger, which involves either a shameful fall or at least an agonizing struggle.

In this connection I beg you to notice the words, *in that He Himself hath suffered being tempted.* Yes, it is a true saying; there is suffering in temptation. That sort of conflict of which I have spoken cannot be endured, end in which way it may, without leaving a dreadful trace behind it. A man may almost be said to carry the scar of every such conflict to his grave. Every man, until he has quite *given himself over*, as it is written, *to work all uncleanness with greediness* (Eph. iv. 19), must find in temptation suffering.

Such then is human life. A time of trial, in all its aspects; in its joys and in its sorrows, its prosperities and its adversities, its days of gloom and its days of brightness. A time, too, in one aspect, not of trial only but of temptation; of efforts directed against our present and eventual good, sometimes from without, in the shape of human solicitation; sometimes from within, in the shape of sinful suggestion, using the natural desires as its engines of attack, but adapting itself, by design and purpose, to the special openings afforded by situation, occasion, and circumstance.

But we turn now, gladly and thankfully, to the other side of this dark picture. We are not left alone. There is another Person too in sight. There is One of whom the latter text reminds us, who, being from eternity one with the Father, yet for us men, and for our salvation, became Himself man, and this in order *that through death He might destroy him that had the power of death, that is, the devil;* might *deliver those who through fear of death were all their lifetime subject to bondage;* might become *a merciful and faithful High Priest* between God and man, *to make reconciliation for sin* (Heb. ii. 14, 15, 17); and finally, having Himself suffered under temptation, might be able, in all time to come, from His place at the right hand of God, to aid and *to succour them that are tempted.* We have to think, not of temptation only, but of Christ made through temptation the Strength of the tempted.

I fear that many of us, if we speak the truth, must confess that we know less of this side of the case than of the other. But may God grant that some even of these may be instructed to-night in His great salvation, and may learn, if never before, what Christ is ready to be to them, and how near at hand He is if they will but *feel after Him* till they *find Him* (Acts xvii. 27).

How is Christ the strength of the tempted? Tell over in your minds the various items, so to speak, of His gracious help.

1. Think of His counsel. What wise directions He gives us in His Word as to the way in which we should walk! In particular, what strong motives does He supply to us for avoiding or else overcoming

temptation! How He shows us the sinfulness of sin by Himself bearing it with such sorrow and at last dying for it! How He offers to us the greatest happiness, the greatest rest and comfort of soul, even now, on the simple condition of coming to Him; coming to Him to be forgiven, and coming to Him to be kept safe! How He seeks, as it were, to preoccupy us with Himself, to cover us with the shadow of His wing, so that, when the tempter comes for us, he may not find us, but only Him of whom he is afraid, by whom he has been conquered, from whose face he always flees away! What inducements are these to a poor tempted soul to take refuge in Him; to *flee for refuge*, as it is said, *to the hope set before us* (Heb. vi. 18)! Which if we do, and if we will keep within the refuge, we shall have a sure safeguard.

2. But counsel alone, advice alone, even inducements alone, may fail of their object. Therefore Christ is the strength of the tempted in this way also: that He has given us His own example. The Gospel for this day tells us how He was Himself tempted, in all points and in each point, like us; in body, through appetite; in mind, through ambition; in soul, through presumption; and how in every particular He met the temptation with its appropriate thought and word of discomfiture; how He used that *sword of the Spirit which is the word of God* (Eph. vi. 17), turning its edge, with the most exact discernment, against the particular form of attack; and thus

was not only made accessible to temptation by being in every respect very man, but also foiled each temptation by means equally available, were there but the will to use them, for every human being. My brethren, we all feel the force of example. For evil, it is all but omnipotent. Where is he who does not readily follow the evil example of those around him? But has it not some power with us too for good? If a man can say, not only, I advise you to do this, but also, I have done this myself; I have found this or that serviceable to me, and, if you try the same means, you will reach the same end; we all feel that there is a force in the words beyond that of mere advice, a force which makes itself felt, as well as a force which convinces and constrains.

3. Again, Christ is the strength of the tempted through His Providence for them that trust in Him. *All power is given unto me*, He says, *in heaven and in earth* (Matt. xxviii. 18); in the spiritual as well as the temporal affairs of His creatures, in the arranging of their circumstances as well as the influencing of their minds. In the exercise of this power, we are expressly told, that He *will not suffer us to be tempted above that we are able;* that is, above the strength which He imparts to meet the temptation; *but will also with the temptation make a way for us to escape, that we may be able to bear it* (1 Cor. x. 13). O, my brethren, what should we be without this assurance? Who could manage the affairs of his own life but for one day? What mistakes, what follies, what dan-

gers, what confusion, what discomfort, what desolation of heart, would be the result! But Christ holds all the threads which make up the web of life in His own hand: and He takes care so to weave them, for those who will trust Him so to do, as that all shall be well; no one shall be overpowered, no one shall be overwhelmed, with disproportionate or resistless temptations, unless he goes in quest of them for himself, and breaks loose from Him who has him in His charge.

4. And Christ is the strength of the tempted, once more, in this sense: that He ministers to them His Spirit. I have asked, what we should be without His Providence: well may I add, what would any of us be without the Holy Spirit? O, my brethren, I have spoken of sudden suggestions of evil coming into our minds we know not whence, and which we ascribe, under the warrant of Scripture, to the immediate agency of a spiritual tempter: and now may I not speak, and will not you all understand me when I speak, of suggestions and impulses of good coming into our hearts we know not whence? thoughts of the wonderful forbearance of God towards us, of the marvellous love of Christ, and of the long patience of the Holy Spirit in striving with our evil and in endeavouring to call us to a better mind; and, along with these, such a sense of our own sinfulness and ingratitude and unprofitableness as seems to constrain us henceforth to live not unto ourselves, but unto Him who so loved and has so borne with us?

Do not these things illustrate to us the reality of a Holy Spirit? Do not these things encourage us to believe that He is very near us, that He is within call, that He is desirous of our good? and do they not teach us to commit our ways to His special guidance day by day, that He may supply us with the needful strength in every foreseen and in every unexpected access of temptation?

5. But, my brethren, we all feel that the consideration of this subject would be most imperfect, if I did not press upon you one remaining sense in which Christ is the strength of the tempted; that, namely, which the latter text speaks of when it says, *In that He Himself hath suffered being tempted, He is able to succour them that are tempted.* Yes, the sympathy of Christ; that sort of sympathy which alone is worthy of the name, the sympathy of experience, the fellow-feeling, the community of feeling, which results from having borne the same; that sympathy which was made possible for Him only by His becoming man, man in every part of man's nature, man in bodily wants and appetites, man in the capacity of being solicited to evil, man in the necessity of choosing between right and wrong, between self-gratification and obedience; it is this sympathy, acquired, in great part, in His longest and sorest temptation commemorated at this season, but for the exercise of which the whole of His earthly life was one continued preparation; this it is which, more than any one thing, makes Christ Himself, Christ personally,

the help and the strength of tempted man. It is the knowledge that in the heavenly places themselves there is One who cares whether we yield or conquer; One who has taken the accurate measure of all our difficulties and all our infirmities, not as a benevolent spectator, but as one who Himself has taken part in all, as one, in short, who has *Himself suffered being tempted;* it is the remembrance of Him, and of His personal interest in our victory over each particular temptation, which often leads him who would else have despaired, to rise yet once more and renew the conflict; this which, more than anything else, touches that softer chord within, which is also the most powerful, the chord of grateful love responsive to that love which loved first. I know, my brethren, that no mere sentiment will ever be found strong enough to resist actual temptation. A man may discourse beautifully, and at times feel tenderly, as to the self-sacrificing and ever sympathizing love of Christ, and yet fall as soon as the tempter comes to him, and yet even live in sin, and yet even have his portion with the unbelievers. I know that nothing but the presence of the living and life-giving Spirit of God within can communicate that practical strength of soul and of life, which is needed *to withstand in the evil day, and having done all, to stand* (Eph. vi. 13). But I am speaking, as my subject leads me to do, of Christ personally as the strength of the tempted. And I say that in the influences exerted by the Holy Spirit upon the will of man, amongst the motives by which He, Spirit acting upon spirit, affects the mind and regulates the conduct and moulds the life, there is none so powerful as the thought of the minute and tender sympathy of Christ Himself with tempted men, a sympathy learned by suffering, a sympathy acquired by having been first tempted.

I hope that the subject on which we have dwelt to-night may be your meditation, your comfort, your help, through the coming week. I wish to say two words before I close my Sermon.

i. The first is, Do not confuse the two things, temptation and sin. It is no sin to be tempted. Christ Himself was led up by the Holy Spirit Himself into the wilderness to be tempted of the devil. And yet He *knew no sin* (2 Cor. v. 21). *In all points tempted like as we are, yet without sin* (Heb. iv. 15). Sin begins, not where temptation begins, but where temptation too often ends; with the yielding to it. In parleying with temptation there is sin: we have no strength to spare; we cannot afford to trifle with temptation, it is a very serious thing, and it is stronger far than we: still more, in going, as it were, to seek for temptation, in going by choice where we know it will assail us, in this there is sin; all the sin, and more than all the sin, of yielding to temptation: but I say again, in being tempted, if it stop there, if we overcome in Christ's strength, there is no sin: Christ Himself was tempted. Some have been grievously injured by confusing the two different things, temptation and sin. From the very fact of a temptation they have inferred that they were out of God's favour: hope has failed them at the outset, and they fell for lack of hoping.

ii. The last word is this. If you would have Christ for your strength when you are tempted, you must not wait to seek Him till temptation comes. You must live in Him always. When temptation comes upon one who is walking carelessly, he has no heart, no will, no desire, to have Christ for his strength in resisting it. It is too late then. The citadel is undefended: of course it will not hold out. O let Christ be in the fortress already when Satan comes! Then you will be safe. Then the desire for Him will be there too. Then, before you call, He will answer. If He waited for the call, you would fall first. *My brethren, be strong in the Lord, and in the power of His might* (Eph. vi. 10). *Put on* beforehand *the whole armour of God, that ye may be able to stand against the wiles of the devil. Your life is hid with Christ in God* (Col. iii. 3).

SERMON IX.

ST PAUL TO PHILEMON.

EPISTLE TO PHILEMON.

1 PAUL, *a prisoner of Christ Jesus*, and Timotheus the
2 brother, *to Philemon the beloved and our fellow-labourer, and
to the beloved Appia, and to Archippus our fellow-soldier,*
3 *and to the congregation at thy house: Grace to you and*
4 *peace from God our Father and the Lord Jesus Christ. I
thank my God always making mention of thee in my pray-*
5 *ers, hearing of thy love and faith which thou hast towards*
6 *the Lord Jesus and unto all the saints, that the communion
of thy faith might become active in the further knowledge*
7 *of every good thing that is in us unto Christ Jesus. For
we have much blessing*[1] *and encouragement on* [*the ground
of*] *thy love, because the hearts of the saints have been re-*
8 *freshed through thee, brother. Wherefore, having much*
9 *confidence in Christ to enjoin upon thee that which is becoming, because of that love I rather beseech; being such as*
10 *Paul*[2] *an old man and now also a prisoner of Christ Jesus:
I beseech thee concerning my child, whom I begat in my*
11 *bonds, Onesimus, who was once profitless to thee, but now*
12 *to thee and to me of good profit; whom I send back: and do*
13 *thou* [*receive*[3]] *him, that is, my own heart*[4]*: whom I was
wishing to retain with myself, that in thy behalf he may*
14 *minister to me in the bonds of the Gospel; but apart from
thy opinion I was unwilling to do anything, that thy good*

---

[1] Or, according to the received text, *joy.*

[2] *In my personal character, and with reference to my present age and circumstances, rather than in virtue of my apostolical authority.*

[3] The construction is broken by intervening clauses, and the verb must here be anticipated from verse 17.

[4] *Dear to me as my own self.*

may not be as if by necessity but by free will. For per- 15
haps for this cause he was parted for a season, that thou
mayest possess him for ever, no longer as a slave, but beyond 16
a slave, a beloved brother, most greatly to me, but how much
more to thee both in flesh and in the Lord. If then 17
thou hast [in] me a partner, take him to thee as myself.
And if he wronged thee or oweth anything, charge this to 18
me. I Paul write it with my hand, I will repay it: not 19
to say to thee that thou owest besides to me even thyself.
Yes, brother, may I have profit of thee in the Lord: 20
refresh my heart in Christ. Confiding in thy obedience I 21
write to thee, knowing that even beyond what I say thou wilt
do. And at the same time prepare me also hospitality: for 22
I hope that through your prayers I shall be granted to you.
Epaphras saluteth thee, my fellow-prisoner in Christ Jesus, 23
Marcus, Aristarchus, Demas, Lucas, my fellow-labourers. 24
The grace of our Lord Jesus Christ be with your spirit. 25

SERMON IX.[1]

ST PAUL TO PHILEMON.

PHILEMON 15.

For perhaps he therefore departed for a season, that thou shouldest receive him for ever.

I HAVE sometimes thought that it might be interesting to a Christian congregation, and that it might turn to the glory of God in unfolding some of the less obvious treasures of His Word, to direct their attention occasionally to one of the very briefest of the Epistles of the New Testament; to one of those Epistles, whether of St Paul, St John, or St Jude, which are comprised each in a single chapter, and which yet, within those narrow limits, bear a glorious testimony to the Gospel in its doctrine and in its practice, in its effects alike upon the mind, the heart, and the soul, of them that believe.

[1] Sermons IX. and XI. were a departure from the course proposed in Sermon I. But I have not thought this a sufficient reason for omitting them here.

In this hope, and with humble prayer for God's blessing, I would ask you to turn this morning to the Epistle of St Paul to Philemon. A brief remark upon the occasion of the letter will be followed by a paraphrase of the letter itself, and that, in its due order, by a few remarks of a practical kind upon the letter as a whole.

The writer of the letter before us, as of all those on which we have before commented, is the great Apostle St Paul. The period of his life with which we are now concerned is one later than the last record of it contained in the Acts. That Book leaves him a prisoner at Rome: dwelling, for two whole years, in a hired lodging, under the charge of a soldier that kept him; not debarred from the sight of persons desiring his counsel or teaching, but in a condition justifying the constant description of himself as a prisoner, and to terminate only in a trial, of which the issue was, humanly speaking, most precarious.

To this period of his life belong the Epistles to the Ephesians, to the Philippians, and to the Colossians. Between the first and the last mentioned of these three Epistles there exists, as every reader must remark, a very strong resemblance. The topics are to a great extent the same, and even the phraseology. The chief difference, beyond that of greater or less amplification of doctrine, lies in this; that the Epistle to the Ephesians appears to have been designed as a circular letter to several of the congregations of Asia Minor, and is almost wholly destitute (in consequence,

L

we may suppose, of that intention) of personal allusions; while the Epistle to the Colossians has a very distinct reference to the circumstances of that particular Church, and contains many messages to and from individual persons there or with the writer.

Along with the Epistle to the Church of Colossæ there was despatched one of a more private character to a resident in that town. Philemon, known only in this one connection, and whose place of abode would have been left in uncertainty but for a single point of contact between this Epistle and that to the Colossians, was a person of sufficient position amongst the Christians of his city to have his house selected as their place of meetings for worship. *The church in thy house.* It appears that a slave of his household, Onesimus by name, had secretly left his service, and made his escape eventually to Rome. There, by one of those chances, as men speak, which God who ordereth all things both in heaven and earth is ever turning to an important account in human life, he was brought to hear and to listen to St Paul's teaching. He became a convert to Christ. *My son Onesimus, whom I have begotten in my bonds.* The effect of this conversion was, as it ever has been and ever will be, a change of life; and, as a prelude to this, the frank confession, to his new teacher, of the circumstances of the past, and an unqualified submission to the will of God as to his conduct in the future.

There was that in the character of Onesimus which appears to have strongly attracted the regard of the imprisoned Apostle. He would gladly have retained him in his company at a time when his Christian society was reduced within very narrow limits. But a stronger sense of duty forbad. There was a debt first to be discharged to Christian morality. Onesimus was not his own master. By the laws of the world as then constituted, he was the property of another. He was the slave of Philemon of Colossæ. And, before he could with a clear conscience attach himself to the company even of an Apostle, he must return to his master and obtain a just discharge.

Whether at Colossæ itself, or on some casual absence elsewhere, Philemon himself, as Onesimus now, had been the convert of St Paul. There existed between the master (as well as the slave) and the Apostle that strong tie, of an inestimable benefit received and conferred, which ensured a ready hearing for any remonstrance or for any intercession. St Paul availed himself of this argument in the present instance. He sent back Onesimus to Colossæ; sent him in company with Tychicus, the bearer of his Epistle to the Colossian congregation: but he sent by him also a separate letter to his master, which, under God's superintending Providence, has become for all time one of the heirlooms, not of a single family or a single congregation, but of the universal Church of Christ. Listen now to the letter itself, with a few words of necessary amplification.

Paul, a prisoner of Christ Jesus, and Timotheus the (our) brother, to Philemon the beloved friend *and our fellow-labourer, and to the beloved Appia, and to Archippus our fellow-soldier, and to the congregation at thy house.* Appia may be supposed to have been the wife of Philemon: Archippus, possibly, his son or near kinsman, but at all events a minister of the Colossian Church; as we read in the Epistle to the Colossians, *And say to Archippus, Take heed to the ministry which thou receivedst in the Lord, that thou fulfil it* (Col. iv. 17). The congregation at Colossæ met in the house of Philemon, just as that of Laodicea, for example, in the house of Nymphas, or that of Ephesus at one time, and that of Rome at another, in the house of Aquila and Priscilla (Rom. xvi. 5. 1 Cor. xvi. 19. Col. iv. 15).

Grace to you, and peace, from God our Father, and from the Lord Jesus Christ. What a Gospel is contained in that brief, that commonest form of Apostolical greeting! What a confident reference to existing relations between us and God, between us and Christ, and what a fulness of satisfaction in the blessings assured to us in that relation!

I thank my God always in *making mention of thee in my prayers.* The salutation was for all: now Philemon is addressed alone. *Hearing* as I do *of thy love and faith which thou hast towards the Lord Jesus, and unto all the saints;* all those who have upon them the mark of the Christian consecration; all who have been dedicated to God through Christ on the confession of a true faith. And now what is the object of that thankful prayer which St Paul is always offering for him? *That the communion of thy faith,* that fellowship with others which belongs to thy faith, *might become active*, operative, energetic, *in the further*, the increased and progressive, *knowledge of every good thing that is in* (or *among*) *us* Christians *unto* the glory of *Christ Jesus*. The prayer is, that his Christian fellowship may be made more and more practically vigorous, as alone it can be, by his entering with a deeper and fuller knowledge into the realities of God's gifts to us in Christ. Take a single parallel expression from the second Epistle of St Peter. *To those who have obtained like precious faith with us:* there is the first thing here expressed, *the communion of thy faith:* then, *Grace and peace be multiplied unto you in the further knowledge of God and of Jesus our Lord, according as His Divine power hath given to us all things that pertain to life and godliness through the further knowledge of Him who called us by His own glory and virtue; whereby*, by which glory and virtue of His, *He hath given to us all those precious and vast promises, that by means of these ye might become partakers of a Divine nature, having fled away from the corruption that is in the world through lust* (2 Pet. i. 1—4): there is the remainder of the text before us; the possession of the faith *becoming effective by the increased knowledge of every good thing that is in us*. My brethren, if we would *grow in grace*, it must be by growing in *the knowledge of our Lord and Saviour Jesus Christ* (2 Pet. iii. 18). But remember what alone is knowledge, in God's sense of the word; a knowledge, not of abstract truths, but of a living Person, of whom all that we really know must be known also from Him, with Him, and in Him.

For we have much blessing (or *joy*) *and encouragement on* the ground of *thy love, because the hearts of the saints have been refreshed through thee, brother. Wherefore,* knowing what thy Christian love is, *having* (though I have) *much confidence in Christ*, as Christ's Apostle, *to enjoin upon thee that which is becoming*, yet *because of that love* of thine *I rather beseech; being such as Paul an old man*—in my personal character, as a man full of years—*and now also a prisoner of Christ Jesus.* I, who might well command, beseech. And for whom? on what subject?

I beseech thee concerning my child (an expression often applied by St Paul to his converts), *whom I begat in my bonds, Onesimus, who was once profitless to thee, but now to thee and to me of good profit; whom I send back* with this letter. *And do thou* receive *him, that is, my own heart,* one dear to me as my own self; *whom I was wishing to retain with myself, that in thy behalf*—even as thou wouldest have done, if present— *he may minister to me in the bonds of the Gospel,* in my imprisonment for the Gospel's sake. *But apart from thy opinion*, without thy consent, *I was unwilling to do anything* in this matter, *that thy good*, thy benefit to me in allowing me to keep him, *may not be as if by necessity (compulsion) but by free will.* Well may the choice be given thee: he is now not less but more than ever thine: *for perhaps for this cause*, under

God's overruling hand, *he was parted* from thee *for a season, that thou mayest possess him for ever; no longer as a slave, but beyond a slave, a beloved brother, most greatly,* in a very high degree, *to me, but how much more to thee both in flesh and in the Lord,* both in a natural and in a spiritual relation. *If then thou hast* in *me a partner,* if there is any fellowship between me and thee, *take him to thee as myself,* as if he were I myself. *And if* in former times *he wronged thee or oweth* thee *anything, charge this to me. I Paul write it with my hand, I will repay it; not to say to thee that thou owest besides to me even thyself:* that is, this promise may suffice thee, without my reminding thee that, even were I to leave the debt undischarged, it would be rather a debt from thee than to thee, when thou rememberest that thou owest to me, under God, something far above money, even thine own self, even every hope and every comfort of a Christian. *Yes, brother, may I have profit of thee in the Lord;* may I have the comfort of finding in thee all that a Christian should be: *refresh my heart in Christ.*

Confiding in thy obedience, I write to thee; knowing that, even beyond what I say, thou wilt do. And at the same time prepare me also hospitality; prepare to receive me as thy guest: *for I hope that through your prayers,* the prayers of you all, *I shall be granted to you,* my life will be spared, and I shall be released from my imprisonment.

Epaphras saluteth thee, my fellow-prisoner in Christ

Jesus, Marcus, Aristarchus, Demas, Lucas, my fellow-labourers. A brief but pregnant record; reminding us, by the mention of Marcus, that *the last shall sometimes be first* (Matt. xix. 30); that he who once departed from St Paul and deserted the work is here again with him, faithful, and *a comfort unto him* (Acts xiii. 13. xv. 38. Col. iv. 11); and by the mention of Demas, that *the first shall* sometimes *be last;* that he who is now, in St Paul's first imprisonment, his fellow-labourer and comforter, shall be spoken of in his second imprisonment as having then forsaken him because he *loved this present world* (2 Tim. iv. 10). *Let him* amongst us *that thinketh he standeth take heed lest he fall* (1 Cor. x. 12).

The grace, the favour and blessing, *of our Lord Jesus Christ be with your spirit.*

And now I would gather into very small compass a few obvious reflections upon this brief Epistle.

1. Observe the naturalness and the consistency of the Scriptures. It is an old topic, and I will spend few words upon it. But just notice, in passing, how confidently we have spoken of Philemon as a Colossian. Is he so described here? Is there one syllable in this Epistle, taken by itself, as to his home or birthplace? Not one. The letter was sent by a private hand, and needed no such superscription. And yet the inference can be drawn, not less certainly than simply. Archippus, who is here described as residing with or close to Philemon, is saluted in another Epistle as being a Colossian. And, as

Onesimus is here described solely in his relation to the person of Philemon, so elsewhere, in the Epistle to the Colossians, he is distinctly said to belong to that place: *All my state shall Tychicus declare unto you...whom I have sent unto you for the same purpose...with Onesimus, a faithful and beloved brother, who is one of you* (Col. iv. 7). The observation of these points of close yet perfectly inartificial concidence between different books of Scripture adds much to the interest of their study, and has its due place, though it be a subordinate one, amongst the proofs of their Divine origin.

2. How large a testimony does this brief Epistle bear to the essential doctrines of the Gospel! Suppose that this one short chapter were all that had come down to us from the first days of Christianity. I do not say that we should not have been losers beyond all calculation by the loss of other and more copious inspired writings. But should we not have possessed something, even in this one letter, to aid us in the ascertainment of evangelical and apostolical doctrine? God our Father: and our Lord Jesus Christ associated with Him in the communication of gifts to man: and those gifts what? grace and peace; free favour, and spiritual repose and tranquillity in the sense of it: faith in Christ the starting-point of all progress; knowledge the means of progress; and love to Christ and to Christ's redeemed the effect and the aim of all. Yes, my brethren, with these few verses alone in our posses-

sion, we should not have been destitute, we should scarcely have been poor, in Christian knowledge or in the materials of Christian life.

3. . But still more strongly may I ask you, in the third place, to notice, what a beautiful exhibition we have in this Epistle of that which in every age has been the distinctively Christian character. Do look closely at the indication of mind and feeling here given. Do reflect upon the grace of God as here shown forth in the mature character of an individual man; a man who was once, as he himself tells us, with reference at least to Christ and His servants, *a blasphemer, and a persecutor, and injurious* (1 Tim. i. 13). What a combination of opposite qualities is here revealed to us in one person! Dignity, and humility. *I might be much bold in Christ to enjoin thee that which is convenient...I do not say to thee how thou owest unto me even thine own self besides.* There is no masking of real claims to respect and gratitude. There is no degradation or disparagement of the holy office which was entrusted to him. He was an Apostle of Christ, and, as such, he had a right to speak, yes, a right to dictate. Yet, on the other hand, how graceful too, how becoming, the humility with which he would by preference take a lower ground; would beseech rather than enjoin; would bring forward, if possible, only that which was most persuasive, most attractive, and keep in the background, if it could be done without neglect of duty, all that was

merely authoritative, official, and imperative. *For love's sake I rather beseech thee, being such an one as Paul the aged, and now also a prisoner of Jesus Christ...If thou count me a partner, receive him as myself...Yea, brother, let me have joy of thee in the Lord.* There is no touch of weakness in all this. There is no necessary connection between tenderness and feebleness. The greatest strength of man—for may we not say, the greatest strength of Him who is God as well as man?—is shown, not in command, but in sympathy. *We have not an High Priest who cannot be touched with the feeling of our infirmities, but was in all points tempted like as we are, yet without sin* (Heb. iv. 15).

4. This, however, might be said of St Paul's character, wherever it is presented to us in his writings. But I would notice here, more especially, in the fourth place, an illustration of the manner in which St Paul, and St Paul's Master, brought the Gospel to bear upon the defective or corrupt parts of the mass of human society. Onesimus, for whom this letter was written, was a slave. He had run away from his master. Some modern philanthropists would have applied Christianity to the case in this manner. They would have said, Slavery is unjust; slavery is against the will of God; slavery is an infraction of the original law of man: therefore let every slave quit his master at once, if he can; therefore, if any slave has succeeded in running away from his master, shelter

him, foster him, recognize his freedom at once, and at once break the chain which he has shaken off. My brethren, you will not suppose that I am either advocating the rights of the slaveholder, or palliating in the slightest degree the sinfulness of a slave-system. But I am concerned—the Epistle before us requires it of me—in showing you that the Apostles, and their Divine Master and Inspirer, did not deal with matters of this sort in detail, but in principle; not in individual cases, the only effect of which would have been, as it always has been, to aggravate for the many what was lightened for the one, but rather by the infusion of a new principle of life into the dead and putrefying mass of fallen humanity; a principle which would certainly work, though slowly and secretly, and would eventually do safely and surely what the haste of an inconsiderate zeal would have done partially and imperfectly because prematurely and because superficially. St Paul sent the slave Onesimus back to the slave-master Philemon. St Paul never said to the individual slave, Quit your master; nor even to the individual master, Liberate your slave. To the one he said, *Slaves, be obedient to them that are your masters according to the flesh, with fear and trembling, in singleness of your heart, as unto Christ* (Eph. vi. 5). To the other, *Masters, give unto your slaves that which is just and equal; knowing that ye also have a Master in heaven* (Col. iv. 1). The abolition of slavery followed in due course upon the reception of Christianity: but it was with the system of slavery, and not with the individual case, that Christianity waged its warfare; and even that, only when it had first succeeded in so penetrating society with its own deepest principles, that the original equality of all men in the sight of each other became the natural consequence of the original equality of all men in the sight of God. Till then, an Apostle would himself restore to a master his fugitive slave, though the master, like the slave, was a Christian, and though the Apostle *might have been bold in Christ to enjoin him that which was convenient.*

I have yet two remarks to add.

5. The Epistle before us is a model of Christian correspondence. It is not below the dignity of this place, because it is not alien to the daily life of Christian men and Christian women, to speak of an occupation which in these days fills up no small part of the brief span of human existence. Have we ever reflected upon what letters may be, or may not be, for good or for evil? St Paul is here writing a letter to a friend, on what we might call by comparison an every-day topic. He is urging a request, and supporting it with the earnestness of a very real man, upon a subject affecting another and (humanly speaking) a very insignificant person. Now I ask no one to write a letter, or to attempt to write one, in the phraseology of St Paul or of any other inspired writer. Phrases imported even from Scripture into modern letters seldom fit in naturally;

seldom give that impression of heart-to-heart simplicity, which is the first condition of persuasiveness. But, on the other hand, I am quite sure that great opportunities of usefulness are daily lost by our neglect of this engine. People write so hastily, so impulsively, with so slight a sense of responsibility, and, I must say, with so little desire to do good, that it is not to be wondered at if little good is thus done, or if letters come to be regarded only as necessary evils, lying altogether out of the reach of the inspired direction, *Whatsoever ye do, in word or deed, do all in the name of the Lord Jesus* (Col. iii. 17). I call attention to the subject, being convinced that a want of attention to it is more than half the fault. Which of us cannot testify that he has been more struck, and more influenced for good, by a few letters than by many books? There are still a few persons in the world—perhaps (God grant it) just one or two for each of us—who evidently write their very commonest letters under the constant guidance of a sound judgment, a Christian principle, and a religious as well as loving motive. These are things which make themselves felt. As we read such letters, we are reproved or comforted, quickened or sobered, but in every case insensibly influenced, according to our own present need. Not elaborate, not studied, not dictatorial, not hortatory, perfectly natural and perfectly level to common life, they yet affect us in a mode peculiar to themselves; a mode altogether different both from words and from books, yet a mode which the Holy Spirit Himself has vouchsafed to consecrate, and for the use of which every one of us is deeply and seriously responsible.

6. Finally, the Epistle before us is an example of the way in which God has been sometimes pleased to bless a condition of obscurity. It was St Paul's imprisonment which gave to the Church the most touching and soothing of all his letters. Those to the Ephesians, to the Philippians, to the Colossians, the second to Timothy, not to mention the one now before us, were all written from a prison. Perhaps he little knew at the time what was in store for these works of his seclusion. But God foresaw it all. God saw that in thus laying His servant aside, and giving him what he might have been tempted to call useless years, He was providing for the everlasting good of ten thousand times ten thousand souls. He judges not as we judge, and measures not as we measure. Great and small, with reference to earthly things, are terms unknown in heaven. Happy he who is in God's hand. Happy he who devotes to Him what he has, and looks to Him to prosper and to use it. In this sense, and perhaps (on earth) in this sense only, both rich and poor, both sick and well, both high and low, may rejoice together.

SERMON X.

CHRIST IN HIS WORD.

GOSPEL FOR THE THIRD SUNDAY IN LENT.

St. Luke XI. 14—28.

14 *Jesus was casting out an evil spirit; and it was dumb: and it came to pass, when the evil spirit was gone out, the*
15 *dumb man spoke: and the multitudes marvelled. But some of them said, Through Beelzebub the ruler of the evil spirits*
16 *He casteth out the evil spirits. And others, making trial of*
17 *Him, sought from Him a sign out of heaven. But He, knowing their thoughts, said to them, Every kingdom divided against itself is desolated; and a house divided against a*
18 *house falleth. And if Satan also was divided against himself, how shall his kingdom be established? because ye say*
19 *that through Beelzebub I cast out the evil spirits. And if I through Beelzebub cast out the evil spirits, through whom do your sons cast them out? Therefore they shall be your*
20 *judges. But if through the finger of God I cast out the evil*
21 *spirits, then is the kingdom of God come upon you. When the strong man fully armed guards his palace, in peace are*
22 *his possessions: but when the stronger than he hath come upon him and conquered him, he taketh away his full*
23 *armour in which he trusted, and divideth his spoils. He that is not with me is against me, and he that gathereth not*
24 *with me scattereth. When the unclean spirit hath gone out from the man, it passeth through desert places, seeking rest; and, not finding it, saith, I will return into my house from*
25 *whence I came out; and, when it cometh, it findeth the house*
26 *swept and arranged. Then it goeth, and taketh to it seven other spirits more wicked than itself, and they come and dwell there, and the last things of that man prove worse than*
27 *the first. And it came to pass, as He spake these things, a certain woman from among the multitude lifted up her voice and said to Him, Blessed is the womb that bare Thee, and*
28 *the breast which Thou didst suck. But He said, Nay rather, blessed are they who hear the word of God and keep it.*

SERMON X.

CHRIST IN HIS WORD.

St. Luke xi. 28.

But He said, Yea rather, blessed are they that hear the word of God, and keep it.

I HAVE chosen a large subject for this evening: *Christ in His Word.* The Gospel for the day suggests it, in the clause just read to you. It may be that some hearts will welcome it. For I know that there is nothing which lies more heavily on the consciences of many Christians, than their slowness of heart to enjoy and to use their Saviour's Word. It is familiar to them; in one sense, too familiar. But, though familiar, it is not dear to them as it ought to be. It does not *dwell in them richly in all wisdom* (Col. iii. 16).

What can I say on such a subject? Let us humbly meditate together, on this His day, in this His house, on the Word of Christ as a whole; holding, as it were, the Book reverently in our hands, and weighing it; gathering into one view all the separate things that we have before learned of its contents, and speaking to one another of what we have ourselves found it to be, or have even heard of it from others; in the language whether of thankfulness, or of self-condemnation, or of awakening curiosity; praying to Him whose word it is, to give us His own help hereafter in the use of it.

I shall make no attempt at arrangement to-night. I would rather throw out, almost as they occur to me, a few leading hints as to the chief characteristics of Christ's Word, whether spoken by Himself or by His Apostles after Him; in the hope that they may find an echo in your hearts, and may bring forth fruit in the inner life of every one of us.

1. Christ speaks, then, first, as it was remarked when He was upon earth by those who listened to Him, *with authority* (Matt. vii. 29). There are many things that we look for in a teacher: some of these we shall speak of presently. But there is one thing which we cannot dispense with: he must speak, if he is to do us any good, as one who has a right to speak; as one who knows that which he speaks of, and knows that it is thus and not otherwise. In a sense beyond that in which any man could be said to do so upon any subject, Christ taught, Christ teaches us still, with authority. He said of Himself to Nicodemus, *Verily, verily, I say unto thee, we speak that we do know, and testify that we have seen* (John iii. 11). There is no guessing and no supposing, no vacillation and no vagueness, in the words of Christ. When He tells

us of God's will, of His requirements or of His purposes, we feel that He is not only *a teacher come from God* (John iii. 2)—though that is a great thing—but that even upon earth He was still present with God, and God with Him; according to those words of apparent but not real contradiction, *No man hath ascended up to heaven, but He that came down from heaven, even the Son of Man which is in heaven* (John iii. 13). That oft-repeated preface, *Verily, verily, I say unto you*, ought ever to sound in our ears—I think it commonly does so—when we read the words of Christ. He who speaks knows what He says, and says it always with authority.

2. There is another point: Christ speaks *with insight*. We feel that He knows us. *He knew all men, and needed not that any should testify of man; for He knew what was in man* (John ii. 24). Many teachers, even Christian teachers, do not give us this feeling. Their instructions sound unreal. They make us out, in their descriptions, to be, not so much worse, and not so much better, than we are: that is not exactly the point: but other than we are. If they would paint to us the very worst of real human characters, we should not complain of it: all of us who know anything of our hearts know that there is in them the germ at least, the· possibility at least, if not the actual experience, of every fault, of every sin: in the blackest representation of real human character we could find some points of profitable warning for ourselves. And if they would paint to

us the very best of real human characters; if they would hold up before us the real inner life of the greatest of saints, of the most devoted of martyrs; we would not quarrel with them: little as we may know of such heights of goodness, still we know that there is in us that little germ at least of good desire, of heavenly aspiration, which God's grace might by possibility foster into great attainments in His service; and in the portraiture of the perfect man in Christ we might see something to encourage us, as well as much to condemn us. But Christian instruction (so called) often misses the mark of reality altogether. And then it is that we may turn back to our Bibles with so strong a sense of relief. There all is real. If the disclosures there made of human wickedness and of Divine judgment are sometimes appalling, still we know that they do but unveil human nature as it is, and warn us lest we, being partakers of that same human nature, should suffer it to run to the same excess of sin and of misery. And if, on the other hand, the exhibitions of human nature in its possible exaltation seem often far above out of our reach, yet these too, being all true and real, serve rather to humble, to quicken, and to stimulate, than to dazzle, to confuse, or to discourage us. Christ teaches with insight. He knows us well, for He made us, and He became man. He knows us in our weaknesses, He knows us in our difficulties, He knows us in our sorrows, He knows us in our temptations. And, as He knows, so He teaches. He charges us with nothing but what is true, and He calls us to nothing but what is possible.

3. I will add that He teaches *with conviction*. I know that it is very easy to evade conviction. We may refuse to read; or we may so read as to answer the same object more effectually. One who does not read his Bible has an uneasy sense of sin in that neglect: the closed Book itself convinces of sin. But one who reads his Bible as many read it, as all of us probably have, at some time or other of our lives, read it, can combine two things in his reading; he can lull his conscience by the idea of a duty done, and yet keep every arrow of conviction away from his reading. We must always remember that, in everything said of Christ's teaching, there is presupposed a learner; one who comes to be taught, and that, not as a form, but with a purpose. O, my brethren, where is that purpose in many of us? We all think how sad it was, and how wrong, that any one should listen to Christ Himself, when He was upon earth, with indifference, or prejudice, or perverseness, or scorn: but is it not more sad, and more wrong, that we should any of us do so in our hearts now; we who do profess to know what He is, and to be concerned in the salvation which he bought for us with His own blood? I am sure it is the case that to many of us the Bible, even Christ's own words in it, carry practically no conviction. Alas, how is it? Because there is not in us a willing, a desiring mind; that mind of which He spoke Himself when He said, *He that is of*

God heareth God's words: ye therefore hear them not, because ye are not of God (John. viii. 47). It is a very responsible thing to be taught of Christ.

4. Again, Christ teaches *with variety*, and teaches *with abundance.* Some springs are soon dry. It is so with all merely human teaching. Every man has his topic; has his favourite doctrine; has his special case in view; has, at best, his strong point or two in dealing with human consciences. When you have heard him a few times, you are in his secret; you see the skill, or the weakness, as it may be, and you know how he will treat almost any given subject. The stream is shallow; you can touch the bottom. But it is not so with the teaching of Jesus Christ. His words are various. There is not a case, not a kind of case, in human character or in human life, which He has not a medicine for. Is it carelessness? Is it worldliness? Is it the love of applause? Is it hypocrisy? Is it presumption? Is it a bosom sin? Or is it (to change the point of view) sickness? Is it sorrow? Is it want? Is it persecution? Is it loneliness? Is it an accusing conscience? Is it a fear of the wrath to come? You all know that for every one of these circumstances, and for every other circumstance that human experience can suggest, there is some word of suitable warning or counsel to be found in Christ's Gospel; some word which goes to the very root of the evil, and deals with it in a manner at once appropriate and thorough. There is this in our Lord's teaching, which makes it both these things; that

every special instruction runs up into that which is the very highest of all; every special comfort has beneath it the one groundwork of all comfort, namely, the free forgiveness, the eternal love, of God, the assurance of His will that none should perish, that all should be saved, that all should be brought to holiness here and to happiness hereafter. Therefore there is no sense of straitness, of narrowness, of circumscription, in any one of Christ's special words: His counsels are not like those of the friend who has certain circumstances in view, and counsels with regard to these; how to avoid this difficulty, or to remedy that inconvenience; but leaves you at last uncertain how many other uncontemplated contingencies there may be behind, to be met as they arise, or perhaps not to be met at all. Christ counsels for the present, with an exact adaptation of His wisdom to the particular exigency of to-day; but, in so doing, He takes into view also the boundless interests which as yet we cannot comprehend, and in comforting for to-day saves for eternity.

5. It is another remarkable point in Christ's words, that He teaches *by principles*, and teaches *by illustration.*

We must all have remarked that the Bible is not a book of rules. There is no index to it. We cannot turn to a particular page which tells us exactly what we are to do in this or that peculiar position. As a guide to duty, the Bible is of little use to one who turns to it only in emergencies. It is vocal only to its friends. Any man, blessed be God, may become its friend: but I mean that a man who habitually neglects Christ's Word must not expect to find it a lamp to his feet the first time that he is in darkness. The wisdom of Christ is shown in nothing more than in this, that He teaches in course, and not by single lessons. His instruction is a process of gradual initiation into mysteries hidden from the earthly-minded and from the sin-bound. He teaches by taking men aside, day by day, to tell them His secrets. He teaches by communing with us; by letting us into His methods of procedure, into His principles of judgment, whether of things or persons, into His estimate of the relative importance of this and that, of the present and the future, the earthly and the heavenly. This instruction takes time: it takes a lifetime. This instruction precedes rather than follows the emergency to which it is to be applied. It consists in so moulding the will, the judgment, the affections, in so disciplining the faith of men, that, when trial comes, they may understand its meaning; that, when difficulty arises as to the path of duty, or a heavy demand is made upon our patience or our submissiveness or our hopefulness, we may need but a more urgent and a more intense application to One with whom we are already acquainted, to enable us to withstand in the evil day, and at last, having done all, to be found standing, stricken perhaps with the storm but not uprooted, because the Word of Christ was dwelling in us beforehand, and we had only to call it to mind, to apply, and to use it.

Christ teaches by principles and not by formal rules. He teaches by a gradual assimilation of our judgments and feelings on all points to His own. A man cannot supersede, by a special and sudden recourse to his Bible on an emergency, that continued and patient study of it which another has pursued through days and years of ordinary and unmarked life. Let him indeed turn to it at any time; let that sudden turning to it be the beginning of a new life to him; but let him not complain, let him not be disappointed, if the Bible be not all at once to him guiding and comforting, if he has to pass, as others have done, to that stage of Christian experience through another less bright and bringing a less immediate recompense.

But I added that Christ teaches by illustration. No doubt the Bible contains many direct precepts; exhortations to certain specified duties, warnings against certain definite sins. But by far the largest part of the Bible is occupied by a different mode of teaching. We are left to learn how we ought to act, by having the actions of others, with their consequences, detailed to us. Lives of the good, lives of the sinful; the troubles of the one, the judgments of the other, the motives, principles, and end of both; fill, to a great extent, the pages of God's Holy Word. If we are ever tempted to complain of this, yet let us see and feel the wisdom of it. It is in action that a man is seen. That is the real proof of his motives and of his principles. Most important is it that we should be again and again reminded of the hollowness of a faith that will not work, of the deceptiveness of a comfort that does not prompt to duty. Nor indeed could the workings of Christian principle be made intelligible to us by general or even by minute precept. We must know what life ought to be for us, by being shown what life has been to others like us. Above all, let us recognize the wisdom of that kind of teaching which consists in setting before us one perfect example. In the life and death of Christ lies the sum of all the teaching of Christ. In *leaving us an example, that we might follow His steps* (1 Pet. ii. 21), He left us that which alone could perfectly guide us in the way in which we should go; that way which an Apostle has briefly described in these words, *that I may know Him, and the power of His resurrection, and the fellowship of His sufferings, being made conformable unto His death; if by any means I might attain unto the resurrection of the dead* (Phil. iii. 10).

6. Once more, let me speak to you of the *tenderness*, and of the *holiness* of Christ's teaching.

I know indeed that there is an aspect of severity in it. Christ is not tender in His teaching, even as He is not tender in His judgments, towards that which is evil in us, nor towards those of us, if there be any, who are determinately choosing that evil. But towards the weak, towards the ignorant, towards the suffering, towards the tempted, towards sinners, yes, the very chief of sinners, when they truly pray to Him for mercy, He is most tender. To them He says indeed, *My yoke*, the yoke of my service, *is easy: my burden*, the burden of my commandments, *is light* (Matt. xi. 30). There is one way, in particular, in which the Scriptures illustrate to us the tenderness of His teaching: its gradual character. *With many such parables spake He the word unto them, as they were able to hear it... and when they were alone, He expounded all things to His disciples* (Mark iv. 33). He does not present to us, all at once and in one view, the whole of His instruction, and bid us fulfil it all or turn away. You remember how, when it was said to Him, *Why do the disciples of John and of the Pharisees fast, but Thy disciples fast not* (Mark ii. 18)? He replied by another question; *Can the children of the bride-chamber fast, while the bridegroom is with them?... but the days will come when the bridegroom shall be taken away from them, and then shall they fast in those days.* Do we not see that saying mercifully fulfilled now in each generation of human life? Is it not still the case that Christ, by that Providence which is as much His as the kingdom of grace is His, adapts His yoke to the strength of those who are to bear it; sanctioning the cheerfulness of childhood and youth, and those interludes of calm and sunshine which occur now and then in the roughest and stormiest life, as one part of His own loving discipline, just as much as the sadness, the anxiety, or the anguish, by which in later years He finally fits the soul for its great and solemn change? And more than this: is it not also true, that the very same portion of His Divine Word will convey either a lower or a higher lesson in His school according to the experience and proficiency of His disciple? A passage which in the earlier days of a Christian's life seemed to be satisfied by one sort of obedience to it, will suggest perhaps at a later stage a more difficult, or what would once have been a more difficult, duty, and He who tempers His treatment to the condition of those who are its subjects has in this case, we cannot doubt, as in that mentioned in the Gospel, spoken His word to each *as they were able to hear it*, addressing Himself to the elementary learner as in a parable, and then, in the solitude of an individual communion, *expounding all things* to a more experienced disciple. His object is to attract, not to terrify; and while He deals truly with all, He deals also wisely with each; keeping ever in view the great object, that He may at last *present each faultless before the presence of His glory with exceeding joy* (Jude 24).

I have spoken of the tenderness of Christ's teaching: I must add óne word upon its holiness also. My brethren, I suppose there is no feeling which is more instinctively present to us in opening the Bible, than that we are in a holy atmosphere. It is this which makes us shrink from the Bible so long as we do not wish to be holy; so long as there is anything in us on which we do not intend to let God's light shine. But when, by His great mercy in preventing or else in chastising, we have learned anything really as to the bitterness and wretchedness of sin; when we have truly felt that not only *is this the will of God, even our sanctification* (1 Thess. iv. 3), but that in that will is our one hope of present and ultimate happiness; then the holiness of Christ's teaching becomes, not repulsive to us, but most attractive; then we feel, not only that this is the feature which most distinctly proves its heavenly origin, but that it is also the one in which we most long to resemble it; and that it is something, in a world of so much corruption, and with a heart so largely partaking of it, to be permitted, in one place at least, in the study of one book at least, to breathe for the time a purer air, to dwell for the time in the very presence of the Holy One, and to come forth from it refreshed and invigorated for a renewed conflict, within and without, with evil.

I deeply feel, my brethren, that there is, in any such attempt to enumerate some of the characteristics of Christ's teaching, a dryness and a hardness most uncongenial to that teaching itself. But there may be, under God's blessing, some use in an occasional survey, rather as from without than from within, of the great blessing which He has given us in His Son's teaching. If it should lead any one of us to a more earnest and constant study of his Bible, it will not have been thrown away. If it reminds any one of us that what he is to look for, in his use of Christ's words, is, not sudden but gradual illumination, not express direction for a particular case of doubt, but rather the information of his conscience and the regulation of his heart so that he shall be able, under the teaching of the Holy Spirit, to judge rightly for himself when the special occasion arises; if it should impress upon any mind in this congregation the affecting sentence read as the text of my sermon, in which our Lord, in answer to a natural but ignorant remark as to the blessedness of one who had held to Him a near earthly relation, turned the thought into a truer and a more practical channel by saying, *Yea rather, blessed are they that hear*, as all may hear, *the word of God, and keep it;* we shall have no cause to regret the time spent in listening to the words now spoken, however small a part of the great subject may have been touched upon, or however cold and feeble the language in which it has been embodied.

But O, my brethren, let us all lay to heart these two concluding words.

i. *The word of Christ* must never be dissociated in our thoughts from *Christ the Word.* The Bible itself will profit us nothing, unless we not only read it as from Christ, but also read it in Christ; read it as those who belong to Him, as those whom He has taken for His own redeemed and for His own disciples and servants, and whose life, and hope, and Saviour, and Lord, He Himself is.

ii. Lastly, the word of Christ can only really act upon us through the Spirit of Christ. *If any man have not the Spirit of Christ, he is none of His* (Rom.

viii. 9). And in each particular instance, whether of learning or of acting, it is the Holy Spirit within who can alone make the one profitable or the other consistent. Whenever the Holy Spirit is honoured, Christ is honoured. Whenever the Holy Spirit is left out of our thoughts, in public or in private, Christ is forgotten. *Through Christ we both have access by one Spirit unto the Father* (Eph. ii. 18). *Built upon the foundation of the Apostles and Prophets, Jesus Christ Himself being the chief corner stone: in whom all the building, fitly framed together, groweth unto an holy temple in the Lord: in whom ye also are builded together for an habitation of God through the Spirit* (Ibid. 20—22).

SERMON XI.

THE ELDER TO THE ELECT LADY.

THE SECOND EPISTLE OF ST JOHN.

1 THE elder to an elect lady and her children, whom I love in truth; and not I only, but also all who know the truth;
2 because of the truth which abides in us, and [which] shall be
3 with us for ever. There shall be with you grace, mercy, peace, from God the Father, and from Jesus Christ the Son
4 of the Father, in truth and love. I rejoiced greatly, because I have found [some] of thy children walking in truth,
5 even as we received commandment from the Father. And now I beseech thee, lady, not as writing thee a new commandment, but that which we had from the beginning, that we
6 love one another. And this is the love, that we walk according to His commandments. This is the commandment, even as ye heard from the beginning, that ye walk in it.
7 Because many deceivers went out into the world, who confess not Jesus Christ coming in flesh: this is the deceiver and
8 the antichrist. Look to yourselves, that ye lose not the things which ye wrought, but that ye may receive a full
9 reward. Every one who goes forward, and abides not in the teaching of Christ, has not God: whosoever abides in that
10 teaching, he has both the Son and the Father. If any one comes to you, and brings not this teaching, receive him not
11 into a house, and bid him not welcome: for he who bids
12 him welcome partakes in his evil works. Though I might write many things to you, I did not wish [to do so] by means of paper and ink: but I hope to come to you, and to talk
13 face to face[1], that our joy may be fulfilled. The children of thine elect sister greet thee.

[1] Literally, *mouth to mouth*.

SERMON XI.

THE ELDER TO THE ELECT LADY.

2 JOHN 8.

Look to yourselves, that we lose not those things which we have wrought, but that we receive a full reward.

I BROUGHT before you last Sunday morning a brief and private letter from St Paul to one of his converts. I desired to realize to you the idea of one of these Apostolical writings as it first came from the pen of its author. I desired, if I might so express it, to translate an Epistle into a letter; to get rid of its more formal aspect, and to present it in its more natural and original character; hoping thus to assist you, if it were but in the slightest degree, in reading the various portions of the Word of God with greater intelligence and greater interest, as at once Divine and human; human, in reference to the circumstances and mind of the writer; Divine, in reference to the Providence which occasioned, and to the inspiration which breathed in each.

To-day I have selected with the same view one of the similar writings of another Apostle; the second Epistle of St John. I shall enter into none of those questions, as to the author, and as to the person to whom it was addressed, which are at all times more ingenious than profitable, and which, here certainly, would be entirely out of place. We can quite understand that an Epistle so brief, and containing so little apparently of new matter, might have been longer in winning its way to general use, or even general acceptance, in the Church, than one of the obviously commanding importance which attaches to St John's first Epistle. And yet, none the less, when time had been given, first for wider circulation, and then for closer examination and enquiry, it may have taken its place amongst the true treasures of the Church of Christ, as the genuine work of an Apostle's hand, a genuine expression of the mind of that Divine Spirit which illuminated, pervaded, and guided, for the benefit of the Church, each one of those on whom Jesus after His Resurrection had *breathed, saying, Receive ye the Holy Ghost* (John xx. 22).

The elder, then, *to an elect lady and her children.* It is in the manner of St John to speak of himself otherwise than by name. In his Gospel, when he has occasion to speak of himself, it is as *the disciple whom Jesus loved* (John xix. 26. xx. 2. xxi. 7, 20); *that other disciple* (John xviii. 16. xx. 3, 4, 8); *the disciple which testifieth of these things and wrote these things* (John xxi. 24). In his first Epistle there is no mention of the name of the writer. Here he describes himself as *the elder;* just as St Peter, in his first Epistle, says, *The elders which are among you I exhort, who am also an elder, and a witness of the sufferings of Christ* (1 Pet. v. 1). It was a lower title than his highest of all; but, in a mixed sense, as denoting partly his actual age, and partly his general ministerial character, by no means inappropriate even to an Apostle, and carrying with it a peculiar force, of humility and of tenderness, which perhaps no other title could have conveyed.

The elder to an elect (chosen, or *Christian) lady and her children. An elect lady.* Either of the two terms which I have thus rendered has been taken by some persons as a proper name. But I have already said that I should not dwell on a point so doubtful—I might almost add, so trifling. Nor shall I allude further to another interpretation, which makes the expression denote, not a person, but a Church or Congregation. After many such discussions, we shall return, I think, in the end, and with a sense of great satisfaction, to the familiar words, associated, I can well believe, in some of your minds, with the evening services of the last days of the year, *The elder to an elect lady and her children, whom I love in truth; and not I only, but also all who know the truth.* The eminent character of the person addressed was a matter, St John says, of general and thankful recognition amongst the Christian communities of the time. *Because of the truth which abides in us, and* which *shall be with us for ever.* The ground of Christian love is the common possession of Christian truth. Christian love is not mere benevolence. It is not a merely natural feeling of good will towards all men. It is founded on something; something certain and something definite. And that something is *the truth;* Christ, who calls Himself the Truth; and the revelation of Christ, which embodies that truth. That truth, St John adds, is a permanent possession. *It will be with us for ever.* Death itself will not rob us of it. Therefore is it that Christian love, or charity, also is indestructible. It is founded upon a rock. *There shall be with you*—and the prediction is a prayer also—*grace,* spontaneous favour; *mercy,* kindness to the undeserving and the lost; *peace,* comfort and repose of mind in the sense of that mercy; *from God the Father, and from Jesus Christ the Son of the Father, in truth and love.* The last words may remind us of those in the opening of St John's Gospel; *grace and truth came by Jesus Christ* (John i. 17): the gifts of God in Christ to those who believe are all given *in truth;* that is, in reality, and without vacillation or pretence; *and in love,* as their source and spring.

And now we reach the subject of the letter. *I rejoiced greatly, because I have found* some *of thy children walking in truth, according as we received commandment from the Father.* It is a letter of congratulation to a Christian parent on the consistent conduct of some of her children who had lately come under the observation of the Apostle. Let us, he says, exchange an affectionate congratulation on such a cause of rejoicing. And let it call forth and increase in us a spirit of genuine love. *And now I beseech thee, lady, not as* if I were *writing thee a new commandment, but* only *that which we had from the beginning,* from the very days when Christ was amongst us on earth, *that we love one another.* And this love is not a matter of feeling only. Nor is it a thing by itself. It is a practical love of which I speak; and it is only another side, as it were, of the love of God. *And this is the love* spoken of, *that we walk according to His commandments,* the commands of the Father. And what are these? Nothing new. *This is the commandment, even as ye heard from the beginning, that ye walk in it,* in the original command. Not a new command, I say; and yet the necessity of attention to it is not on that account the less urgent. There is great cause for it. *Because many deceivers went out,* are gone forth, *into the world, who confess not Jesus Christ coming in flesh;* persons who deny the real Incarnation of Jesus Christ; persons who deny the simple Humanity of Christ, and talk of Him (as different schools of false doctrine did in those days) as a mere emanation, perhaps, from the Divinity; or else as having only seemed to do and to suffer, to be born and to die; thus, in either case, losing all hold upon plain tangible realities, and wandering into ideal and fantastic regions in which there is no resting-place for mind or heart or soul. Such were some of the early corruptions of the simplicity of the faith. *This*, St John says, *is the deceiver and the antichrist.* This doctrine, which would rob us of the human nature of Christ; and with it of His sacrifice, and of His sympathy, and of His union with man; and with it of all sense of truthfulness and simplicity and reality in God's dealings with us for our redemption and salvation; is indeed, by comparison with every other form of error, worthy to be called *the* deceiver of man, and *the* enemy of Christ.

And yet, he adds, however grievous, however fatal, this form of error has an attractive side. *Look* therefore *to yourselves*—to thyself and thine—*that ye may not lose the things which ye* once *wrought, but that ye may receive a full reward.* Do not forfeit, by turning aside now, the fruits of former service. *Every one who goes forward;* that is, every one who, instead of resting within the limits of the truth, professes to advance beyond and to improve upon it; every one who thus errs, *and abides not in the teaching of Christ, has not God: whosoever abides in that teaching, he has both the Son and the Father.* To part with Christ, the true Christ, Christ as He is revealed to us in simplicity, is to part with God. Do not suppose that you can err, for example, about the true nature of your Saviour, and yet retain your God: it is only through Christ that you can come to God: it is in Christ that God is made known to you: therefore, if you lose Christ, you lose God also, and, if you retain Christ, you retain also the Father with Him.

And therefore you are called to decision, to plain speaking and downright acting, on a point so vital. *If any one comes to you, and brings not this true teaching, receive him not into a house, and bid him not welcome: for he who bids him welcome partakes in his evil works.* Be quite sure that doctrine will always react upon conduct. A man who is teaching a visionary, a delusive, a false Christ, is sinning as much against Christian practice as against Christian truth. Therefore take heed lest in admitting him to your company you be drawn on to imitate, as you certainly will be encouraging, an unchristian and a sinful life.

Though I might write many things to you, I did not wish to do so *by means of paper and ink: but I hope to come to you, and to talk face to face, that our joy may be fulfilled;* that we may enjoy to the full the happiness of a Christian converse. *The children of thy elect* (that is, *chosen*, or *Christian*) *sister greet thee.*

Some of the more general remarks which I might have wished to make upon this Epistle were anticipated last Sunday. But the Word of God, even in its smallest and least marked portions, is a living spring of thought and counsel: we shall not be the poorer to-day for our use of it yesterday.

1. Remark, in passing, first of all, that this letter is addressed to a Christian woman.

In Christ Jesus, St Paul said, *there is neither male nor female* (Gal. iii. 28). Men and women alike share in the help and hope of the Gospel. What pains did Christ Himself take, upon earth, to show that this was His purpose! He disdained not to be found by His disciples *talking with a woman* (John iv. 27); bringing her to the knowledge of herself, and so to the knowledge of Him. Some of His most consolatory words on earth, some of His most wonderful acts on earth, were addressed to, or done for, women. Upon the Cross, His last earthly thought was for a woman: *Behold thy mother* (John xix. 27). And although the ordinary language of a Congregation, whether as addressed by its Minister, or in its own addresses to God, must necessarily be, in outward form, suggestive of the idea of a congregation of men, yet it is wisely ordered that one portion of the daily service should be borrowed from the words of a woman—*He hath regarded the lowliness of His handmaiden* (Luke i. 48); and that that which is always implied should thus sometimes be expressed, that a Christian woman is as honourable in the sight of God as a Christian man; her wants, no less than his, cared for; her anxieties shared, her sorrows borne, her sins forgiven, her services accepted, by the common Creator and Redeemer and Sanctifier of the whole race of man.

2. Again, we learn from this letter what vital error is.

We have often had occasion to remark how great a readiness there is in our days to make men offenders for a word. It adds much to the difficulties of a Christian teacher, that he has to be so constantly on his guard against perverse as well as reasonable misapprehensions of his statements of doctrine. And I fear that it sometimes tempts a man to repeat with a wearisome exactness what may be called the stereotyped form (on certain subjects) of theological precision, instead of infusing a new life into them by drawing afresh, with however careful a hand, from the well-spring of his own deep feeling and experience. God forbid that we should any of us be indifferent to the accuracy, as well as the force, of our enunciations of His truth! But I cannot refrain from turning sometimes with relief to those tests of true and false doctrine which are furnished to us in the inspired Word itself. With one, if one, exception, how far less fearful are the deviations from what we believe to be the true doctrine, amongst persons calling themselves Christians in our days, than they were in the days of the Apostle whose words are now before us! Differences about Church discipline, about the proper age for Baptism, about the amount of blessing to be looked for in the Sacrament of the Lord's Supper, about the lawfulness or the duty of confessing sins to human advisers; how small do such questions appear when we place them side by side with that kind of error to which St John applies the language of condemnation here! Both here and elsewhere he gives this as the test of true or false doctrine in its highest sense, *Every spirit that confesseth that Jesus Christ is come in the flesh, is of God; and every spirit that confesseth not that Jesus Christ is come in the flesh, is not of God…Hereby know we the spirit of truth and the spirit of error* (1 John iv. 2). My brethren, we may be a little more charitable than we are, without any risk of injury to the cause of truth. Those whom we condemn have not yet reached the point of denying or doubting the proper Humanity, no, nor the true Divinity, of our Lord and Saviour Jesus Christ. Within those limits, let us not be indifferent, but let us not be cruel. Let us hold fast that which is true, but let us also hope something with regard to persons who on minor points may be in error.

3. Not wholly unconnected with this is another remark suggested by this second Epistle of St John, as to the simplicity of the Christian life. *This is love, that we walk after His commandments: this is the commandment, that, as ye heard from the beginning, ye should walk in it.*

My brethren, some of us are always on the lookout for new commandments; fancying that, unless they do this or that, they cannot be Christians; distracting themselves with questions of difficult duty, or inventing for themselves novel and untried methods of service. St John's advice is very different. He says to us, You all know what is right. Love to God, and love to man, these are the old commandments, and these also are the new commandments: there are none other. O, if there were such a heart in you, as to desire to know God's will that you might do it, be assured that His will is very near you; nothing abstruse, nothing intricate, nothing (with His help) so very difficult; only that you love Him with all your heart, and for His sake love all men also. O, my brethren, when we go astray, it is not through the difficulty, but rather through the very simplicity, of God's commands. We think there must be something more, something beyond, something kept back: we do not go forward with a trusting heart into the little trivial duties of the day's life, but are rather looking this way and that to see who will bid us *do some great thing* (2 Kings v. 13); something which shall be all heavenly, all for God; and missing meanwhile that real presence, which is ever with him that is of a humble spirit, willing to *abide with God in the* very *calling*, whatever it be, *wherein he was called* to be a Christian (1 Cor. vii. 24). *Surely the Lord is in this place, and I knew it not...This,* the common home, *this,* the trivial duty, *this is none other than the house of God and this is the gate of heaven* (Gen. xxviii. 16).

4. There is a fourth point suggested throughout the Epistle, and more especially by the verse read as the text: the constant danger of drawing back. *Look to yourselves, that we lose not the things which we have wrought, but that we receive a full reward.*

Look to yourselves: there is danger then. *Those things which we have wrought;* that is, the exertions of past days and years in the Christian life. *That we lose not* these: then if we turn away, or turn aside, from Christ at last, all that has gone before will be vitiated and destroyed. It is just as Ezekiel said of old, *When the righteous turneth away from his righteousness, and committeth iniquity...all his righteousness that he hath done shall not be mentioned; in his trespass that he hath trespassed, and in his sin that he hath sinned, in them shall he die* (Ezek. xviii. 24). And it is as St Paul wrote too to the Galatians, *Have ye suffered so many things in vain? if it be yet in vain* (Gal. iii. 4). Did ye undergo *affliction or persecution* once *for the Word's sake*, and are ye now *offended?* (Mark iv. 17). *But that ye receive a full reward.* I know not that the hope of a reward, in the common sense of that term, exercises much influence upon Christian minds. We think rather, and must think, of safety. If we can only have our *life given* us *for a prey* (Jerem. xlv. 5); if we can only be *saved*, though it be as *through fire* (1 Cor. iii. 15); it is all that we care about, for ourselves. Still we know that the figure of a reward, as that of a prize, of a crown, of a throne, of commendation and praise, of authority and dominion, is used in the Scriptures with reference to the awards of the great day. And, taking all these in their very simplest and most certain sense, as promises of admission into full communion with God Himself, into the sight of Christ, into the comfort and joy of a rest found, of a haven won, of dangers for ever escaped, of unspeakable happiness finally attained, there is no one who can be insensible to the force of the appeal, that we take care not to forfeit the past, that we take care not to miss the full recompence of the reward.

And how anxiously does St John here press upon

us the peril of doing so! O how easy it is to become weary of well doing! How easy to be daunted by the discovery, made ever more and more, of the corruption within, which has to be mortified, transformed, eradicated! How discouraging is the opposition, the coldness, and still more (in these days) the deadening acquiescence, of those who surround us, of our friends, of our own household! How tempting, oftentimes, the offer of the world, if we will only cast in our lot with it, of ease, of honour, of advancement, of fame! Still more, how insidious are the snares spread for us by the tempter within; the *little cloud, like a man's hand* (1 Kings xviii. 44), *arising out of the sea* of human nature in some unexpected and unsuspected quarter, and destined, before we are aware, to overwhelm the whole heart with a perfect tempest of sinful passion! These causes, and a thousand others, will explain the anxiety of the holy Apostle; the earnest caution to be ever looking well to ourselves, lest by going back from Christ after walking with Him, we should lose even those things which have been wrought for Him, and miss the attainment of our full reward.

5. I add a fifth and last observation upon the Epistle before us: that it shows us what Christ Himself is in the Christian scheme. *He that abideth not in the teaching of Christ hath not God: he that abideth in that teaching hath both the Son and the Father.*

To many of us, my brethren, I greatly fear that Christ is not thus the sum of Christianity. It is only in dark days that we turn to Him as being Himself the Gospel. It is only when the sense of sin lies very heavy upon us, that the Lamb of God who takes away the sin of the world stands out before us as the head and the front, the first and midst and last, of all God's revelations. At other times, beyond a general trust in God's mercy through Christ, a correct doctrine of the Atonement, and some reverence for His great example, we live on from day to day much as we should have done if Christ had never come in the flesh, had never died and never risen. My brethren, this ought not so to be. This was not so in the first days of the Church; the days of St Paul, the days of St John. Then, though He was no more upon earth than He is now, yet Christ was a living Person to His disciples, and to be a Christian was to love Him. Then *to live* was *Christ* (Phil. i. 21). Then to live was to *live by faith in the Son of God who loved*, not the world only, but each one himself; loved him, *and gave Himself for* him (Gal. ii. 20). Then to be faithful was to *abide in Him* (1 John ii. 28). Then to die was *to depart and to be with Christ*—known and felt to be *far better* than to live here away from Him (Phil. i. 23). *Whether we live, we live unto the Lord; and whether we die, we die unto the Lord: whether we live therefore or die, we are the Lord's. For to this end Christ both died and rose and revived, that He might be Lord both of the dead and living* (Rom. xiv. 8, 9).

SERMON XII.

THE EFFICACY OF THE BLOOD OF CHRIST.

EPISTLE FOR THE FIFTH SUNDAY IN LENT.

HEBREWS IX. 11—15.

11 BUT *Christ, having arrived, a High Priest of the future good things; through the greater and more perfect tabernacle, not made with hands, that is, not of this creation;*
12 *nor through blood of goats and bullocks, but through His own blood; entered once for all into the holy place, having obtained*
13 *an eternal ransoming. For if the blood of goats and bulls, and ashes of a heifer sprinkling those who have been defiled,*
14 *hallows with a view to the purity of the flesh; how much more shall the blood of Christ, who through an Eternal Spirit offered Himself faultless unto God, purify our conscience from dead works that we may serve a living God?*
15 *And for this cause He is the Mediator of a new dispensation, that, a death having taken place unto redemption of the transgressions which related to the first dispensation, they that have been called may receive the promise of the eternal inheritance.*

SERMON XII.[1]

THE EFFICACY OF THE BLOOD OF CHRIST.

HEBREWS IX. 14.

How much more shall the blood of Christ, who through the eternal Spirit offered Himself without spot to God, purge your conscience from dead works to serve the living God?

I CANNOT turn aside from that deeply instructive passage of the Word of God which is selected as the Epistle for this day. Rather would I bespeak for it your closest attention, the attention at once of the mind and of the heart—for without both these it must remain a hidden secret—while I endeavour humbly and patiently to unfold to you its meaning, and to draw from it those lessons of truth which it is so directly calculated to convey.

We shall have no time to bestow upon the context of the passage, or upon the general objects of the Epistle from which it is taken. I may say, in a few words, that the Epistle to the Hebrews was written in the near prospect of that last crisis by which the

[1] A collection was made after this Sermon for the Scripture Readers' Society.

Old Dispensation was brought, in God's Providence, to a compulsory close. Jerusalem was about to be *trodden down of the Gentiles*, as it was written (Luke xxi. 24). Ordinances of local worship which would otherwise have continued in force, to distract and to mislead the children of the New Covenant, were to be shattered and destroyed by the stroke of Him who established them. And now, when that event happened, what would be the feelings of the Christian Israelite? Would he recognize, as he ought to do, the proper and orderly withdrawal of the shadow because the substance was come? Would he say to himself, The material temple is gone, but the spiritual temple remains to me? Would he say to himself, The priesthood of Aaron is abolished, but the priesthood of Melchisedec shall stand fast for ever? Would he say to himself, The sacrifices of a typical expiation are no more offered, but there is one sacrifice, once offered, the efficacy of which is indestructible and eternal? If he could not say these things, and say them with a clear conviction and a confident hope, there was every reason to fear lest, in that last struggle of expiring Judaism, he should be found casting in his lot with the enemies of Christ, resisting alike the work of God's Providence and the express prediction of the Divine Master, who said, when He was called upon to observe the beauty of the Temple and its surrounding adornments, *When ye shall see the abomination of desolation, spoken of by Daniel the prophet, stand in the holy place . . . then let them which be in Judea*, not join the standard of a false and fatal patriotism, but rather recognize in the sign before them the fulfilment of the declared purpose of God, and *flee into the mountains* (Matt. xxiv. 16), where they may hide themselves for a little season until the storm of that vengeance be overpast.

Now it was to answer this purpose that the Epistle to the Hebrews appears to have been written. It consists of a series of contrasts between what the Mosaic Law had of comfort and of glory, and what the Gospel offered in its stead. In each case Christ is presented on the one side, and on the other the exalted persons or the magnificent institutions connected with the history or ritual of the Levitical dispensation. Christ, and the Angels amidst whose agencies on Mount Sinai the Law was promulgated; Christ, and Moses the lawgiver and mediator of that covenant; Christ, and the Aaronic priesthood; Christ, and the Mosaic tabernacle; Christ, and the Levitical sacrifices; such are some of the subdivisions of that great argument by which it is sought to establish the faith of the Christian Israelite in the superior, the incomparable value of that which he has over that which he loses, of that which is the possession of the faithful, over that which was, but no longer can be, the possession of the despiser or the apostate.

The point at which the passage now before us is introduced is that at which the Mosaic Tabernacle has been brought into view, with its accurate and significant distribution of parts, and equipment of each part with its proper apparatus of service. One peculiar institution has been referred to—that of the great day of Expiation or Atonement. On one day, and on one day only throughout the whole year, the High Priest alone was permitted to penetrate within the veil which hung between the two parts of the Tabernacle, carrying with him the blood of slain victims, which he sprinkled before the mercy-seat in the most holy place, in typical atonement for the sins of the people and for his own. Now let the Hebrew Christian reflect for a moment on that which the Gospel offers to him in place of this solemn and mysterious rite. Was he asked to forego that comforting hope which must have glimmered, to a thoughtful and pious mind, in this annual service of a so-called expiation? Listen to that reality, of which the other was but a shadowy emblem.

The High Priest went once a year within the veil, indicating quite as much of exclusion as of admission; an exclusion for all but himself, and even for himself through all the year save one single day; for the rest of the year, and for all but himself, a rigid, a discouraging, an all but hopeless prohibition.

But now *Christ, having arrived,* having appeared, having entered, as it were, on the scene—His whole work is summed up in one single act of manifestation; for it is the completed work, not the Incarnation alone, and not the Sacrifice alone, that we are here to take into view—*Christ, having arrived, a High Priest,* not of typical and representative rites, but *of the future good things;* introducing and realizing to us those spiritual and eternal blessings to which the Levitical law could only darkly point as afterwards to be revealed; *through the greater and more perfect tabernacle,* one *not,* like the Mosaic tabernacle, *made with hands, that is, not of (belonging to) this* visible *creation; nor through (by means of) blood of goats and bullocks,* like that which the High Priest had to carry with him on the day of Expiation as his passport into God's presence; *but through (by means of) His own blood; entered once for all,* not, like the other, with an annual repetition of the act, *into the holy place, having obtained an eternal ransoming;* not a temporary expiation, and even that but ceremonial and external, like the Mosaic atonement which has been described, but a liberation real, spiritual, and enduring, yea enduring for ever, in behalf of all that believe.

I call your attention for a moment, before we pass on, to the expression, *through the greater and more perfect tabernacle.* It depends upon the word *entered* below. Christ entered into the Most Holy Place, that is, into the very presence of God Himself, *through the tabernacle;* through what is called in an earlier verse *the first tabernacle,* the Holy Place, by distinction from the second or innermost tabernacle, the Holy of Holies. Just as the High Priest had to pass through the outer division of the Tabernacle before he penetrated within the veil on the great day of Expiation, so Christ *passed through the heavens* (according to the correct rendering of the passage to which I refer, Heb. iv. 14) into the highest heaven of all, in which God dwells. And this outer heaven, if we might so express it, is described as *greater and more perfect* than the earthly tabernacle, as *not made with hands* like it, as *not belonging to this creation*, that is, to that part of the created universe which belongs to man, or of which the human senses can take account.

Through (by means of) His own blood. The blood poured out is, as elsewhere, the emblem of death. It is in virtue of His death, as the final and completive act of His life-long sacrifice, that Christ enters the presence of God for us. It was His perfected sacrifice which gave Him redemption for us.

And lastly, the word *redemption* or *ransoming;* deliverance by the payment of a ransom; including the three ideas, of a previous captivity, the interposition of a price or valuable consideration, and the consequent liberation of the prisoner; is one of the most significant, as it is also one of the most frequent, of all the figures by which the work of Christ, and its effect, is designated for our instruction. Let us all sometimes ask ourselves whether, as we believe in the ransom paid, so also we are personally delivered by its interposition from that chain of sin and self from which, if it is to avail anything, the sacrifice of Christ must set us free!

For if the blood of goats and bulls, and ashes of a heifer sprinkling those who have been defiled— according to the direction of the Levitical law for the removal of pollution arising out of contact with a grave or a dead body—*hallows with a view to the purity of the flesh,* removes defilement so far as it is external and ceremonial; if, in other words, the blood or the ashes of an animal could by God's appointment have a certain value assigned to them in reference to the removal of an outward impediment to a person's joining in His outward worship; *how much more* —it is an argument *à fortiori,* as we call it: if an animal's blood could have any value at all in relation to religious matters even of an external kind, *how much more* shall that which has an intrinsic, an inestimable worth, avail for its purpose, the cleansing of a soul—*how much more shall the blood of Christ, who through an Eternal Spirit offered Himself faultless unto God, purify our conscience from dead works that we may serve a living God?*

Through an Eternal Spirit. It is scarcely needful to say that the Person thus designated is the Holy Ghost. If the Greek idiom in such a phrase omits the definite article, it is for the purpose of laying stress upon the quality rather than the substance; in this case, for the sake of giving emphasis to the attribute *Eternal.* The same remark applies to the last clause of the verse, *that we may serve a living God;* that is, One whose characteristic attribute it is to have life in Himself. This is one remark.

Again, as to the connection of the words *through an Eternal Spirit* with the statement that Christ *offered Himself faultless unto God.* We are introduced here into the very heart of that mystery of mysteries, the humiliation of the Lord Jesus Christ in taking upon Himself man's nature, and, in that nature, *becoming obedient even unto death*. It was of the essence of that *self-emptying* of which St Paul speaks in a passage just referred to (Phil. ii. 7, 8), that the Divine Son laid aside the exercise of the powers and prerogatives of the Godhead, and submitted to take upon Him a perfect Manhood; not only a body capable of suffering, and liable to all the accidents of mortal being, but a human soul also, endowed with the faculties, susceptible of the feelings, and exposed to all the temptations of mankind; and into that perfect Humanity condescended to receive the all-pervading presence of the Holy Ghost, for the informing, enabling, elevating, and strengthening of His life, in all its exercises of spiritual communion, and in all the various efforts, trials, and sufferings of His ministry and sojourn below. In the condescension of that marvellous self-sacrifice, it was the Eternal Spirit who made His life perfect, and the offering up of that life on the Cross *faultless* in the sight of God. *Jesus being full of the Holy Ghost returned from Jordan, and was led by the Spirit into the wilderness ... Jesus returned in the power of the Spirit into Galilee ... The Spirit of the Lord is upon me, because He hath anointed me* (Luke iv. 1, 14, 18). *God giveth not the Spirit by measure unto Him* (John iii. 34). *How God anointed Jesus of Nazareth with the Holy Ghost and with power* (Acts x. 38). On the

Cross itself was the obedience perfected, when Christ through the same Spirit offered Himself a faultless offering.

Again, *the blood of Christ shall purify our conscience from dead works.* Dead works are the opposite of living works. They are the works which have no Divine life in them. They are the acts of one who, having separated himself from God, either wholly or in the particular instance, cannot please Him, and whose best works, while he is so, *have the nature of sin* (Art. xiii). And these dead works are represented as lying upon the conscience, dragging it down and defiling it, so that there is no freedom in the life within, no conscious and peaceful intercourse between the soul and God, no strength for service because no release from guilt. For such a state the remedy here mentioned is the only medicine. *The blood of Christ shall purify our conscience from dead works to serve*—and the expression indicates the nature of that service; the service of a priest, dedicating his life, and every act of that life, to Him whose he is—*to serve a living God.* Believe that Christ died for thee; believe that by that death He put away sin, even thy sin; and in the strength of that faith dismiss the irrevocable past, and turn to the available future; by one act, or by repeated acts, of self-dedication to God, take up the priestly office, whosoever thou art, however humble, however sinful, and exercise that office in the discharge, as unto God, of all the various functions of thy common calling. *To whom coming*, even to our Lord Jesus Christ, *ye also* (addressing all Christians) *are built up a spiritual house, an holy priesthood, to offer up spiritual sacrifices, acceptable to God by Jesus Christ* (1 Pet. ii. 4).

And for this cause, because He has thus died for us, and because His death is of such everlasting efficacy, *He is the Mediator of a new dispensation, that, a death having taken place, unto redemption*, for removal by a ransom, *of the transgressions which related to the first dispensation, they that have been called*, they to whom the call and invitation of the Gospel has come, *may receive the promise of the eternal inheritance*.

The term here rendered in our Version *testament*, and elsewhere (as by many persons here also) *covenant*, properly denotes an arrangement or disposal, as of property, whether by deed in the lifetime of the disposer, or by will at his death. In the passage which follows, we can scarcely doubt that the latter notion, that of a testamentary disposition, is at least partly involved. The same word in the original language having the two senses, and those senses running very naturally into each other, it is not surprising that there should be a less clear line of demarcation between them in a particular passage than would have been entirely satisfactory in our own language. The word *dispensation* appears to express, more nearly than any other, that which is the fundamental thought in the Scriptural use of the word everywhere; namely, a disposition or arrangement of God's spiritual blessings to man according to certain terms, whether those, for example, of the Law of Moses, or those of the Gospel.

When we read that the death of Christ took place *for the redemption of transgressions relating to the first dispensation*, we are not to suppose that it was not also designed for the remission of sins committed under the second or Gospel dispensation. It is rather to be read as though it were, *even* for the redemption of those sins which were committed before it took place, as well as, more obviously, for the redemption of those for the pardon of which it could be pleaded as an accomplished fact.

And lastly, the words, *may receive the promise of eternal inheritance*, mean, may receive the fulfilment of that promise; may actually enter, now by faith, hereafter in possession, into that eternal inheritance which God has promised to them that believe.

Let me then briefly sum up to you the great and deeply important truths contained in this paragraph of the Epistle. This is the substance of it.

I spoke of an earthly tabernacle, minutely as well as divinely ordered, by which the Holy Spirit of God typified certain revelations before they were vouchsafed in their fulness. I reminded you of one imposing rite of the Mosaic dispensation, by which the High Priest entered once a year, and once only, into that innermost shrine of the Tabernacle in which the light of God's presence shone visibly displayed. Let me remind you that that Tabernacle was but a sign of one greater, more perfect, and of no human workmanship. The holy place without the veil was the figure of that lower heaven through which the risen Saviour passed in His Ascension. And the most holy place, that within the mysterious veil, was the figure of that heaven of heavens in which we are taught to conceive of God Himself as in a more especial manner present and enthroned. And the High Priest passing through the veil of the earthly tabernacle once a year, with blood of senseless victims, to be sprinkled by him upon the mercy-seat within, was a figure of the true High Priest of man passing through the heavens on His return into God's presence, there to appear, no longer as the Eternal Son alone, but as the Redeemer of sinners; as though He actually carried there that blood of the cross by which He made peace and gained access for us through one Spirit to the Father. Now, if God was pleased ever to use for any sacred purpose the life-blood of irrational creatures, accepting it in behalf of sinners, as a sign and token of a better sacrifice, and allowing it to restore them, after ceremonial defilement, to a ceremonial purity; judge ye if the blood of the Son of God may not well have a virtue far more powerful, reaching to the very secrets of the human conscience, relieving the sinner from that oppressive sense of defilement which was before inseparable from guilt, and setting him free to run with a brave and loving heart the remainder of the race set before Him. Thus it is that Jesus *becomes, in deed and in truth, the Mediator of a new and a better dispensation; by first dying to put away sin, yea, even the sins of those who never lived at all in the age of His revelation, and then admitting all those to whom His gracious call comes, into the secure possession, if only they be faithful, of an eternal inheritance.*

My brethren, the weighty importance and (in some respects) serious difficulty of the passage brought before us to-day, so appropriate to the near approach of our annual commemoration of the great sacrifice itself, has constrained me to devote more than a usual share of my whole Sermon to the explanation of the words, and less to general comments upon them. But I must not end without a brief enforcement of one or two of the principal thoughts here suggested.

1. *An High Priest of good things to come.* Such is Christ's office as here set before us. What use are we making of Christ's Priesthood? It is the office of a Priest, not only to make one atonement, but to be always at hand for the work of intercession. Whenever any one of us has sinned against God, even in word or in thought only, we have need of the help of our Intercessor. We need that He who entered into the Most Holy Place, as it were, with His own blood, should, by a fresh application of that blood to our special need, remove, over again, the sense of guilt, and enable us to set out yet again in the way of our Christian duty. Does every one in this great congregation make this use of Christ?

2. *Having obtained eternal redemption for us.* We have heard what redemption is: O are we yet, all of us, in the effectual sense redeemed? I know we are in that sense, that primary and most true sense, in which we give thanks to God for His inestimable love in the Redemption of the world by our Lord Jesus Christ. We are redeemed in that sense: the ransom has been given, the price has been paid, for us all; and upon all of us the Redemption itself has been personally sealed in Baptism. But I say again, for well may the Minister of Christ ask this question seriously and even sorrowfully, Are we all, is each one of us, personally redeemed? Are we all set free from sin? Have we all remained from childhood in that *liberty wherewith Christ hath made us free?* (Gal. v. 1.) Or, if not that; if we have been again enthralled by him who has no right over us, by him whom a stronger than he once cast out, but who is ever on the watch to re-enter the inheritance by the first unguarded door; if, I say, we have thus been taken captive; if some portion of life has been passed through in that captivity to self and sin; are we yet delivered again? O let our earnest, solemn, searching enquiry this day be, Am I sinning on with Christ in sight? Am I still trifling? Am I still living for the world? Am I still tied and bound with the chain of any particular sin? For, if I am, then, for me, Christ is as yet *dead in vain* (Gal. ii. 21); I am *crucifying to myself the Son of God afresh, and doing despite to the Spirit of grace* (Heb. vi. 6. x. 29).

3. Yet let me not end here. Let me rather say to each one present to-day in God's House of Prayer, Rise, I beseech you, to the height of your Christian standing, as persons possessing, while your day of grace lasts, everything that can be required to make you safe, to make you happy, to make you holy. Think what it is to have a Divine High Priest. Think what it is to have had the blood of Christ Himself shed for your sins. Think what it is to have a Mediator in the very presence of God for you day and night. Take into account the grandeur of such a position. Consider what a power there is in such knowledge; how it should shame us out of our degradation, out of our worldliness, out of our depression, out of our sinfulness, and rouse us to a spirit of courage, and a spirit of hope, and a spirit of energy, and a spirit of a sound mind. That is what we want; and, behold, it is here; it is in the Volume of God's Revelation; it is in the few verses just read to you; it is in the knowledge of the death of Christ, and of the life of Christ after death as our High Priest and our Mediator as well as our Redeemer.

4 You have not forgotten that a request of a practical kind is made to you to-day; namely, that you will give your effectual aid in carrying this Gospel, with all its merciful and healing consequences, into the homes of the poor, by means of the ministrations, in due order and measure, of lay members of the Christian Church. No one who reads the New Testament can doubt that, as there are functions appro-

priated to the agency of ordained ministers, so there are also offices of private instruction and of active charity in which Christ accepts and will bless the work of any man, of any woman. Do not fear lest any work be entrusted to those for whose support I ask your alms to-day, which would be inconsistent with the strictest interpretation of ecclesiastical order. But you all know well that, in the vast multitude of human beings congregated around us in this enormous city, it is idle to suppose that clerical ministrations alone can meet the demands made upon them in the name of humanity or in the name of God. While we stand by hesitating, discussing questions of propriety, of form or precedent, bodies and souls are perishing, and He who *will have mercy and not sacrifice* (Matt. xii. 7) is loudly summoning us to *do what we can* (Mark xiv. 8). You, my brethren, will cherish no such scruples. You will admit, before it is pressed upon you, the urgency of the necessity; and you will give of your abundance, or, if it be so, of your penury, in aid of any lawful agency by which consciences may be cleansed from dead works, through the blood of Christ, to serve the living God.

SERMON XIII.

THE DISINTERESTEDNESS OF CHRIST.

GOSPEL FOR THE FIFTH SUNDAY IN LENT.

St. John VIII. 46—59.

46 JESUS *said, Which of you convicts me of sin? If I*
47 *speak truth, why do ye not believe me? He that is of God heareth the words of God; on this account ye hear them not,*
48 *because ye are not of God. The Jews answered and said to Him, Say we not well that Thou art a Samaritan and hast*
49 *a devil? Jesus answered, It is not I that have a devil; but*
50 *I honour my Father, and ye dishonour me. But it is not I that seek my glory: there is one that seeketh it and judgeth.*
51 *Verily, verily, I say to you, If any one keep my word, he*
52 *shall not behold death for ever: The Jews said to Him, Now we know that Thou hast a devil. Abraham died, and the prophets; and Thou sayest, If any one keep my word, he*
53 *shall not taste death for ever. Art Thou greater than our father Abraham, who died? and the prophets died: whom*
54 *makest Thou Thyself? Jesus answered, If I glorify myself, my glory is nothing: it is my Father who glorifieth me, of*
55 *whom ye say that He is your God, and know Him not: but I know Him; and, if I should say that I know Him not, I shall be like you, a liar: but I know Him, and keep His*
56 *word. Abraham your father rejoiced to see*[1] *my day, and*

---

[1] Literally, *rejoiced in order that he might see, &c.* The same particle is used, for example, after words expressing *worthy, expedient, to will, need, suffice*, &c., in other passages of this Gospel, where the English idiom requires *to*. *Abraham rejoiced to see beforehand by faith the promised coming of Christ.*

Gospel for the Fifth Sunday in Lent.

he saw it, and was glad. The Jews therefore said unto 57
Him, Fifty years old Thou art not yet, and hast Thou seen
Abraham? Jesus said to them, Verily, verily, I say to you, 58
Before Abraham became[1], *I am. They took up therefore* 59
stones to cast at Him: But Jesus was hidden[2], *and went*
out of the temple.

[1] That is, *came into being, was born.*

[2] So in Chap. xii. 37, *These things said Jesus, and departed, and was hidden from them.*

SERMON XIII.

THE DISINTERESTEDNESS OF CHRIST.

ST. JOHN VIII. 50.

I seek not mine own glory.

THE Gospel for this day, in which the text occurs, is taken from a Chapter of St John's Gospel which stands in somewhat marked contrast with the general tone of that inspired Book. Every one in trouble turns to that Gospel. It is so full of thoughts of peace. Each Chapter of it has its own special passages of deep spiritual comfort. The third, the fourth, the sixth, the tenth, the eleventh, the thirteenth and those which follow it containing the last Discourse, each is associated in our minds with everything that we have ever known, less or greater, of Christian faith and strength; and the whole of this Gospel is the very treasure-house of those revelations which God has sent for the illumination of this dark world with a hope full of immortality.

But the eighth Chapter of this book, like the twenty-third, for example, of St Matthew's Gospel, is for the most part of a different character. There is indeed, at its opening, one short passage which has done as much as any part of Christ's Word for the revival and re-establishment of the sinful and fallen. But the bulk of it contains a record of the severest words which Christ ever uttered. It describes an occasion on which the most perverse, the most insolent, and the most obstinate attack was made upon our Lord, of all those which He endured upon earth from the *contradiction of sinners against Himself* (Heb. xii. 3). In the same degree, perhaps, it is a Chapter which less attracts us. It is not the one which we should fly to for encouragement in depression, or for strenthening in weariness.

And yet, when we look more closely into it, what an amount of grace and of wisdom shines even here! What a manifestation of dignity, of majesty, of self-control, of judgment, of Divine authority and Divine power, is made to us in this Discourse of Christ! I select out of it for consideration this evening the few and simple words of the text, *I seek not mine own glory*. And I propose to you as the subject of this Sermon, *The disinterestedness of Christ*, first as shown in His own teaching and conduct, and next as furnishing an example for our reproof, correction, and guidance.

I seek not, He says, *mine own glory*.

The word *glory* is one of very frequent occurrence in Scripture. To many of us it is a vague and inexpressive sound. *The glory of God—Mine own glory—Manifested forth His glory—Do all to the glory of God*—these expressions convey perhaps to few minds a very definite and explicit meaning. And yet it is a very important expression; the glory of God. Let us try to understand it.

We read often in the Historical Books of the Old Testament, of *the glory of the Lord appearing—appearing in the cloud—resting upon the tabernacle—filling the house of the Lord.* In those days it was a visible sign; a bright light indicating to the senses the more immediate and intended presence of God Himself. But when the day of type and emblem was gone by; when many ages of a more elementary teaching had prepared men's minds, as doubtless they were designed to do, for conceptions of truth less carnal and more spiritual; then the glory of the Lord ceased to denote a bright light from heaven indicating where God was, and began to signify rather the manifestation of God's attributes, whether of power, truth, or love, the revelation of Himself as He is, the showing forth, by act or word, before the minds and souls of men, of His Divine character in some one or more of its real and distinctive features.

To leave this explanation impressed upon your memory, let me refer you to one or two examples of the use of the expression in this Gospel of St John.

The Word was made flesh, and dwelt among us; and we beheld His glory, the glory as of the only-begotten of the Father; full of grace and truth (John i. 14). *We beheld His glory;* that is, we who were permitted to live in constant intercourse with Him during His earthly ministry, saw His Divine character manifested day by day; saw in Him just that disposition, that wisdom, that power, that goodness, which was suitable to the character of the Son of God.

This beginning of miracles did Jesus in Cana of Galilee, and manifested forth His glory; and His disciples believed on Him (John ii. 11). By this first miracle He showed Himself in His true character, as one possessed of the Almighty power of God Himself.

When Jesus heard that, He said, This sickness is not unto death (John. xi. 4), not designed to terminate finally the earthly life of the sufferer, *but for the glory of God, that the Son of God might be glorified thereby.* It is designed to furnish an opportunity of showing forth what God is, and what Christ is, by a miraculous restoration from death. And so at a later point in the same narrative, *Jesus saith unto her*, to the sister of the dead man, *Said I not unto thee, that, if thou wouldest believe, thou shouldest see the glory of God?* (John xi. 40.) What He had said was, *Thy brother shall rise again* (John xi. 23): that resurrection was to manifest God as a God of unlimited, of irresistible power, and exercising that power through His Son Jesus Christ.

Now therefore, when we look back to the words of the text, we shall hear Jesus say, *I seek not mine own glory:* I seek not to show forth upon earth what I am; how great, how wise, how good: that is not my aim: but to show, in all these respects, what God is. Such was the elevation, such the extent, of that which I have endeavoured faintly to describe as the disinterestedness of Christ.

When we speak of disinterestedness, we commonly take a far lower view. We have regard rather to man than to God. We think rather of a voluntary foregoing of some advantage, or else of an unselfish motive in using an advantage, with reference to other men who may be·concerned in our actions. But our Lord's disinterestedness was of a higher order than this. His aim in everything was to show forth God; to make God known to man, in some one, or in all, of His Divine perfections, that so, in the sight of these, the soul might be stirred to go forth, as it were, in quest of Him, to *feel after* till it should *find Him* (Acts xvii. 27) in whom, as a real and living Person, all these perfections dwelt as their home and spring. This it was which guided and animated the whole life of Christ. Every word was spoken with this one object; to make God known as He is. Every act was done, every suffering endured, with this one object; to show what God is, in the power, in the peace, in the majesty, in the love, which, having its source and its key in Him, is communicated also by Him to the soul and to the life which is in union and communion with Himself.

My brethren, there were many qualities in our Lord which, used in a certain way, would have made

Him merely attractive, merely (if the word may be allowed) popular, upon earth. Do we suppose that a Person possessing an unconquerable sweetness of temper, an inexhaustible patience, an indefatigable benevolence, would not win his way to esteem and affection coextensive with the circle in which He was known? Do we think so meanly of human nature in its fallen state as to imagine that it is incapable of responding to kindness, that it is incapable of appreciating excellence, that it is incapable of being won by unswerving goodness? Not only did *the common people hear Him gladly* (Mark xii. 37); not only were the friends of the sick and suffering grateful for His healing hand; not only were the outcasts of human society attracted by a compassion which rather sought them out than merely tolerated their approach; but we cannot doubt that even Scribes and Pharisees, Sadducees and Herodians, would have joined in the tribute of a general applause, but for certain features in that gracious character, by which it was made evident that Christ sought not His own glory, but lived singly and solely for the manifestation of the excellence of Him who sent Him.

The discourse from which the text is taken furnishes us with an example of this drawback to the universal acceptance of Christ. If He had sought His own glory, He would have done as many teachers have done in every age, He would have kept back from His hearers unwelcome truths, or He would have so veiled them, so blunted their edge, so generalized and so neutralized them, as that they might be (it is no imaginary possibility, it is scarcely a difficult art to learn) accepted without offence by the very persons who were the objects of their sharpest sting. Christ showed, wherever He went, whenever He opened His lips, that His one aim was to glorify God; that is, to make God known to His creatures, in truth and power, as that which He is, and as all that which He is. Therefore Christ never flattered. He never used address in securing acceptance for the truth. He adapted it indeed most exactly to the particular case; but in that very adaptation He thought not of what would make it acceptable, but of what would make it appropriate. He discerned indeed, with the justest tenderness, the case which needed the balm of the Divine forgiveness: it was not sin which made Him stern: His words of love and consolation were never wanting because guilt was before Him, no, not if it was the guilt of a life, no, not if it was guilt open and notorious and scandalous, provided there was a pause in it which gave time for the voice of love to be heard, provided there was a sense of it which made the accents of forgiveness sweet and not contemptible. But even in these cases, even where sin had brought forth its bitterest fruits, it was not that He flattered when He spoke in love. Then too, then most of all, was He seeking God's glory; seeking, that is, with a single aim, to make God known as that which, as all which, He is. It is no fiction, it is no accommodation to human conceptions, certainly it is no concession to human example, when Christ tells of the love of God to the fallen. It is the simplest truth, as well as the mightiest and the most transforming.

Nay, it was this very truth which so often gave offence; which rendered His desire to glorify God, by showing Him to man exactly as He is, so inconsistent with His own acceptance amongst a certain class of hearers. The freedom of God's mercy has ever been a topic unpopular with the self-righteous. Having had no experience themselves of its marvellous efficacy, in the cleansing of the conscience and the transforming of the life, they ever treat it as language capable of dangerous perversions, and springing out of enthusiastic notions. That which is life from the dead to those who need it, is a stumbling-block and an offence to those who listen to it from what they falsely deem a higher standing-point.

But, if the proclamation of a free forgiveness was one part of that teaching by which Christ especially sought God's glory, the other side of the same truth was yet more contrary to His acceptance with men. He spoke kindly to sinners: but even that might have been forgiven, if He would have spoken softly and smoothly to hypocrites and self-deceivers. His language to these was that manifestation of God which, more than anything else, showed His entire disinterestedness. Instead of bearing a timid or guarded testimony to these, He spoke boldly and without disguise the most unpalatable of all truths. It was not merely that He described hypocrisy, and warned men against it. It was not merely that He detailed the workings of a subtle self-deceit, and bade His hearers examine themselves lest they be the victims of it. This perhaps is as much as an uninspired and therefore fallible man can or ought to attempt in his addresses to a congregation; though even he must take heed, that, by self-observation and by the observation of others, by earnest prayer and by closeness of application, he do indeed show the human heart to itself, and make his warnings as well as his exhortations real. But He who alone knew what was in man could go, and did go, far beyond this. He looked His adversaries in the face, and said—we may borrow our illustrations wholly from this one discourse—*Ye are from beneath. Ye are of this world. Ye shall seek me, and shall die in your sins: whither I go, ye cannot come. If God were your Father, ye would love me. Ye are of your father the devil, and the lusts of your father ye will do. He that is of God heareth God's words: ye therefore hear them not, because ye are not of God.* Terrible words, my brethren! but spoken in zeal for God's glory, and with the determination to make Him known in His truth as well as in His love, in His abhorrence of sin, and, most of all, of the sin of self-righteousness and wilful blindness of heart, as well as in His readiness to give repentance to the most sinful and to save to the uttermost all that turn to Him through Christ.

Christ sought not His own glory. His discourses

The Disinterestedness of Christ.

showed it; showed it in His language towards self-accusing sinners; showed it also in His language towards the self-satisfied and the harsh-hearted.

And did not His life show it too? There were moments even in that life of humiliation at which He might have converted it into one of immediate exaltation. As in the first and most prolonged temptation He was shown all the kingdoms of the world and offered the possession of them on the condition of doing homage for them to the tempter; so, at a later time, we read of His perceiving a design in the people to *come and take Him by force to make Him a king* (John vi. 15), which He frustrated by a resolute retirement into a position of solitude and seclusion. If He would only have listened to the advice of His disciples, if He would only have stood aside and suffered them and the multitude to carry out their own prepossessions and wishes concerning Him, He might have known what it was to be the idol of His nation, and to appear to have reached as by a short road that Sovereignty which was otherwise to be attained only through the deep waters of suffering and by the rugged road of self-denial and self-sacrifice. But He sought not His own glory. He came to manifest God. He came *to bear witness to the truth* (John xviii. 37); to the realities of the world of substance against the appearances of the world of shadow. And therefore He looked only at the work which had been given Him by His Father, at the lessons which He was to teach by first obeying them, at the cup which He was to sweeten for others by drinking it Himself in its bitterness, of the joy set before Him, not in the time that was, but in the eternity that was to follow.

And this was His reward; that, not seeking His own glory, another sought it for Him. *I seek not mine own glory: there is One that seeketh, and judgeth.* There is One that seeketh to manifest me to the world, even as I to manifest Him, and who exercises in my behalf that judgment which I refuse to exercise for myself. According to the testimony borne in two other passages of this Gospel: *I have glorified Thee on the earth; I have finished the work which Thou gavest me to do: and now, O Father, glorify Thou me with Thine own self, with the glory which I had with Thee before the world was* (John xvii. 4): and again, *If any man hear my words, and believe not, I judge him not; for I came not to judge the world, but to save the world: He that rejecteth me, and believeth not my words, hath one that judgeth him: the word that I have spoken, the same shall judge him at the last day* (John xii. 47).

And now, my brethren, a few concluding words must be given to the bearing of the subject upon ourselves in the way of example.

I seek not mine own glory. If Christ laid down for Himself this rule, have not we tenfold cause to do so? to say, each one for himself, My aim in life is not to show how great I am, or how wise, or how good; how many talents have been committed to me, or how faithful I am in the improvement of them: no, none of these things: my aim is, to seek the glory of Him who placed me where I am, who entrusted to me certain gifts, great or small, few or many, and whom, to a certain extent, less or greater, I can either, by His help, make better known and more loved upon earth, or else, by my fault and sin, help to hide and obscure from the sight and recollection of His creatures?

Does any one ask, How can I do this? how can I make God better known on earth, or, on the other hand, how can I obscure God upon earth? for this is the meaning of living, or not living, to God's glory: I might answer him by another question, Do not you find that there are some persons with whom— I might almost add, certain houses in which—you have a far livelier recollection of God and eternity, than with other persons, or in other homes? It is not always in the society of those who talk most of religion that this is so on the one hand, nor in the society of those who talk least of religion that this is so on the other hand. There is a kind of talking about holy things, which acts upon us not for good but for evil in this respect. But, depend upon it, a person who really loves God above all things— and it is possible to do so—does show it, beyond mistake, though it may be almost without words. Such a person is God's witness on earth, though he may never call himself so, though he may shrink from claiming that character or fancying that he possesses it. Yes, to possess a care for God is the thing. It cannot be counterfeited. It is God's seal; inward first, then outward. O, if we loved God with all our hearts, do you think it would not appear? Do you think that words are the only or the chief way in which it would show itself? Would it not be, far more, by the peace, by the tenderness, by the patience, by the charity, which God's Holy Spirit breathes into the souls of those who love Him through Christ?

Therefore, my brethren, it is a great and glorious ambition to which the Gospel calls us. To love God first, and then to live for God; to have God within us first, through Christ, by the Spirit, and then to let the light within shine out through the various openings which connect the life within with the life without; this is that to which we are called; this is that which is offered to us; and we know not, any one of us, before the experiment, how very near this glorious attainment is to us, and by what a very simple process—that of merely believing, merely grasping, what we all hold loosely as a truth—that attainment is to be made our own. Let us try, every one of us—for we cannot give it to one another—whether this habitual desire for God's glory may not powerfully, and even speedily, become in some degree really ours.

The rule is very plain; given to us briefly in one passage of St Paul's Epistles: *Whether therefore ye eat, or drink, or whatsoever ye do, do all to the glory*

The Disinterestedness of Christ. 229

of God (1 Cor. x. 31); in such a way as to make people think of God, and not in such a way as to lead them to forget God; in such a way as to show that we ourselves believe in Him, and believe in Him as that altogether holy and great and merciful God whom Christ has made known to us.

The rule is plain: but O how insidious are the lower and baser motives which seek to obliterate this rule in our hearts! How many of us do really live with a view to God's glory in the sense just explained? Have we not almost agreed together to regard that as an impossible, as a fantastic thing? a thing altogether of other times and other circumstances than our own? Disinterestedness in its lower sense, as an absence of selfishness towards one another, we may perhaps now and then see exemplified: even this how rare is it! how poor and intermittent our own efforts after it! how far more often do we live on from day to day thinking only of ourselves, seeking only our own interests, our own reputation, our own advancement, in some shape or other our own glory! But why, chiefly, is this? Because even those who have some thought for others, some benevolence, some charity, yet do not base it all on the love of God, and therefore can only love their neighbour with a precarious and fluctuating love, liable to be turned aside by every blast of passion or worldliness, and even in its best moments more or less capricious, self-complacent, and self-contained.

If it is a great attainment, one worthy of pains

and prayer and earnestness, to live to God's glory, do not forget, on the other hand, how poor and tame and low is that life which is spent without any such motive. God, for His own glory, but at least as much for our happiness if we will only have it so, has set the mark of vanity upon all that is only earthly. Look at an old man who has always lived for himself: is he happy? does he look happy? are not the lines of care and disappointment and vexation traced almost visibly upon his countenance? is his retrospect satisfactory? is his prospect bright? is the present altogether to his mind? O no! He may try to represent it so to others, and even to himself: but, depend upon it, if you could look within, you would find an aching void there; a void which nothing can fill; not earth, for it has been tried; not heaven, for he will not try it. O, whatever we may think about a youth, or a middle age, spent without God, no one, I suppose, thinks cheerfully of an old age, and a death-bed, and a judgment, and an eternity, without God!

On the other hand, how often is the other half of this verse verified, in its measure, towards Christ's servants as towards Christ Himself! *I seek not mine own glory: there is One that seeketh. Them that honour me I will honour* (1 Sam. ii. 30). *When a man's ways please the Lord, He maketh even his enemies to be at peace with him* (Prov. xvi. 7). Often has the old age of a Christian been indeed glorified by Him whom he has served. *Peace at the last*

(Psalm xxxvii. 38), after many conflicts; honour at last, after many misconstructions; rest at last, after many wanderings; safety at last, after many misgivings; and then, a quiet departure; and then, Paradise with Christ; and then, the resurrection of the just; and then, the sight of God—*His name in the forehead —no night there—no more death, neither sorrow, nor crying, nor any more pain—the former things passed away, and, behold, all things new—this is the heritage of the servants of the Lord, and their righteousness is of me, saith the Lord* (Isai. liv. 17).

SERMON XIV.

THE MYSTERY OF THE CHRISTIAN LIFE.

EPISTLE FOR EASTER DAY.

COLOSSIANS III. 1—7.

1 *IF then ye were raised with Christ, seek the things above,*
2 *where Christ is, seated on the right hand of God. Mind the*
3 *things above, not the things on the earth. For ye died, and*
4 *your life has been hidden with Christ in God. Whensoever Christ is manifested, our Life, then shall ye also with Him*
5 *be manifested in glory. Deaden then the members that are upon the earth; fornication, uncleanness, passion, evil desire,*
6 *and that grasping which is idolatry; on account of which*
7 *things cometh the wrath of God. In which things ye also once walked, when ye were living in them.*

SERMON XIV.

THE MYSTERY OF THE CHRISTIAN LIFE.

COLOSSIANS III. 1.

If ye then be risen with Christ, seek those things which are above, where Christ sitteth on the right hand of God.

WE can have no doubt where to turn for our Easter subject. No passage gives in a smaller compass or in a more attractive form the doctrine of this day, and its proper and natural effects upon the life of those who believe, than that selected as the Epistle. A brief examination of the passage itself will not only introduce but contain those lessons which the recurrence of our great Christian Festival is designed to impress upon our hearts.

St Paul writes from Rome. He is suffering, he says, and rejoicing in his sufferings. Hard as it was to be condemned to a life of inaction, to feel that opportunities of extended usefulness were denied, and that he was wearing out in imprisonment days which might have been full of labours and triumphs in his Master's cause, he could yet see that all was well both for himself and for the Gospel: he was *filling up* (as he expresses it) *in his own person that which was behind of the afflictions of Christ, for His body's sake, which is the Church* (Col. i. 24); and he doubted not that in some way or other even these sufferings would redound to God's glory. Meanwhile his heart was not inactive. He could still struggle and combat, if it were but in prayer, for congregations known to him personally or unknown. *Though absent in the flesh*, he could still *be with them in the spirit, rejoicing to behold their order and the stedfastness of their faith in Christ* (Col. ii. 5): he could still reach them, from time to time, with a word of written admonition, charging them, *as they had received Christ, so to walk in Him* (Col. ii. 6); to beware lest a false philosophy should rob them of Him *in whom dwelt all the fulness of the Godhead bodily* (Col. ii. 9); to remember the several items, as it were, of that *completeness* which was theirs in Christ, and to take heed lest either a system of *will-worship*, recommending itself by its show of reverence and humility, or of ceremonial observance, altogether beside the mark of a Christian perfection, should tempt them to let go the Head, from whom alone all spiritual nourishment can be derived, and in union with whom alone can any progress be made, worthy of being described truly as *increase of God.*

And now he enters with them yet more deeply into the mysteries of the Christian life. Warnings against error are flat and unpersuasive, except so far as they spring out of positive truth revealed, apprehended, cherished, and lived by. Hence the considerations introduced in the opening of the third Chapter, the Epistle for this day.

If then ye were raised with Christ. You will notice here a somewhat important deviation from the Authorised Version. Much, very much, of St Paul's deepest teaching is involved in it. I will refer you presently to one or two passages of His Epistles in which the interpretation given is warranted and confirmed. For the moment, we will confine our attention to the words before us. *If then ye were raised with Christ, seek the things above, where Christ is, seated on the right hand of God;* invested, that is, with all the honour and all the authority of God Himself; *reigning,* as it is elsewhere said, *until God hath put all enemies under His feet* (1 Cor. xv. 25).

Set your affection on the things above: more exactly, *mind the things above; have the things above for your thoughts and sentiments:* let them be at once your subject and your object, that which occupies your mind and satisfies your heart. *Mind the things above, not the things on the earth.*

For ye died; not *are dead,* but, with reference to one particular time, *ye died; and your life has been hidden with Christ in God.*

Whenever Christ is manifested, our Life, then ye also with Him shall be manifested in glory.

Deaden then the members of the body *which are upon the earth; fornication, uncleanness, passion*—that is, any inordinate, ungoverned, violent affection, whether of emotion or longing, love or hatred, sorrow or fear—*evil desire, and that grasping*—that selfishness in coveting, seeking, and getting, whatever be the particular object of desire, whether money, pleasure, or honour—*which is idolatry*.

On account of which things cometh the wrath of God. The last words of the verse, *on the children of disobedience*, are supposed to have been added from a corresponding passage in the Epistle to the Ephesians: *For because of these things cometh the wrath of God upon the children of disobedience* (Eph. v. 6).

In which things ye also once (at one time) walked, when ye were living in them. When your life was self and sin, no wonder the separate acts of your life were selfish and sinful.

Now, before I endeavour to draw from this passage the doctrine which it so distinctly expresses, let me, as I proposed, set before you one or two parallel passages which will be the best interpreters of this.

One of these occurs in the Epistle to the Galatians; also, like this, a little obscured in our Version. In reality it stands thus.

I have been crucified with Christ; and it is no longer I that live, but Christ liveth in me: and as for my life now in flesh, I live in (through) faith of (in) the Son of God who loved me and gave Himself for me. I have been crucified with Christ ... I live no longer, but Christ lives in me (Gal. ii. 20). Compare these expressions with those of the passage before us:

The Mystery of the Christian Life. 239

Ye were raised with Christ ... Ye died ... Your life is hid with Christ in God.

Turn now to the Second Lesson for this morning, the sixth Chapter of the Epistle to the Romans; in which the same doctrine is more fully drawn out, and which I would commend to the patient and thoughtful study of all who would know what Easter-Day is in its deep comfort and in its practical consequences. I will make no apology for running through a few of its verses with a brief word of comment.

What shall we say then? If God's grace is so abundant as it has just been declared to be—*where sin abounded, grace did much more abound* (Rom. v. 20)—*must we continue in sin that grace may abound? God forbid. We who died* (not *are dead:* one particular act is referred to) *to sin, how shall we any longer live in it? Or know ye not that all we who were baptized into Christ Jesus, were baptized into His death;* were baptized into Him, were introduced into Him by baptism, not as a Man living on earth, but as One who has already died, and with especial reference to His death? *We were buried, then, with Him, by means of that baptism, into death: that, like as Christ was raised from among the dead by the glory,* the manifested power, *of the Father, so we also should walk in newness of life.* Our baptism, by means of which we were united to Christ, was, like burial, a solemn act of consigning us to death: that, as Christ rose again from death, so should we, in this world, live as men who have already died and risen again. *For, if we have become united with the likeness of His death,* if we have become so united with Him in His death as to be like Him in it, *we shall be also* united with the likeness *of His resurrection;* we shall be so united with Him in His resurrection as to be like Him in it: *knowing this, that our old man,* our old natural self, *was crucified with Him, that the body of sin,* the material body with its proneness to sensual and other evil, *might be destroyed, that we should no longer be slaves to sin: for he that has died is,* by that very fact, as though by a judicial sentence, *set free from sin;* he cannot commit sin again. Even so he who is united to Christ crucified and risen is to live as though he had already laid aside his body in death; mastering its sinful promptings in the power of a new life derived from Christ in heaven. *And if we died with Christ, we believe that we shall also live with Him,* both now and hereafter; *knowing that Christ, raised from among the dead, dieth no more: death hath no longer the dominion over Him. For in that He died, He died in relation to sin, once for all: but in that He liveth, He liveth in relation to God,* and therefore for ever. *Thus do ye also consider yourselves dead men,* insensible, immovable, *in relation to sin; and living men,* full of energy and vigour, *in relation to God, in Christ Jesus,* that is, by virtue of your union with Christ Jesus. *Let not sin therefore reign in your mortal body, that ye should obey the desires thereof,* that is, of the body: *neither present ye your members to sin*—personified, as one of two possible masters—*as instruments of unrighteousness, but present yourselves to God, as persons alive from among the dead, and your members to God as instruments of righteousness. For sin shall not have dominion over you: for ye are not under a law, but under grace;* under a system, not of working for life, but of free, unmerited, gratuitous acceptance.

And now we can return with a fully prepared mind to the direct subject of discourse. Now we perceive something of the real meaning of St Paul when he wrote the words—

If ye then were raised with Christ, seek the things above, where Christ is, seated on the right hand of God. Mind the things above, not the things on the earth. For ye died, and your life has been hidden with Christ in God. Whensoever Christ is manifested, our Life, then shall ye also with Him be manifested in glory. Mortify then, deaden, reduce to a state of death, *the members that are upon the earth.*

O, my brethren, in proportion as we can enter with understanding and heart into the mystery of the Christian life as here disclosed to us, we shall be happy and we shall be holy. See what St Paul regarded as the essence of it. Union with Christ. A Christian is a person who is united to Christ. How united? By having one spirit with Christ: the same Holy Spirit dwelling in him, who is also the Spirit of Christ and the Spirit of God. That is union with a person; the having the same spirit with that other person. It is what no two earthly persons, no two human beings, can have: each man has his own spirit, and *what* other *man knoweth the things of the man, save the spirit of the man which is in him?* (1 Cor. ii. 11). But that union which is impossible for human beings is possible between a man and Christ: and he, he only, is a Christian, who has it. *If any man have not the Spirit of Christ, he is none of His* (Rom. viii. 9).

This is the essence of that union of which St Paul speaks, which St Paul himself experienced, which St Paul describes as the common property of all Christians. It is the having Christ's Spirit for our spirit. It is the having our whole being directed, and as it were pervaded, by that Holy Spirit who is one with Christ in heaven.

Now St Paul traced the commencement of this union to the time of Baptism. You heard in the sixth Chapter of the Epistle to the Romans the warrant for this statement. I am going into no doubtful questions here: we have no time for them. I only call your attention to the fact, that, addressing persons who had, no doubt, for the most part, received Baptism in mature life, when already penitent, already believing, he bade them trace back their union with Christ to that public and real transition from a state of Judaism or of heathenism to a life of faith and of holiness, and said to them, *Know ye not that all we who were baptized into Christ Jesus were baptized into His death?* or, as he elsewhere expresses it, in writing to the Galatians, *All ye who were baptized into Christ did then put on (clothe yourselves with) Christ* (Gal. iii. 27).

The Mystery of the Christian Life. 243

We in too many cases, need to seek a vital union with Christ at a far later point of earthly life. Let me say of that necessity, It is a real one: be not deceived into putting anything else in the place of a vital union with Christ; that union which consists in having the Holy Spirit of Christ to dwell in you. But let me add, Let no one teach you to despise the comfort and the promise contained in that simple ordinance of Baptism, which is as much of Christ's ordaining, of Christ's sanctioning, of Christ's blessing, as any human institution ever was the ordinance of any human institutor. If unhappily in our days the outward ordinance and the highest gift have too often parted company, yet remember, that ordinance is still a standing pledge, to every person who has been subjected to it, and to the whole world which stands by and looks on, of Christ's willingness, of Christ's will, to convey the inward gift to each soul that desires it, yes, to that soul when and if it desires it. Baptism the outward ordinance, and the promise in words that He will give the Holy Spirit to them that ask Him, are two harmonious and co-ordinate assurances from the throne of Christ in heaven that, if we have not, it is because we ask not; if we perish, it is not His will, but our own; if we will only turn to Him, though it be late and timidly and sorrowfully, He is most ready to receive us, yea, even before we call, He will answer.

And let me say one other word with regard to Baptism, at whatever age and under whatever circumstances administered; that it leaves no one exactly as he stood before it; that it is the act which appropriates Redemption to the individual man; that it seals upon the person what Christ did for the world, places him within that community to which every promise is made, and gives him a right, of God's free gift, to every blessing for which his heart is ever stirred to ask.

Such is the Christian standing. It is a condition of union with Christ. Every baptized person ought to have that union; for to every baptized person who shall desire it is the gift of the Holy Spirit promised. But no person must take it for granted that he has received that gift, that availing gift, of the Holy Spirit. He has it not unless he asks for it; asks humbly, asks earnestly, asks perseveringly. He has it not unless it is working a change in him; a gradual, a growing conformity to the mind of Christ and to the life of Christ. By these signs shall he know himself: *examine yourselves whether ye be in the faith: prove your own selves* (2 Cor. xiii. 5).

But now we are taught the consequences of this real union with Christ; that union of which He Himself spoke, when He said to His disciples, *I am the vine, ye are the branches—Without me (apart from me) ye can do nothing—Abide in me, and I in you* (John xv. 5).

If you are united to Christ—such is St Paul's argument—then whatever has happened to Christ has also happened to you. Did Christ die? then you, who are one with Christ, died also. *The love of Christ constraineth us; because we thus judge, that, if one died for all, then* (not, *were all dead,* but) *did all die* with Him and in Him; *and that He died for all, that the living might no longer live in relation to themselves,* as the object of their life, *but in relation,* with constant regard and reference, *to Him who for them died and was raised* (2 Cor. v. 14, 15). Did Christ, then, die? you, who are one with Christ, died also. Was Christ raised from death? then you, who are one with Christ, rose also. Did Christ ascend into heaven? then you, who are one with Christ, ascended also: then is heaven your home; not your future home only, but your present home also: then is your treasure there: then is your happiness, your comfort, your strength, your life, there also; hidden, stored away, out of sight, out of reach of attack, of accident, of change; safe, perfectly safe; yea, *hidden with Christ in God.*

What a view is thus opened! how wide, how lofty, how glorious! What an antidote to care and fear, to restlessness and anxiety, to minor ambitions and to unworthy vanities! The Christian is one with Christ: Christ has passed safely through this life, Christ has overcome the world, Christ has died and risen and ascended; then you, who are one with Him, may well be bidden to seek the things above and to mind the things above, to have your heart and your aim and your interest and your affection firmly fixed in heaven, where true joys are to be found, because Christ Himself is there; Christ who once died for sin, Christ who now and ever liveth unto God.

And we are reminded too, in the passage before us, not only of the present position, but also of the coming change, of a Christian. *Whensoever Christ is manifested, our Life, then shall ye also with Him be manifested in glory.* At present, though Christ is, and though the inner life of a Christian is a real thing, yet there is a veil over both, which hides the reality from the eyes of men, and makes it possible for the unbelieving to doubt and to deny it.

There is a veil between us and Christ. *We walk by faith, not by sight* (2 Cor. v. 7). *Blessed are they who have not seen and yet have believed* (John xx. 29). But that veil will be taken away: *in a moment, in the twinkling of an eye* (1 Cor. xv. 52), when the appointed time comes, He will be revealed; unveiled, disclosed, manifested; *every eye shall see Him* (Rev. i. 7); and wonderful, incredible, will it then seem to the now most incredulous, that they could ever for one moment have gainsaid or forgotten His glory.

And there is a veil too over the life of a Christian. Men see not his connection with One within the veil. They hear not his communings with that invisible world and with Him who dwells there. They know not in what strength he walks, through whom he conquers, by what supplies his inner life is fed, or what is the intrinsic dignity of a position oftentimes so humble. But they shall see, they shall know.

Whensoever Christ is manifested, our Life, then shall ye also with Him be manifested in glory. That is the time elsewhere spoken of as *the manifestation of the sons of God* (Rom. viii. 19). That is the time for which St Paul describes the whole creation, rational alike and irrational, as instinctively looking and longing. At present there is a veil over human character: men move about among their fellows, and know not with whom they mingle; know not the hidden vileness of one, know not the hidden majesty of another. But, when that day comes which is sometimes briefly called *the adoption* (Rom. viii. 23), that is, the manifestation of a sonship which has before been veiled, then will the disclosure of Christ be the signal for the disclosure of those who are one with Christ, and the careless and the hardened will suddenly awaken to the consciousness of a glory which has been about them unperceived before, and say, *Surely the Lord has been in this place* (Gen. xxviii. 16), in my neighbourhood, in my family, in my home, in my very presence, *and I knew it not.*

Finally, let the thoughts on which we have dwelt, not only quicken in us an earnest longing after that union with Christ of which such glorious things are spoken, but also turn to a very practical use this high and holy commemoration. *Mortify therefore*, St Paul says, *the members which are upon the earth.* If your position is that of persons whose home is in heaven, of persons who have already with Christ and in His person died and risen again and ascended, take heed lest your life here below should belie that glorious gift. If men see you, or, let us rather say, if God sees you, to be still self-indulgent, still selfish, still eager for worldly advantage, still grasping after worldly shadows, still proud, still vain, still resentful, still ungoverned in temper, still unrenewed in heart, or (yet worse) still sinful in life, O, these things will be a witness against you that you are either deceived or else a deceiver, still a stranger to that gift of Christ which is the one infallible mark of all who are His. O carry the light of conscience, the light of the Word, the light of the Spirit, into these hearts and lives of yours! Spare nothing that offends in you: you will be glad and thankful one day to have swept it clean away. It will not bring you peace at the last, to have spared one darling lust, one rebellious temper. It will be your tormentor, be quite sure, before all is over. And O the deep peace, the bright hope, the sense of strength, the consciousness of being cared for and helped from on high, which springs out of one resolute conflict waged and carried through against the power of sin!

For the sake of these things cometh the wrath of God. Yes, *cometh, and is come.* There is no doubt, even now, even in this sinful world, on which side God is in the great strife of good and evil. He leaves not Himself without witness. *He hath bent His bow, and made it ready* (Psalm vii. 12), not for a future day of recompence only, but even already, even now. He has not wholly deserted the world which would fain isolate itself from Him: in conscience He still speaks, in human life He already sometimes judges.

But the Lord is risen, risen indeed, risen as on this day; and risen for this one purpose, *that He might be Lord both of the dead and living* (Rom. xiv. 9). Let every heart in this Congregation own Him as such! If never before, yet now, yet on this day, yet before you go forth from this place, I would beseech you to do Him homage. No man who has once spoken to Him from the heart, will again willingly be silent. No man who has paid one visit to that heaven where Christ is at the right hand of God, will ever rest without seeking Him again. The veil which hangs between you and Him is slight and shadowy: push it aside, and enter! Let faith pierce it! Reality is within, shadows without. Believe yourself to have entered: behold, worship, pray, as if you were within, as if you were in His presence: He will hear, He will answer! The spiritual world is not local: it is near, it is present, it is within you. *Say not in thine heart, Who shall ascend for me into heaven? as though to bring Christ down from above: or, Who shall descend for me into the deep? as though to bring up Christ again from the dead: no, the word is nigh thee, in thy mouth, and in thy heart; that is, the word of faith which we preach; that, if thou shalt confess with thy mouth the Lord Jesus, and shalt* believe in thine heart that God hath raised Him from the dead, thou shalt be saved. For with the heart man believeth unto righteousness; and with the mouth confession is made unto salvation (Rom. x. 6—10).

SERMON XV.

THE RETURN FROM THE SEPULCHRE.

GOSPEL FOR EASTER DAY.

St. John xx. 1—10.

1 *On the first day of the week cometh Mary Magdalene early, while it was still dark, to the sepulchre, and seeth the stone*
2 *already taken away from the sepulchre. She runneth therefore, and cometh to Simon Peter, and to the other disciple, him whom Jesus loved, and saith to them, They have taken away the Lord out of the sepulchre, and we know not where they*
3 *have placed Him. Peter therefore went forth, and the other*
4 *disciple, and they set out to the sepulchre. And they ran, the two together: and the other disciple ran on more quickly*
5 *than Peter, and came first to the sepulchre, and, stooping to*
6 *look in, seeth the linen clothes lying, but went not in. Simon Peter therefore cometh following him, and went into the sepul-*
7 *chre, and beholdeth the linen clothes lying, and the napkin, which was on His head, not lying with the linen clothes, but*
8 *wrapped up in one place apart. Then went in therefore the other disciple also, who came first to the sepulchre, and he*
9 *saw, and believed: for not even yet knew they the scripture,*
10 *that He must rise from among the dead. The disciples therefore went away again to their home.*

SERMON XV.

THE RETURN FROM THE SEPULCHRE.

ST. JOHN XX. 10.

Then the disciples went away again unto their own home.

THESE words close the Gospel for Easter-Day. Viewed even historically, they are full of interest. The contrast between the two Disciples as they awoke that morning and as they slept that night, as they ran to the Sepulchre and as they returned from it, is one which we cannot think of without emotion. That sudden change, from the darkness of sorrow and disbelief and self-reproach; from the state of one who has lost his best Friend and never expects to see Him again in this world, and not only so, but who in parting with Him has to remember that his own unkindness, his own desertion, aggravated the pain of death and must for ever embitter the remembrance of the separation; to that of one who has had the evidence of his own senses that the tomb is deserted, that the dead Friend is living, that all His words which told of Resurrection, however unintelligible, however incredible, at the time, were intended literally and have literally been fulfilled, so that now it is not too much to hope that even on earth there may yet be converse, there may yet be reunion, and at all events that the hope of Redemption which had been awakened by years of intercourse and companionship with Him was no fable, no delusion, but a real and certain truth; this change, this transition, from darkness to light, from sorrow to joy, from despair to confidence, has ever been a delightful subject of Christian meditation, and is here brought within the compass of ten short verses and presented to our view as a topic most suitable to that great commemoration to which this holy day is consecrated.

But, if interesting and attractive as the record of a historical fact, as suggesting the idea of an unspeakable joy vouchsafed long ages ago to Christ's first Disciples, does not the same verse which has just been read to you speak also to us and of us as those who have been permitted once again to celebrate the anniversary of His Resurrection, and are now about to return from it to the various homes and to the various occupations in which and amidst which it has pleased God that our earthly life should be spent?

The disciples then went away again unto their own home. They went, we know, with hopes revived and hearts comforted. They went, to expect further communications from Him whom they now know to be alive from the dead. They went to recall to mind the words which He had so lately spoken, but to which they had listened at the time with hearts so deaf that it was as if they had never heard them. They went, to talk one to another of the things which had happened. They went, to give thanks to God for all that they had been permitted to hear and to see of their Divine Master, and to try to carry out in their daily lives the instructions which He had given and the example which He had set them.

I will not attempt an elaborate subdivision of the subject which I desire to-night to press upon you. But I would show you how just and how forcible an application the text has to our own circumstances. I would ponder with you the senses in which we may be said to-night to resemble the Disciples here spoken of as returning from the sight of the deserted Sepulchre, which was to them the assurance of Christ's Life after Death, to their several homes and occupations, with feelings so much altered from anything they had known before.

1. Let me say then, first of all, that we ought to return to our homes and to our occupations with hopes revived and hearts comforted.

The fact of Christ's Resurrection is not indeed a new knowledge to us. We have said over and over again, all of us, in our Creeds, *The third day He rose again from the dead.* But it is wisely ordered, in our Church, that the separate truths of Christ's Doctrine, the successive steps, if I may so express it, of Christ's Redemption, should be presented to us every year one by one, for distinct and definite contemplation, as well as that they should all be always recognized, always commemorated, in their aggregate and combination, whenever we come together on the commonest occasion for the purposes of prayer and praise. And we miss a great blessing, when we allow either indolence or self-will to deprive us of this separate contemplation of the several events of His life, and more particularly of the several stages of that progress by which He passed through humiliation to glory. Our minds are so constituted, and, we may add, the method of our Redemption is so arranged, that we ought to view each part in its turn singly and separately, as well as the whole work, at other times, in its object, its combination, and its result.

To-day then the part of the truth which has been presented to us thus distinctly is the Resurrection of Christ: the fact, the simple yet marvellous fact, that, after really dying, by that death which we have looked upon during the past week in its circumstances and in its details; after being buried in a particular place and before several witnesses; after lying in the state of death, His tomb guarded and watched, through a portion of three days, by those who were interested to prevent the removal of the body by any secret or collusive means; and after passing, as to His soul, into that condition, whatever it be, which men's souls pass into when separated from the body; a condition expressed in our Creed by the words, *He descended into hell*, that is, into Hades, into the place or the state of departed spirits between death and resurrection; the fact, I say, that, after these realities of death, burial, and sojourn in the Paradise of the departed, He did rise again out of death; His soul returned to the lifeless body, and He became again a living Man, invested with that transformed, that immortal body, which dieth no more, which needs no more the things which are necessary to the life of this world, but is ready to take its place above in the everlasting presence of God.

This is the fact which has been presented to us to-day. And now can we go away again to our own homes, like the first Disciples, with hearts comforted by this faith in Christ risen? Why are we here to-night? Why have we taken part in the services of this day? Why did many of us partake this morning of the Lord's Supper? O surely it has not been as a mere form! Surely it has not been in irreverence: surely not in utter ungodliness, carelessness, or hardness of heart! I know how subtle the tempter is, how capricious are the alternations of feeling, how powerful the workings of sin. But I do not, I will not, doubt that all of us who are here assembled do acknowledge Christ as their Saviour, do desire His mercy and help, do wish, however faintly, to live to Him. I am sure that very many are not in any sense His enemies: rather are they His humble disciples, though they may be very faint-hearted, very lukewarm, very sinful. Now all these—and God grant that the description may embrace all who are

S

here present—have great cause to rejoice in the Resurrection of Christ. O what should we be if Christ had died for us—*even* if Christ had died for us—and not risen? Put yourselves for a moment out of sight of Christ risen; imagine that you were without a living Intercessor, a living Mediator, a living High Priest; and do you not feel that life would be for you far darker, far more dreary, far more hopeless, than even with the faintest Christian hope it is? Then I say that we ought to go home to-night with hopes revived and hearts comforted by having gazed to-day upon the Resurrection of Christ. I am sure you are glad that He has risen. Cherish that feeling. It is a good one, for all of us. It is a sound and a safe and a salutary one, for all of us. Thank God for His inestimable love in the redemption of the world by our Lord Jesus Christ; for the means of grace, and for the hope of glory. All these things are inseparably bound up in the assurance that Christ who died lives again. Go home rejoicing that it is so: and be assured that in that very rejoicing lies for you the germ of life.

2. And this brings us naturally to the second point touched upon. We should return home, as did the first Disciples, to expect further communications from Him whom we believe to be alive from the dead.

I would earnestly press upon you this consideration. The Disciples, when they saw the tomb empty, and were thus convinced that Christ was risen, yet were in a most imperfect state as regarded their knowledge of Him. We all know that during forty days He was from time to time visiting them; visiting one here, another there, then several, then all of them together; speaking to them, as the beginning of the Acts of the Apostles expresses it, *of the things pertaining to the kingdom of God* (Acts i. 3); familiarizing them with the thought of Himself as risen, and habituating them, at the same time, to His being no longer constantly with them; in short, as before, so now also, manifesting to them His truth *as they were able to hear it* (Mark iv. 33), and preparing them, by a most wise as well as loving discipline, for the work which they were afterwards to accomplish for Him in the world.

My brethren, we should be ill off if we too might not expect further communications, beyond what we have already received, from our risen Saviour. I do not mean that we expect, or ought to expect, new revelations from Him. In His Word we have all that we need of this kind. But new communications from Him we do greatly need; and they who ask for them shall have them. I would have you go back to-night, and enter again to-morrow upon your common occupations, with the full expectation, even as the Disciples doubtless did, of hearing and seeing more than you have yet heard and seen of your living Lord.

What is your case? Which of the cases described in the Chapter before us does it most resemble? I will venture to say, whatever your case be, there is a parallel for it here; in the mind of some one of those first disciples to whom Jesus appeared after His Resurrection.

Are you a doubter? Are you one of those, of whom there have been some in every age, who find a great difficulty in apprehending, in grasping and handling, the truth of the Gospel? to whom the Incarnation, or the Resurrection, the idea of a spiritual communion with God, or of a spiritual influence derived from God, presents much that is puzzling and baffling to their human comprehension? one who would give all that he possesses and all that he is for one ray of absolute conviction as to the revelations made to us in the Gospel? one who doubts, not because he wishes to doubt, but because the simple Gospel seems to him too good to be true? Then for you there is the case of Thomas; who said that he could not believe unless he actually saw, and who was so tenderly dealt with by his Saviour that he was permitted to see, and yet, in the very moment of this indulgence, was made to be the encourager of all those who by the nature of the case could not equally enjoy it, when it was said to him, *Thomas, because thou hast seen me, thou hast believed: blessed are they which have not seen, and yet have believed* (John xx. 29).

Or are you, again, one whose past life has been defiled by much sin, and who in the remembrance of that guilty past is often tempted to say, No, the Gospel cannot be for me? Then remember to whom it was that Christ after His Resurrection first appeared; even to Mary Magdalene, *out of whom*, it is expressly added, in the same connection, by one of the Evangelists, *He had cast seven devils* (Mark xvi. 9). Read the record of that appearance, as it is given us in this very Chapter: and then you will see that none are quite so near to Christ as the self-abased and self-accusing penitent; that, so far from coming last to them, He comes to them first, and with His most gracious words of comfort; that there is no state of mind in which we so truly *see the heavens opened, and Jesus standing on the right hand of God* (Acts vii. 56), as that in which we are most deeply humbled by the sense of sin, and driven, as it were, by very necessity, to cry aloud for a salvation altogether of grace and altogether from above.

But what I am urging upon you at this moment is, that, whatever be the present state of your knowledge, or faith, or conviction, you ought, in returning home from that sight of the empty Sepulchre which is your assurance of the Resurrection, to expect further communications, according to your need, from One who is alive from the dead. Do not imagine that the whole of the Gospel is communicated to any man at once. Its great basis and groundwork, the Death and the Resurrection of Christ, is soon stated: but that is but the beginning of knowledge; of that knowledge which lies not in the head only but in the heart; of that knowledge which is not so much the knowledge of things as the knowledge of a Person; of that knowledge which is life eternal because it is communion with the only true God through Jesus Christ whom He hath sent (John xvii. 3). Expect every day to see more of Christ, by communicating directly with Him, and with God through Him, by the Holy Spirit.

3. I mentioned as a third point in the condition of the Disciples spoken of in the text—and it is one equally applicable to us—that they returned from the Sepulchre to remember Christ's words.

They had heard Him say many things, careful as He was to teach them gradually and appropriately, which at the time they did not understand. This very fact of the Resurrection was an instance of it. Again and again it had been foretold to them during His earthly life. And yet in the verse before the text we are expressly told that *as yet they knew not the Scripture, that He must rise again from the dead* (John xx. 9). It is a striking instance of the way in which all truth affects the human mind. It requires that there should be something in us to which it can assimilate itself. We all know that one of the higher discoveries of a science is altogether unintelligible to us, its statement a merely unmeaning sound in our ears, until we have learned the principles of that science, and risen step by step to the particular truth in question. So was it with the Disciples, during the earthly ministry of Christ, in reference to the things that were to befall Him at its close. They had their own idea of what it was likely and of what it was becoming that He should be, and, so long as they retained that prejudice, they could not learn what He was and was to be. It was not until after the Resurrection that His words began to come back upon them as voices and not sounds. Then indeed, in that interval between the Resurrection and the Ascension, they had occupation enough in recalling to themselves the things which He had spoken, in pondering their unsuspected meaning, and in marvelling at their own unbelief in having listened as it were without hearing.

Even thus is it with us after every real apprehension of the Resurrection and immortal Life of Christ. We go back to our homes to remember His words. Revelations which lie like dead things on the pages of the Bible, while we read them, I do not say with carelessness or with indifference or with prejudice, but yet, if I might so express it, apart from Christ; as things spoken or written, rather than as the living voice of a Person; become instinct with life and meaning when we kneel over them as in Christ's presence, beseech Him to speak them to our consciences, and let the light fall full upon them from His abode in heaven. We ought to go back from every such celebration as that of this day, to read the Holy Scriptures with a double interest. If there is one word of truth in the fact which we to-day commemorate, it means that *Christ, being raised from the dead, dieth no more* (Rom. vi. 9); it means that *He ever liveth to make intercession for us* (Heb. vii. 25); it means that *God has exalted Him* with His own right hand *to be a Prince and a Saviour, to give repentance* to each of us *and forgiveness of sins* (Acts v. 31); it means that the time is come, of which Jesus Himself said to His Disciples, *Because I live, ye shall live also* (John xiv. 19).

4. Once again, the Disciples went away to their own home to talk one to another of the things which had happened.

Thus were two other Disciples occupied, as they walked that same day to the village of Emmaus, and were joined in their walk by Him of whom they communed. I need not say how in all times this ought to be descriptive of those who believe in Christ's Resurrection. He Himself came upon earth, died and rose again, not to redeem to Himself individual souls only, but also to *gather together in one the children of God that were scattered abroad* (John xi. 52). He knew that the spiritual life needs communion, as with Himself above, so also with partakers of the same benefit below. That is the very meaning of a Church. Every ordinance of public worship is instituted on that principle. The Lord's Prayer itself asks every blessing for others also as well as for the person praying. And as in these most obvious ways, so in a more private manner also, we all know, by experience of it, or by the want of it, how important is communion, human communion I mean, to the life within. How often has a word of hearty encouragement, spoken by one who knew and felt what he said, cheered and animated our onward way!

How often has a word of deep sympathy, the disclosure, from some loving heart, of an infirmity, a fault, a coldness, a backwardness, an unbelief, just such as we were conscious of, been the means of raising us from a deep depression, or of guiding us to a point of rest and strength! Those who have together commemorated the reality of Christ's Resurrection, can scarcely go home to be silent altogether, from day to day, as to the faith and the hope which are deeply cherished within. Or, if they speak not, at least they will indicate one to another, by signs not to be misunderstood, that they are pursuing the same end, by the same means, through the same difficulties, in the same strength.

5. I add yet one last particular. The Disciples went back to their own homes full of thankfulness to God for all that He had permitted them to see and hear of Christ, and desirous to show that thankfulness by obeying the directions and by following the example of their beloved Master.

And surely this, my brethren, ought to be the parting word, the abiding impression, of our Easter Day. If we at all enter into its great subject, can it be otherwise? Christ raised for our Justification; Christ raised to be our Intercessor; Christ raised to be our Life; Christ raised to be hereafter our Resurrection; these things are either true, or they are empty sounds: if, as we all hope, as we all believe, they are true, surely they are matters for thankfulness, and surely they are calls to exertion; exertion within, as well as exertion without. The soul needs energy to take hold of these things. They must not lie on the surface of the mind: they will do no good there. The eye of the soul must be firmly fixed upon them: they must be taken into view: they must be handled: they must be leaned upon, tried, and used. O there is a great backwardness in us in believing any spiritual truth! How often does it seem to elude us when we have just grasped it! How often does the question recur, What if it be all a dream? We must not be daunted by these misgivings. They are easily to be accounted for. We live in a world of sense. What we cannot see with our eyes and handle with our hands, there is much to make us deem visionary. God knows our difficulties. Jesus Christ Himself seems to have recognized them in the words, before referred to, addressed to His doubting Apostle. But these things are not motives for disregarding spiritual truth, for acquiescing in doubt, for hoping that doubt is venial and will be forgiven. Rather should they be attractions to belief. The knowledge that God sees, that Christ feels for, our difficulties in believing, should arouse us to throw ourselves upon His help in overcoming them. There is great strength in sympathy. It is not enfeebling: it is invigorating. Most of all, when that sympathy is Divine; when it can not only feel for us, therefore, but help also. And God will help us to believe. Faith is His gift: but it is given to all who ask it. Not all at once strong faith, undoubting assurance:

The Return from the Sepulchre.

this may come after: but humble faith, hoping faith, trusting faith: the faith which says, *Lord, to whom shall I go? Thou, Thou only, hast the words of eternal life* (John vi. 68); none else, in heaven or in earth, even professes to have eternal life to offer to a sinner like me: the faith which says, *Lord, I believe: help Thou mine unbelief* (Mark ix. 24): the faith which accepts thankfully a little light, and waits trustingly for the perfect day.

It is with this kind of faith that almost all Christians have begun: and their sincerity has been shown in accepting it, in thanking God for it, and in waiting upon Him for more. Now have we not all a little faith? It may be very little: but there is probably in all of us just enough to begin with; just the germ, just the seed, of true faith: and if not, yet, even then, God can give it from the very beginning to those who ask it. I think we can all just thank Him, in some way or other, for Christ crucified and for Christ risen. I think we all believe that the tomb was once seen occupied, and that the tomb was afterwards seen empty. O let us begin with that! Begin with thanking God for giving His Son to die for us. Begin with thanking God for raising His Son from death, in token that that death was accepted, was effectual. This we can do, if it be but a small thing. And one other thing we can do, God helping us. We can say to ourselves each morning, What would be the conduct to-day of a person who really believed that Jesus Christ had died for him, and that

Jesus Christ had risen for him? What would be my life to-day on that supposition? Let me refer everything in my acts and words to that belief. Often I may, often, I am sure, I shall, contradict that belief in both; but let me try, let me watch, let me pray, and perhaps in some part, in some degree, I shall succeed, by God's grace, in so living.

And remember, that is the way in which faith grows. Every little thing done, or forborne, because Jesus Christ is; because He died, because He lives; reacts upon ourselves as a real strengthening of our faith. In time, we shall know what it is to say, *The life which I now live in the flesh, I live by faith in the Son of God, who loved me and gave Himself for me* (Gal. ii. 20). In time we shall be able to say, *To me to live is Christ* (Phil. i. 21). Well may that hope, the hope of being at last a Christian indeed, the hope of being altogether believing, altogether faithful, reconcile us to many a dark day, and many a stumbling step, in the way to it. That is the path that all Christians have trod: and in proportion to their earnestness and to their submission in treading it, has been the speed at which they advanced, and the hour at which they arrived.

Remember, St Paul says to Timothy, *that Jesus Christ, of the seed of David, was raised from the dead according to my Gospel* (2 Tim ii. 8). That was his motto for one charged with the oversight of souls. It is indeed a fit motto for us all. Remember, day by day, remember in your acts, remember in your

The Return from the Sepulchre. 269

words, remember in your thoughts, that Jesus Christ, first made Man for you, then dying for you, was at length raised from death for you. Remember this, in all your estimates of the life that is; remember this, in all your estimates of the life that shall be. Live as if, not Christ only, but you yourself, had already died. *He that is dead is freed from sin* (Rom. vi. 7). Live as if, not Christ only, but you yourself, were already risen. *In that He liveth, He liveth unto God* (Rom. vi. 10). *If ye then were raised with Christ, seek the things above, where Christ is, seated on the right hand of God* (Col. iii. 1).

SERMON XVI

THE VICTORY OF FAITH.

EPISTLE FOR THE FIRST SUNDAY AFTER EASTER.

1 JOHN V. 4—12.

4 *EVERYTHING which has been begotten of God overcomes the world: and this is the victory which overcame the*
5 *world, our faith. Who is he that overcomes the world, but*
6 *he who believes that Jesus is the Son of God? This is He who came through water and blood, Jesus the Christ; not in the water only, but in the water and in the blood: and the Spirit is that which testifies, because the Spirit is*
7 *the truth. For there are three who testify; the Spirit, and*
8 *the water, and the blood; and the three are at*[1] *one. If we*
9 *receive the testimony of mankind, the testimony of God is greater: for this is the testimony of God, [namely,] that*[2]
10 *He has testified concerning His Son. He who believes in the Son of God has the testimony in him: he who believes not God has made Him a liar, because he has not believed in the testimony which God has testified concerning His Son.*
11 *And this is the testimony; that God gave us eternal life,*
12 *and this life is in His Son. He who has the Son has the life: he who has not the Son of God*[3] *has not the life.*

---

[1] Literally, *the three (persons) are unto the one (thing).*

[2] According to the reading of the revised text. Not *which.*

[3] Why are the words, *of God,* omitted here in the Prayer-Book?

SERMON XVI.

THE VICTORY OF FAITH.

1 JOHN v. 4.

Whatsoever is born of God overcometh the world: and this is the victory that overcometh the world, even our faith.

SUCH are the opening words of this day's Epistle; a passage presenting some points of peculiar difficulty, yet abounding also, as I trust we shall see, in lessons of peculiar interest, importance, and power. May the wisdom of God guide us in the endeavour to meet the former, and to profit by the latter.

The verse read as the text is not the beginning of a paragraph. In our Bible Version it is prefaced by the word *For*. This consideration will carry back our thoughts to the beginning of the Chapter.

Whosoever believeth that Jesus is the Christ hath been begotten of God: and every one that loveth Him that begat loveth him also that hath been begotten of Him. A child of God is he who believes that Jesus is the Christ, the Saviour of the world. A child of God will be sure to love his Father: and he who loves

God as his Father will love all other children of God as his brethren. Such is the simple yet sound argument of the great Apostle of love. He who truly loves God will certainly love his brother also.

But the converse of this is equally true. *In this we know that we love the children of God, when we love God and do His commandments.* If you doubt whether you love God, ask yourself whether you love the children of God; that is, true and simple believers in Jesus Christ. If you doubt whether you love the children of God—for that also is a question which has caused anxiety to many hearts, knowing the vast importance attached in Scripture to Christian love—ask yourself whether you love God, and guide yourself to an answer to that further question by seeing whether you are keeping God's commandments; whether, in heart and life, you are and are doing what conscience and Scripture concur in pointing out as the will of God for you.

For this is the love of God, that we should keep His commandments: and His commandments are not grievous; literally, *are not heavy,* or *burdensome:* and the reason follows in the text. God's commandments are burdensome, are a yoke too heavy to be borne, to those who are not His children: but, where He is known as a Father—in other words, where there is a heart which believes in Christ as a Saviour—there they are not so.

For everything which has been begotten of God overcomes the world. It is made as general as possible:

The Victory of Faith.

every thing rather than *every one:* that is, wherever there is anything sprung from God's parentage, there is a thing essentially stronger than anything that is alien or hostile to God: exactly in so far as a man has anything in him of God, in the same degree he is victorious over evil. And what is it, the Apostle goes on to say, which makes a child of God strong to overcome the world? What is that quality, that principle, that thing, in him, which is the means of this victory, which is the weapon whereby it is won? *And this is the victory which overcame the world,* in all who have overcome it, *our faith. Who is he that overcomes the world, but he who believes that Jesus is the Son of God?*

.Before we pass on, let us briefly define these two expressions, *the world,* and *faith.* We shall return presently to that which is said of the conquest of the one by the other.

The term rendered *world* means properly *arrangement;* and is then applied to the universe of created things in its orderly and systematic conformation, as opposed to the confusion of the original chaos. In all this, however, the idea is rather that of God's handywork than of God's antagonist: in this sense, the world is not God's enemy but God's witness. The term passed, however, in the hands of the inspired writers, into a designation of things visible and temporal, the state of things that now is, and the persons who have their treasure, their home, and their all, in it, as opposed to things spiritual and eternal, the state of things that shall be, and the persons who belong, even in this life, as to their home and higher being, to that heaven in which God dwells. *The world* thus became a brief title for all that is not God nor of God, all that is earthly, sensual, and evil, all that tempts to sin, and all those who live without God, apart from God, or in enmity against God.

Of the word *faith* we have the best of definitions in the Scripture itself. *Faith is the substance of,* or rather, *the confidence*[1] *of,* that is, *confidence in, things hoped for; the evidence,* or *test,* or *proof, that which gives conviction, of things not seen* (Heb. xi. 1). Faith is the apprehension, the assurance, the conviction, of things which are unseen, because either spiritual, or future. Faith is that state of the mind, in which it realizes to itself some thing of which, or some person of whom, the senses cannot take cognizance. The Chapter from which this definition is taken is full of examples of its working. *He endured, as seeing Him who is invisible* (Heb. xi. 27): that is the briefest and yet the fullest of all the descriptions of it. Faith is the seeing Him who is invisible. Applicable indeed to many other subjects besides that of religion or of the Gospel; for it is the foundation of almost every act of human life, which would itself come to an end instantly if we attempted to set aside and disregard in our conduct everything which is not before our

---

[1] The same word occurs in this sense in 2 Cor. ix. 4. xi. 17. Heb. iii. 14.

eyes; it is yet in the things of God that we see it in its highest and most remarkable developement, and it is with reference to these things, I need not say, that St John here writes, *This is the victory which overcame the world*, even *our faith*.

This is He who came through water and blood, Jesus the Christ; not in the water only, but in the water and in the blood: and the Spirit is that which testifies, because the Spirit is the truth. The words are difficult, and they have been darkened still further by the perverse ingenuity of men. Let us humbly endeavour to take them in their simplicity.

None of you will fail to remember upon what historical circumstance the sentence is founded. We have in St John's narrative of the Crucifixion the following words: *But one of the soldiers with a spear pierced His side* as He still hung upon the cross after death had taken place, *and forthwith came thereout blood and water. And he that saw it*, the same Apostle on whose words we are dwelling to-day, *bare record, and his record is true; and he knoweth that he saith true, that ye might believe* (John xix. 34, 35). I quote the latter of these two verses to remind you of the importance attached by St John to the incident which he alone has recorded. He saw in it a symbolical significance, which in the Epistle he brings out into view.

This is He who came through (by means of) water and blood: that is, *whose coming was attested by water and blood:* who brought these two things, whatever may be denoted by them, as His credentials, as the authentications of His mission.

I believe that here, as elsewhere, the Scripture will be found to be its own best interpreter. Let me refer you to one or two passages in which, whether separately or in combination, we may find these two figures, of the water, and of the blood.

Christ loved the Church, and gave Himself for it, that He might consecrate it by cleansing it with the laver of water in (through) a word, an utterance, a Divine utterance, the Gospel itself (1 Pet. i. 25), *that He might present the Church to Himself glorious, not having spot or wrinkle or any such thing, but that it may be holy and blameless* (Eph. v. 25—27). The laver of water is spoken of as a means of purifying the Church for presentation hereafter to Christ Himself as His Spouse and Bride.

Again. *Not by works which are* done *in righteousness, which we did, but according to His own mercy, He saved us by means of a laver of regeneration and renewing of (by) a Holy Spirit, whom He poured forth upon us abundantly through Jesus Christ our Saviour* (Tit. iii. 5, 6).

A third illustration is furnished by St John himself. *If we walk in the light, as He Himself is in the light, we have communion one with another, and the blood of Jesus His Son cleanseth us from every sin* (1 John i. 7). The two former passages spoke of the water, this of the blood.

A fourth passage, from the Epistle to the Hebrews,

will combine the two. *Let us draw near with a true heart, in full assurance of faith, having our hearts sprinkled from an evil conscience, and our body washed with pure water* (Heb. x. 22). We have here both the sprinkling of blood upon the heart, and the washing of the body with pure water. The water is that of Baptism; the blood is that of Atonement.

He who came by water and blood is, in other words, He who authenticated His mission by the two seals, of cleansing and propitiation; a cleansing typified by Baptism, and an atonement effected by His own death. *Not by water only;* for a cleansing from sin cannot be effected alone; no thorough change of heart and life can be effected until something else has gone before: *not by water only, but by water and blood;* first the blood that *sprinkles from an evil conscience*, from the consciousness of guilt, and next the water that cleanses from a life of sin.

But then, together with both these, there is the concurrent testimony of the Spirit, the Holy Spirit. No baptism typical of cleansing, and no death efficacious for atonement, could suffice without this to complete the credentials of the Saviour. There must be also the witness of the Spirit. His witness, first, in the life and ministry, the words and the acts, of Christ Himself upon earth. *How God anointed Jesus of Nazareth with the Holy Ghost and with power* (Acts x. 38). The triple seal of power, of wisdom, and of goodness, must be set upon the Person of the Son of God made Man. His witness, next, in those miraculous powers with which He endued the first Disciples and Apostles of the risen Saviour. His witness, thirdly and above all, borne through every age from the first days of the Gospel until now, in the actual transformation of human character by His living presence in the hearts of all who believe.

We have now reached the seventh verse: and it will not startle some of those who hear me, if they observe that I omit a portion of the passage in my comment upon the rest. It has, in fact, crept into the sacred text without sufficient warrant[1]. Those who were eager to discover in all manner of fanciful analogies proofs from Scripture of the doctrine of the Trinity appear to have caught at the words, *For there are three who bear testimony, the Spirit, and the water, and the blood, and these three agree in one*, as furnishing material for such an illustration; and that which was first written in the margin of the latter verse, as a mere illustration of doctrine, eventually crept into the text, and became a chief weapon of controversy in behalf of the orthodox faith of the Trinity in Unity. That faith, my brethren, needs no false supports: and it is a false support, when a text which rests upon no sufficient warrant of genuineness is employed in defence of a truth which God has not suffered to lack its proper evidence.

Therefore we read the passage thus. *This is He who came through water and blood, Jesus the Christ;*

[1] It may be enough to refer to a very lucid statement of the case in Bishop Marsh's well-known Lectures.

not in the water only, but in the water and in the blood: and the Spirit is that which testifies, because the Spirit is the truth. For there are three who testify; the Spirit, and the water, and the blood; and the three are unto, that is, result in, combine in, *the one thing;* bear a consistent, a harmonious, an united testimony.

If we receive the testimony of mankind, the testimony of God is greater, more powerful, more convincing: and such is the case in this instance; *for this is the testimony of God;* namely, *that He has testified concerning His Son.*

He who believes in the Son of God has the testimony in him; gives it entrance, and retains it within him: *he who believes not God*, he who refuses to accept God's testimony, *has made Him a liar*, has imputed falsehood to God, *because he has not believed in the testimony which God has testified concerning His Son.*

What then is that testimony? *And this is the testimony; that God*, in giving His Son, *gave us eternal life, and this life is in His Son.*

He who has the Son has the life, that eternal life which has just been spoken of: *he who has not the Son of God has not the life.*

My brethren, there are many points in this passage of Scripture which might profitably be selected for special remark. But I must content myself with indicating one, that contained in the text, and ask God to bless it to our humble meditation.

Observe the place which faith holds in the Christian life. *This is the victory that overcometh the world, even our faith.* Is this your idea of faith, my brethren? a practical, working, yes, even a fighting and a conquering power?

What is the representation here made of our position? We have an enemy. That is plainly said. Every one of us, who has any of the hopes or aims of a Christian, has an enemy, whose existence, whose ceaseless activity, may well trouble and alarm him. We cannot escape from him. It is a foe of our own household. It is a foe with whom we are compelled to associate every day. *The world:* the things that are seen: the present state: the life that is, with all its cares, its interests, its pleasures: this is our enemy. We do not speak in a fantastic, unreal, or exaggerated sense. We are not counselling a morbid fear of things which God has created for our use and for our enjoyment, as though a serpent lurked in each, and made its very touch deadly. But we do know, every one of us, that, taking the present state as a whole, the world in the aggregate of its influences upon us, it is not a friend to our highest good, if our highest good be that which God seems to represent it to be in His Word of Revelation. Let yourself alone but for one day; surrender yourself but for one day to the guidance, to the operation upon you, of your world less or greater; move about in it, listen and talk, work and enjoy, in it, for one day, without any counteracting and countervailing power consciously evoked and appealed to within; and where would you be at the end of that day? Should you be nearer to, or further from, the goal of life, if that goal be a heavenly one, if that goal be the love of God, the attainment of a Divine rest, a spiritual happiness, and an eternal home?

It is thus that we must test the world, and not by any lower or more arbitrary standard. If this strange complicated thing which we call our being, ourselves, is ever to know unity, repose, complete satisfaction, all its parts having attained their object, and consciously resting in their perfect joy; if this is the hope which Christ came to inspire in all who will have Him for their Saviour; then that must be our enemy which tends to distract and to unsettle us, to turn off our attention from the aim of life, and to bid us find or seek repose in this thing or that thing which is either doubtful of attainment, inferior in nature, limited in extent, or brief in duration.

The world is our enemy, on the supposition that we have any aim or any hope beyond it. Not otherwise. The world is our friend, if all we have ever to look for is bounded by the life that is. If we do not believe in Christ, if we do not desire to be with Him, if we do not wish above all things so to live that that hope, of being with Him hereafter, may not be interfered with; then we cannot do better than get all that this world has to offer us; make peace with it, adopt its principles, claim its friendship, sue for its rewards: else shall we be losing both worlds, the world that is and also the world that shall be.

But this is not so, avowedly, with any of us: God

grant it be not so really! We do wish, every one of us, to get safe to heaven. If by any one great sacrifice or great exertion we could secure this, I do not believe that there is one person in this Congregation who would refuse or hesitate to make it. I scarcely believe there is one here present, who would not willingly lay down even this precious life that is, for the certainty of a sure and instant entrance into a world of safety and of immortality. But it is not thus that our warfare has to be waged. Rather is it by a protracted, a wearisome, often a desultory process, that we must make our way: by wakefulness, by discernment, by discretion, by being always ready, by being patient of delay and disappointment, by willingness oftentimes only to stand and wait, by experience dearly purchased, by rising sadder and wiser from painful falls, by making an onward step when we can, but more often by hardly refraining from a backward one, by being ever prepared to find real foes in fancied friends, or to see the mountain-side, which seemed but now empty and untenanted, bristling on the sudden with armed enemies; it is thus that the Christian conflict is waged; and many a man who could have nerved himself for one brief decisive struggle, however sharp or unequal, fails, faints, and at last deserts, amidst the ceaseless and less heroic exertions by which he must fight his way into the kingdom of God in heaven.

The world: that is our foe. Sometimes the world is made but one of three foes, the flesh and the devil being added to it. But, like each of these also—like the flesh, like the devil—it is sometimes made to embrace all that opposes the Christian warrior. It is the flesh which gives entrance to all; it is the devil who directs and uses all; but the world furnishes the material of all. The world contains everything that can either tempt or harass: and the victory of the Christian, like the victory of Christ Himself, is then completed, when he can say, without enumerating aught else, *I have overcome the world* (John xvi. 33).

Now therefore we can understand why the Apostle should sum up the whole of our victory in the one word *faith*. You have heard what faith is. It is the apprehending of things unseen. It is the grasping of heavenly realities. It is the seeing One who is invisible. It is the having that which is not cognizable by any bodily sense, as real to us, as present, as powerful, as if it were so. One person acted by faith, when he left his own home and country and kindred at the call of God, and went forth simply under His guidance, not knowing whither he went (Heb. xi. 8). Another person acted by faith, when, in obedience to God's command, he sprinkled the blood of the lamb upon the door of his house, and depended upon the destroying Angel's regarding the token (Heb. xi. 28). Another person acted by faith, when, in obedience to God's command, he compassed for seven days the walls of a hostile city, and waited for the miraculous achievement of a victory in which he was not to intermeddle (Heb. xi. 30). In all these, and in ten thousand other instances in every age, Faith has fought for God's servants, and has overcome the world. So long as our eye is steadily fixed on One above, so long as we set God and Christ really before us, so long as we retain the unshaken recollection of God's being, and of His right over us, and of His having spoken to us and loved and redeemed us in His Son, so long the world is powerless to entrap, to seduce, or to terrify. But, alas! here is our weakness; that we look off from God: *the spirit is willing* (Matt. xxvi. 41); the day begins well; the prayer of the morning is earnest and effectual; the blessing has descended as we knelt: the heart has been warmed, the spirit refreshed, the mind strengthened, the will firmly resolved; the communication is open, and we have used it; we think, as we rise from prayer, that, though all should be offended this day, yet shall not we (Matt. xxvi. 33); though all should prove unfaithful to our Divine Lord, yet shall we surely follow Him even if it were to prison and to death (Luke xxii. 33); *but the flesh is weak;* duty itself calls us back into the things that are seen and temporal, bids us work, bids us mix with men, bids us play a manly part amongst the people of our generation, bids us come forth and not hide ourselves in the seclusion of an indolent contemplation: and the result of all is, that, long ere the day is at its height, we have lost the dew of its morning; the world is with us, and we with it; God is in heaven, and we upon earth, and between us and Him there is already a great gulf fixed. Then the very least of temptations may assail us successfully: our strength has departed from us, and man, left alone, cannot but fall. At night, with great difficulty, we force our way back across the barrier which has been interposed: but it is to remember with shame and sorrow how often we have fallen; how much we have walked by sight, how little by faith; how slight a trial has been too great for temper, for humility, for kindness, for charity; how little has been said or done for God's glory, how much for vain-glory, for self-indulgence, for men-pleasing!

My brethren, well might this and every Sermon end with the three words, *Let us pray!* Yes, let us all pray. How little do we know, till we heartily try it, not only the benefit, but the happiness, of Prayer. God is very near us: we are not straitened in Him. God would have us pray, in order that He may answer. He needs not words: He knows what is in us, our sins, our weaknesses, our desires, our wants, even before we ask: yet He would have us ask, He would have us open our hearts to Him, He would have us confide in Him, that He may comfort, that He may soothe, that He may strengthen, that He may bless. *In the evening, and morning, and at noonday, will I pray, and that instantly: and He shall hear my voice* (Psalm lv. 17). *O Thou that hearest prayer, unto Thee shall all flesh come* (Psalm lxv. 2).

SERMON XVII.

THE WANDERING AND THE RETURN.

EPISTLE FOR THE SECOND SUNDAY AFTER EASTER.

1 Peter ii. 19—25.

19 THIS is acceptable[1], if by reason of consciousness of God any
20 one supports griefs, suffering unjustly. For what sort of glory is it, if, sinning and being buffeted, ye shall endure? but [the glory is] if, doing good and suffering, ye shall
21 endure: for this is acceptable[1] with God. For unto this were ye called; because even Christ suffered for us, leaving behind for you a copy, that ye might follow upon His foot-
22 steps: who did not [any] sin, nor was deceit found in His
23 mouth; who, being reviled, reviled not again; suffering, threatened not; but committed [it] to Him who judges
24 righteously: who carried up our sins Himself in His body to the tree, that, having died to sins, we might live to
25 righteousness; by whose stripe-wound ye were healed. For ye were, as sheep[2], straying; but ye turned back now to the Shepherd and Guardian[3] of your souls.

[1] Literally, *grace, favour, acceptance.*

[2] Matt. ix. 36. Mark vi. 34. *They were as sheep not having a shepherd.*

[3] Acts xx. 28. *Take heed...to all the flock, over the which the Holy Ghost hath made you overseers* (or *guardians*).

SERMON XVII.

THE WANDERING AND THE RETURN.

1 Peter ii. 25.

For ye were as sheep going astray; but are now returned unto the Shepherd and Bishop of your souls.

THE first Epistle of St Peter has ever been deeply valued by Christian men. Nowhere have we a more emphatic statement of the work of Christ in redeeming, or of the Holy Spirit in sanctifying us. Nowhere have we a more animating description of the Christian life in this world, or a brighter and more attractive anticipation of the glory that shall be revealed.

It is, throughout, in the truest sense of the word, practical in its character. Not only does it contain many details of duty, but it also never leaves those details separated from the one availing motive.

The Epistle for this second Sunday after Easter is an example of this remark. It is taken from a passage referring to the duties of servants. It states in a very strong form the Christian duty of obedience. This duty was not affected by the character of the master. In those days, you remember, service was servitude. A servant was a slave; the property of his master; with no choice therefore either as to the person whom he would serve or the terms or duration of that service. In all these respects times have changed, with us at all events, greatly for the better. But the injunctions laid upon servants, or slaves, in the New Testament are not therefore obsolete. Much more rather than less justly may it be said to servants now, as it was said to slaves then, Be obedient to your masters, with good will doing service. If your serving at all is a matter of choice, a choice guided by considerations of interest, and followed by results of mutual benefit, surely this is but an added reason why it should be faithfully fulfilled, with strict integrity, with self-denying diligence, with ready obedience. *Servants*—and the term here employed denotes a particular kind of service, that of the house or family, domestic service—*Servants, be obedient to your masters in all fear, not only to the good and gentle, but also to the froward*, the unreasonable, ill-tempered, or perverse.

Such is the connection in which the passage before us stands. But we shall see that, important as is its present bearing upon the case of servants, it is by no means restricted to that one use. Which of us does not stand in a relation of inferiority to some one? Which of us, I might add, has not something to bear at the hands of some one? We shall find here a rule for every kind of subordination, and a motive for every kind of endurance.

For this is acceptable—literally, *this is favour* or *acceptance—if for conscience toward God*—more exactly, *if by reason of consciousness of God;* that is, because he is conscious of God, and of his own relation to God as His redeemed creature—*any one supports griefs, suffering unjustly.* The stress is on the word *unjustly, wrongfully. For what sort of glory is it, if, sinning and being buffeted, ye shall endure;* if, when ye be buffeted for your faults, ye shall take it patiently? *but* the glory is *if, doing good and suffering, ye shall endure;* if, when ye do well and suffer for it, ye shall take it patiently: *for this is favour*, this is acceptable, *with God.* A veiy different estimate of merit is this, my brethren, from that which is either natural to us or even in a Christian country generally taken. More often, I think, do we hear people praised for their spirit in resenting than for their patience in bearing wrongs.

For unto this were ye called: this sort of submissive endurance was that to which God called you when He offered you the Gospel of Christ: *because even Christ,* great as He was, and holy, and sinless, *suffered for us,* and therefore, so far as His own merit was concerned, suffered wrongfully, for no sin and no failing of His own: and this with a special object in view; by way of *leaving behind for you an example*—the word denotes properly a *copy*, like that given to a child to write after—*that ye might follow upon His footsteps.*

And then we have a most beautiful account of Christ's work for us, in its two parts; those two parts which the Collect for this day distinguishes, when it calls upon God as having given His only Son *to be unto us both a sacrifice for sin, and also an ensample of godly life.* Here the other order is followed, and the example stands before the sacrifice, as the context required. We are to bear injustice patiently, because so did Christ, leaving us an example.

Who did not any *sin, nor was deceit found in His mouth.* The words are quoted, you remember, like some of those which follow, from a well-known passage of the Old Testament (Isai. liii. 9). Christ, if He suffered, could not but suffer wrongfully, because He had no sin of His own, in deed or word, to suffer for: and yet He did suffer, and suffered patiently. *Who, being reviled, reviled not again;* did not retaliate with words of reproach or contumely. O how few can say this! How few can resist, even with this example before them, the temptation to return taunt for taunt, sarcasm for sarcasm, anger for anger, scorn for scorn! This is that quality in our Lord to which the prophet Isaiah alludes in the words, *As a sheep before her shearers is dumb, so He opened not His mouth* (Isai. liii. 7). *When He suffered, He threatened not; but committed* it, referred His cause, *to Him who judges righteously.*

Such is the use here made of the example of Christ. If in any way, from any cause, from any quarter, you are suffering unjustly, do not recriminate, do not threaten, but place yourself and all that concerns you in the hands of Him who in His own good time will bring your just dealing to light, and who even now, even while suffering lasts, can mitigate and brighten it by the comforts of His own Spirit within. Happy indeed are they who in their sufferings have no reason for self-reproach; who have a cause which they can commit to a righteous Judge; who have only to keep their own spirit under suffering, and all shall be well with them. But still more cause surely have they to give heed to this exhortation, who know and feel that suffering has been in any part brought upon themselves; still more cause to guard against allowing it to make them morose, fretful, or resentful; still more cause, if it be possible, for committing themselves and it into His hands, who, if in one aspect He is a righteous Judge, is in another a faithful Creator, and in another a gracious and most merciful Saviour.

Who His own self bare our sins in His own body on the tree. The original expression is rather this; *who carried up our sins Himself in His own body to the tree.* The verb is the same with that used in the Epistle to the Hebrews, in the words, *So Christ was once offered to bear the sins of many* (Heb. ix. 28). He carried up our sins, Himself, in His own Person, yes (it may be said) in His own body, to the tree, to the cross as to an altar, that there they, our sins, might be put to death when that body was put to death. Put to death as to their guilt, put to death as to their curse, put to death as to their condemning voice, put to death as to their debasing and enchaining power.

It seems as though the Scriptures would exhaust the very resources of language in the endeavour to reassure and to reanimate them that believe. Again and again, in every possible variety of form, is the completeness of Christ's work shadowed forth to us in the writings of His Apostles. Take a single example from St Paul's Epistles; one which appears to approach as nearly as any to the exact idea here conveyed. *One who knew not sin did God make sin for us, that we might become a* very *righteousness of God in Him* (2 Cor. v. 21). I will not fritter away the force of the term by any paraphrase. God made Christ to be sin for us; and, because He did so, therefore, when Christ was led up to the altar of His sacrifice, lifted up from the earth upon His cross to draw all men unto Him, our sins, yes, all the sins of all of us, were carried up in Him to that altar, and, when He was put to death, they were put to death. What can we say more? Do you ask, What part of them was put to death? was it their guilt, or was it their power? I answer, *They* were put to death: each part and every part of them was put to death. Seize upon that truth, that fact, and live as if it were true; live in the strength of it, yea, in the strength of Him whose truth it is; and, I say not only, *Ye shall be made free* (John viii. 32), but I say also, in the words of the same all-true Witness, *He that heareth my word, and believeth Him that sent me, hath everlasting life, and cometh not into judgment, but hath passed*, has gone across, has passed the boundary line, *out of death into life* (John v. 24)!

I would seek, God helping us, to transfer your

thoughts and your hopes out of the vague future into the living present. I would restore to its right and original place in the scheme of Redemption such passages as those which say to persons who believe in Christ, not, *Ye shall come,* but, *Ye have come, to the mount Sion, and to the city of the living God, the heavenly Jerusalem...and to the spirits of just men made perfect, and to Jesus the Mediator of a new dispensation, and to a blood of sprinkling speaking better things than Abel* (Heb. xii. 22—24). In that difference between, *Ye shall come,* and, *Ye have come,* lies, I am persuaded, for many persons, the whole question of a vigorous or a torpid Christianity. Tell a man, By great efforts, or at a time indefinitely remote, you may attain union with God through Christ—and the world, the flesh, and the devil, are together and singly too powerful for Him. Tell him, This life of union with God is yours already, rise, enter into it, live it, now—and his soul may be stirred within him as by a mighty and resistless power. And the whole of this vast difference lies, for each one of us, in the right appreciation of these few grave words, *Himself carried up our sins in His own body to the cross, that we, having* then and there, as by one act, in His person with whom, as Christians, we are one, *died unto (in relation to) our sins, might* then and there, as by one act—such is the force of the original—*live unto (in relation to) righteousness.*

This was our subject on Easter Day, suggested by St Paul's language to the Colossians, as read in that day's Epistle. A Christian is united to Christ, and is to live as though all that has happened to Christ had happened also to him. Death and resurrection are for him as truly past events as future. *If ye then were raised with Christ... Ye died, and your life is hid with Christ in God* (Col. iii. 1, 3). But observe to-day how exactly the same thing is not only the sense but the very form of St Peter's doctrine also. Let me strengthen the interpretation by a reference to yet one other passage in this same Epistle. *Christ then having suffered for us in* (or, *unto, in relation to*) *flesh, arm yourselves likewise with the same mind*, the same idea or thought; namely, that you also have already suffered in the flesh, have already died, not like Him only, but with and in Him: *for he who suffered in flesh*, he who has once died, *has been made to cease from sin* (1 Pet. iv. 1). It is the very statement of St Paul in the Epistle to the Romans, and applied in precisely the same manner. *For he who died*, he who has once undergone death, *has been set free* (*cleared as by a judicial sentence*) *from sin* (Rom. vi. 7). A dead man cannot sin. He has no body in which to sin. *Arm yourselves* then *with the same idea*, that you died when He died; *that ye no longer should live your remaining time in flesh to* (*in relation to*, and so, *in the indulgence of*) *the desires of men, but to* (*in relation to*, and so, *in the fulfilment of*) *the will of God* (1 Pet. iv. 2). Believe that your sins were upon Christ when He was put to death—that is the expression before us; believe that you were in Christ when He was put to death—that is the expression adduced from the fourth Chapter; and, in either case, as the consequence of this belief, live as if you had done with sin as much as a dead man has done with it, and as if the only life now left to you is that life in Christ, as He now is in heaven, which is altogether above earth, even while, as to its outward scene, it has still to be passed in it.

By whose stripes—or rather, *by whose stripe-wound*, by the mark of whose stripes, the wound or bruise left by His scourging—*ye were healed.* The figure is again borrowed from the prophecy of Isaiah. *The chastisement of (which procured) our peace was upon Him, and with His stripes we are healed* (Isai. liii. 5). His death was our life, and each particular portion of his sufferings was an integral part of the work of our healing. It was the suffering of Christ; His humiliation unto death, as a whole, and in its parts; which brought you back, like lost sheep, to the fold of God. *For ye were as sheep, straying: but ye turned back now*, in these days of grace and the Gospel, *to the Shepherd and Guardian of your souls.*

You will all desire that our last thoughts this morning should be suffered to rest without distraction upon this contrast. Happy are they who can enter into both its parts. Into one of the two we can all enter. Past experience, or else present experience, will impress it upon our hearts in all its significance.

Ye were, like sheep, going astray. Such is the brief description of the life without Christ. It is a perpetual straying. Of all the figures by which it is described to us in Scripture, I know not that there is one more just, or, I may add, more affecting, than this. It is so simple, and, like all the figures of Scripture, so true to experience. There is no exaggeration in it. It does not say of us all, what truth as well as charity may constrain us to feel to be applicable only to some. *Straying, wandering:* whatever else might be exaggerated as a charge laid universally against human nature, certainly this is not so. I believe there is not a heart in this congregation which does not plead guilty inwardly to this indictment. Certainly we all say this of ourselves when we meet for worship. *We have erred and strayed from Thy ways like lost sheep.* It is true not only of those whom we describe as great sinners; persons of profligate life or profane lips. It is true not only with reference to the two or three glaring instances of transgression, known to others or unknown, of which many persons, kneeling before God, may bitterly accuse themselves. No, it is true, almost equally, of many a very decent life, of many a very pleasing character. *Ye were once,* or, *ye are still, as sheep going astray.* I may say it in this congregation almost without wounding the pride, and quite without distorting the history, of any one who hears me. I confine the words to one idea: that which stands most directly in contrast to the parallel and opposite clause. You once had, or else you still have, consciously at least, no Shepherd and no Guardian; and therefore

The Wandering and the Return. 301

you could not help being wanderers. A wanderer may be very far, or very little, out of the right way: now and then he may be for a moment or two almost or quite in the right way: but the point of his condition is, that he is under no guidance: when he is right, he is right by accident: when he is wrong, he is wrong by accident, though by a very natural accident, and one easily to be accounted for: he has no consciousness of a shepherd, a guide, a guardian, a constant and watchful eye over him, and therefore his journeyings have no direction, his race no goal, his exile no home.

Brethren, many a heart says at this moment in its secret place, That is true. I am journeying through life at hazard. I have no plan. One day is very like another, but not because each day is a definite and regular progress towards a known end. Not in that sense. I have many good impulses, many vague hopes, and many just regrets. I often do that which is right. I show kindness, I abstain from falsehood and blasphemy, I give something to the poor, I go where others go to worship. But I am not really at unity within. I do not know rest. I have no sense of being under guidance, under an almighty hand, under an unsleeping, a watchful, a loving eye. If I were to die, I am not sure what would become of me. I cannot feel satisfied with my own inward retrospect. I cannot cast myself upon a tried and proved mercy I am a lonely man; lonely in heart, lonely in reference to any one independent of change and death, lonely in reference to any one like Him of whom I seem to read in my Bible, of whom I seem to hear some few Christians tell, as nearer to them than the nearest earthly friend, a real refuge in trouble, a supporting stay, and an unfailing hope. Tried by this test, I am still a wanderer. If I am going right, it is by chance; if I ever reach a home beyond the grave, accident, not aim, will have brought me thither.

Would to God, my brethren, that it were given to man—but that which is impossible with man is possible with Him—to guide his brother's steps into the way of peace! to give an aim to the desultory, a standing-place to the unstable, a destination, and the right destination, to the purposeless and the vacillating! Listen to the other half of the text. Do not put from you God's teaching: it is for you: it may be true of you to-morrow, if not to-day, *Ye are now returned to the Shepherd and Bishop of your souls.*

Remark that there is One who is this to you, by right and by will of His, even already, even before you turn. The question is in the turning. Shepherd and Bishop of your souls He is already: the question is, Have you yet turned to Him? This it is which so wonderfully marks God's teaching. It is all of things ready, things done, things which are already facts; not visionary prospects, not possible contingencies, but things accomplished, things waiting only to be grasped. See it here. *The Shepherd and Bishop of your souls.* There is a Person so described in reference to us all. Some have turned already to Him, and some not yet: but to all He already bears this relation, if only they will have Him in it. There is no getting, procuring, finding a Saviour: that is not what God sets us to do: that He does, that He has done, for us. There is only this: the Shepherd being ready, the Guardian being ready, but you having your back towards Him, *you must just turn round.* Against your will He cannot assist you. It is against His rule; which always is, *According to your faith, be it unto you* (Matt. ix. 29). Strong faith, much help; weak faith, little help; no faith, no help. But more than this: we can understand just enough of the things of God to see that a salvation against a man's will, or (in one sense) even without a man's will, would be no salvation at all. And therefore we can accept with thankfulness the one condition which is imposed. You must turn—or (which is only another way of expressing the same truth, and perhaps still more Scripturally) you must be turned—and then all is done: the Shepherd, the Guardian, of your souls, stands ready, and salvation is not to be still sought, it is already found.

This is that act of which some unsound things have by some been uttered, and with which some, yet far more perilously, would endeavour wholly to dispense—Conversion. *Ye are now returned, ye now turned back*, or, *were turned back*—it is spoken of as a single definite past act—*to the Shepherd and Bishop of your souls*. True, we ought not to want this. In a Christian country, within the fold of a

Christian Church, we ought to be Christians from the first hour: little children in Christ first, then young men, then in due course men of full age, then old men, fathers, in Christ (1 John ii. 12—14); His all along, growing with a steady and a healthy progress to *the measure of the stature of the fulness of Christ* (Eph. iv. 13). We ought not to want a wrench, a reversal, a convulsion, of the spiritual being, to make us Christians indeed. But, if we do want it, it may be a thing to be regretted, it may be a thing to be ashamed of, but do not let us deny that it is a necessity. Do not let us argue that, because we ought not to want it, therefore we do not want it.

Two things I will say, and then conclude.

The question as to our wanting this change, this return, this conversion, is merely this: Which way are our faces turned now? If towards Christ, then we do not want it. The only object is, that we should, somehow or other, by whatever means it be effected, face towards Him, front towards Him, have our eye fixed upon Him that we may follow Him henceforth whithersoever He goeth (Rev. xiv. 4). I cannot answer the question for any one. But it is a very serious one. Are you still wandering? still living by chance, and therefore going astray? Or is Christ before you? do you set Him before you each day, in His death, in His resurrection, in His life after resurrection in heaven, in His work for you, in His will concerning you, in His unchanging mercy, in His all-availing, His Spirit's, strength?

Lastly, if the answer to this former question be in any case unfavourable or doubtful, then I would beseech you to take a very simple, and a very hopeful, view of the change required in you. Say to yourself, I am like a sheep going astray; but there is One seeking me. There is One whom my wandering has pained, has grieved. There is One whose heart yearns after me still. The moment I come to myself, the moment I want Him, the moment my heart relents, and would fain see Him and have Him for my Shepherd and my Guardian, that moment He will become this to me. To be converted is to turn round. It is a change of direction, not a change of nature. It is a turning back; yes, it is a return. Blessed words! Ye are *returned* to your Shepherd. These persons to whom St Peter writes had not first had Christ and then left Him; and yet when they came to Him, it is called not a coming, but a returning. What does that say? Surely that Christ is (if I might so express it) the natural, the original, Shepherd and Guardian of our souls; so that he who comes to Him, even if it be for the first time consciously, returns in doing so; comes to a place, to a home, to a Person, which or who was his already, and from which or from whom he has been all the time a truant and a wanderer. Does not this speak volumes to us as to the facility of finding Christ when we do turn to Him? God grant that blessing to each one of us who may still need it—and we all need it more or less; in a stronger or a more limited sense we all need it every day—the blessing of this turning round by an act (under His prompting) of the heart and will, and of then discovering that He to whom we thus turn has been all the time, by right and by office, not a stranger to us, but already the very *Shepherd and Bishop of our souls!*

SERMON XVIII.

ONE FLOCK, ONE SHEPHERD.

GOSPEL FOR THE SECOND SUNDAY AFTER EASTER.

St John x. 11—16.

11   JESUS said, *I am the good shepherd. The good shepherd*
12   *lays down his life for the sheep. But he that is an hireling and not the shepherd, whose own the sheep are not, beholds the wolf coming, and leaves the sheep, and flees—and the*
13   *wolf seizes them, and scatters—because*[1] *he is an hireling,*
14   *and cares not for the sheep. I am the good shepherd, and I*
15   *know my own* [*sheep*], *and my own know me, even as the Father knows me and I know the Father; and I lay*
16   *down my life for the sheep. And other sheep I have, which are not of this fold; them also must I bring, and they shall hear my voice, and there shall become one flock, one shepherd.*

---

[1] According to the reading here adopted, the word *because* depends upon *leaves the sheep and flees* in verse 12; the clause *and the wolf seizes them and scatters* being regarded as parenthetical. The words *the hireling fleeth*, with which the 13th verse begins in some manuscripts and in the Authorized Version, were probably added to explain the sense.

SERMON XVIII.

ONE FLOCK, ONE SHEPHERD.

St John x. 16.

And other sheep I have, which are not of this fold: them also I must bring, and they shall hear my voice; and there shall be one fold, and one Shepherd.

THE Epistle for the day, considered this morning, spoke of a return to the Shepherd of our souls. The Gospel, reserved for this evening, tells us more of this Shepherd, in His own words; and, familiar as the subject is to all of us, I know not that it can ever be superfluous to dwell upon it with prayer and praise.

The few verses read as the Gospel are taken from a much longer passage on the same general topic. But the difficulty is rather to choose than to find material for thought, when we dwell upon the character of Christ as the Good Shepherd. And therefore I will confine myself strictly to the six verses which form the Gospel for the day.

Jesus said—for so is the Gospel prefaced—*I am the good shepherd. The good shepherd lays down his life for the sheep. But he that is an hireling and not the shepherd, whose own the sheep are not, beholds the wolf coming, and leaves the sheep, and flees—and (so that) the wolf catches them, and scatters—because he is an hireling, and cares not for the sheep. I am the good shepherd, and I know my own, and my own know me, even as the Father knows me and I know the Father; and I lay down my life for the sheep. And other sheep I have, which are not of this fold: them also must I bring, and they shall hear my voice, and there shall be one flock, one shepherd.*

I know not that it is necessary to say more than one word upon the imagery here employed.

In Palestine, we are told—to quote the substance of a few sentences from the account of a recent traveller—there is a sight often to be seen in the near neighbourhood of Jerusalem, that of the shepherds leading over the hills their flocks of sheep and goats, the white sheep and the black goats intermingled on the mountain-side, yet by their colour at once distinguishable from each other. The shepherds, we know, abode with their flocks, at the time of the Gospel history, at least within a few miles of Jerusalem: it is possible that such a flock may have wandered up the sides of the Mount of Olives, and suggested to Him who was sitting there with His disciples over against the temple, the scene of the Shepherd of mankind dividing the parts of that vast flock, each from each, the sheep on His right hand, and the goats on His left. It was probably on the same Mount of Olives, while conversing with the excommunicated blind man, that our Lord uttered, in the hearing of the Pharisees, another Parable—that which is now before us—the Parable of the Good Shepherd. The sheepfold on the slope of the hill—the wicket-gate—the keeper of the gate—the sheep, as in all southern countries, following, not preceding, the shepherd whose voice they hear—may have been present to His sight then, as in the later parable; and thus it may have been the same outward scene which suggested the image of the mild and beneficent Guardian, and of the stern and awful Judge of the human race[1].

It is with the earlier only of these two Parables that we are now concerned; that which sets before us our Lord Himself under the similitude of the Good Shepherd. I think that the Parable, so far as it is comprised in the six verses just read to you, may be suggestive of three chief reflections.

1. The first of these is, *the care of Christ for those who are His; a care arising out of ownership, and prompting an entire self-sacrifice in their behalf.*

A contrast is presented. Some shepherds are hirelings, paid for their trouble in guiding and guarding the flock. Such a shepherd does not really care for the sheep. He thinks of himself; what he can get for taking charge of them. When danger approaches, it is not of them that he thinks, but of himself. He leaves them to the ravening wolf, to be caught or to be scattered. He thinks only of making

---

[1] See Dean Stanley's *Sinai and Palestine*, Chap. viii. p. 415.

his escape, because he is an hireling, and careth not for the sheep.

The words, my brethren, have a significance for us ministers of the Gospel beyond what they can possibly have for you. It is not that there is any reproach in what St Paul calls *living of the Gospel* (1 Cor. ix. 14); receiving a maintenance from that work which in these days demands a whole life for its performance. It is not this which makes a man a hireling, in the bad sense of that word. That lies in the spirit in which the work is done. And how rare is that solicitude for the souls of men which is here ascribed to the good shepherd! We are called pastors (shepherds) as well as teachers. No figure is more common. *Take heed to yourselves*, St Paul said to the elders of the Church of Ephesus, *and to all the flock over the which the Holy Ghost hath made you overseers, to feed the Church of God, which He hath purchased with His own blood. For I know this*, he adds, continuing the same illustration, *that after my departing shall grievous wolves enter in among you, not sparing the flock* (Acts xx. 28, 29). And in the same terms St Peter addresses the ministers of the Church in his own and in all later times. *Feed the flock of God which is among you, taking the oversight thereof, not by constraint, but willingly; not for sordid gain, but of a ready mind... And when the chief Shepherd shall appear, ye shall receive the crown of glory that fadeth not away* (1 Pet. v. 2, 4). How deeply must a conscientious Clergyman reproach himself for the faintness of his own sense of these things! How difficult is it for him in all things to see himself last; to think more of the welfare of his charge than of his own ease or comfort or honour! Men are severe judges of us: but we must not complain. We ought to be what too often we are not. We have devoted ourselves to a certain work, and woe is unto us if we do it not as we have promised!

But let us now, both for your sake and our own, set in contrast with the conduct of the hireling, that of the true, the good, the Divine Shepherd.

He careth for you (1 Pet. v. 7). I know nothing more deeply persuasive than those four words and the truth which they express. There are those who pass through life in a state of constant depression and discontent, because they think that no one cares for them. It is a pain which lies very deep in hearts that would not be suspected of it. A person may possess power and fame and success and popularity, and yet feel it. Such persons, perhaps even more than others, are slow to believe in the existence towards them of such a thing as disinterested affection. And we are all of us too much guilty of the sin of thinking of God, or of Christ, that He is even such an one as ourselves (Psalm l. 21): slow to realize the idea of there being in heaven a love and a care for us which we have not found upon earth; a love and a care absolutely disinterested, unaffected by distance and difference, unvanquished by coldness and ingratitude, ever ready, throughout our day of grace, to come forth towards us freely and fully with cheering and elevating and transforming power. Such a thought, could we but receive it into our hearts, would, by His grace from whom it comes, convert us, turn us towards God, as in a moment. Is it true? Can Jesus Christ really thus care for us? Can it be anything to Him whether we are happy or unhappy, whether we live or die, are saved or perish? It is difficult indeed to think so. When we look within, to what we are in ourselves; when we look behind, to the time past of our lives; we can scarcely see what there is in us on which the love of Christ can fasten. But He seems to tell us here how it is. The hireling flees because he cares not for the sheep; and he cares not for them because they are not his own. The care of Christ for us springs out of ownership. We are His twice over; first brought into being, then redeemed, by Him. If He thought it worth while to create us, if He thought it worth while to give His own life for us, He may well, He must indeed, care for us. I take the broadest ground of all. I say nothing of personal merit, or of states of mind, of repentance, or faith, or obedience. I speak only of Creation, and of Redemption; that Redemption of which we read that Christ *is the propitiation for our sins*—and, lest any one should say, Perhaps not for my sins, perhaps only for the sins of true Christians; it is then added—*and not for ours only, but also for the sins of the whole world* (1 John ii. 2). Take that ground, and it will not fail you. It is *exceeding broad* (Psalm cxix. 96). Christ cares for you because you are His and with a reality of concern which led Him even to lay down life itself for you.

It is the thought of this care which has in every age opened the flood-gates of repentance, and turned souls to God. While we will not believe in it, we cannot turn. But, if anything should ever, under God's blessing, reveal it to you—and many things may do so; many things, I mean, may be the instrument of doing so—then you will hasten back to Christ, and love Him because you see that He has first loved you (1 John iv. 19). I say, many things may be the means of revealing to you Christ's care about you. Because the same God is the God of Providence and of grace: the same Saviour holds the keys of natural and of spiritual life and death (Rev. i. 18); and I am quite sure that He uses the one function to subserve the other. I am quite sure that our lives are very minutely as well as very powerfully attended to, and that every life has many openings afforded to it for seeing what it has never seen before, and for becoming what it has never become before.

But you must not wait for these things. They come to those who will seize them when they come, but not to those who, if they come, would let them pass by unheeded. This very Service, this very Sermon, has been an opportunity for you of realizing Christ's care that you should be saved: if you let it escape you, you may perhaps never have another.

2. But I must come now to a second topic sug-

gested by this passage; *the intimate mutual knowledge, if I might so express it, which exists between Christ and those who are His,* those who believe in His care and turn to Him.

The words are very remarkable. They are a little obscured in our English Version. In reality they are these. *I know my own and my own know me, even as the Father knows me and I know the Father.* The mutual knowledge of Christ and of His redeemed is like the mutual knowledge of Christ Himself and God. These are deep things, my brethren; secret things, too deep for words. But surely we may call one another to acknowledge and to admire the greatness of the gift offered to us, the closeness and intimacy of that knowledge of Christ which is opened to all who truly believe.

It is very easy to disparage things in which we do not share. And in this way it has come to pass that the world even of professed Christians can despise or deny the mystery of a real and living communication between the soul of a man and the Spirit of his Saviour. But we must cling to that truth, and never let it go. *The secret of the Lord is with them that fear Him, and He will show them His covenant* (Psalm xxv. 14). *My own know me, even as I know the Father.*

My brethren, we are not inquisitive enough, and we are not ambitious enough, in the things of God. Men used to spend a lifetime, hours in each day, in exploring the mysteries of the Christian life; in studying with all their energy the living Word, and in calling upon God with those unuttered yearnings of soul which St Paul recognizes as the very intercession of the Holy Spirit within (Rom. viii. 26). These things are now almost of the past. We demand now a more easy, a more popular, I fear a more superficial, kind of religion; one which shall be compatible with almost any amount of dissipation, and satisfied with almost any slightness of devotion. It is not thus that the words will ever be made good to us, *My own know me, even as I know the Father. Such knowledge is* indeed *too wonderful* for such seeking, and we cannot attain it (Psalm cxxxix. 6).

Yet let me not use words of harshness towards any the faintest enquirers after the life of Christ. It is only for the purpose of arousing that we would ever reprove. We all need the word of exhortation, which bids us enquire more, desire more, expect more, in the knowledge of Christ. We all need to be put on our guard against that perfunctory sort of devotion, which actually runs away from the very communications for which it seems to ask. We cannot know Christ without giving some time to it. There is a work of the understanding to be done, and there is a work of the heart to be done, in acquiring this knowledge. We have to study deeply what God has revealed to us of Himself in Christ. And we have to acquaint ourselves with Christ Himself, even as we would with an earthly friend, by the help of intercourse and of converse. He that has much time at his command may well give liberally of it, and he that has little may well do his diligence gladly to give of that little, in the pursuit of that knowledge of God and of Christ, which alone for any of us is life eternal (John xvii. 3).

There are still two points to be very briefly noticed in the knowledge here spoken of.

(1) The knowledge of the *voice;* the ready recognition of that sound when it summons in this direction or in that. *The sheep follow him; for they know his voice ... A stranger will they not follow, but will flee from him; for they know not the voice of strangers.*

This is one reason why we should be well acquainted with Christ; that we may always hear when He calls, and be able to distinguish His call from the many other sounds which counterfeit it in this world. It is the first condition of obedience. If we know not whether a certain sound be the voice of the Shepherd or of a stranger, we cannot be sure whether we are right or wrong in following it. Hence that frequent hesitation in matters of duty, which marks the course of so many of us. We have allowed other lords to have dominion over us (Isai. xxvi. 13); inclination, passion, the world, self-love, self-interest; till at last we can scarcely distinguish our real owner's voice when it reaches us; there is no promptitude in our response to it, and no stedfastness or consistency in our obedience.

(2) The intimate personal knowledge which Christ has of each one of us. *He needed not,* St John says,

that any should testify of man; for He knew what was in man (John ii. 25).

Is the thought of Christ's knowledge of us, ought it to be, can it be, in any degree a comforting thought? What can that knowledge be but a knowledge of infirmities, faults, and sins; a knowledge of the clearness of the light against which we have sinned, of the perverseness of the spirit in which we have walked before Him?

It does not seem as if He represented His knowledge of us quite in this aspect. He seems rather to speak of it as a privilege of His servants, that He should know them as He does. And if the knowledge spoken of be that which we understand by the knowledge of a Friend, we can all comprehend this. To be acquainted, even amongst men, with the great, with the good, with those who are honoured in their generation, is felt by every one as an object of ambition: in this sense, how much more to be permitted to say that we know and are known by Christ!

But even if the other kind of knowledge be intended; the knowledge of insight, apart from that of acquaintance; it ought not to be, it is not meant to be, terrifying or confounding to any of us. If Christ knows, as no man can know, our shortcomings and our backslidings, our follies, faults, and sins; on the other hand He knows, as no man can know them, our difficulties, our temptations, our struggles, our aspirations, our reluctant defeats, our all but victories, our bitter anguish of repentance, our earnest efforts after amendment, our sincere confessions, our humble prayers. I do not say this in excuse for sins: God forbid. I only say that Christ's judgment, though ten thousand times more holy, is also ten thousand times more merciful, than that of the world. Well may His servants say, *Let me fall now into the hand of the Lord, for His mercies are great, and let me not fall into the hand of man* (1 Sam. xxiv. 14). They need not fear the searching penetration of that discerning eye, if only they can appeal to Him, as His fallen Disciple did of old, and say, Lord, though I have fallen, though I have forgotten, though I have denied, though I have forsaken Thee, yet, *Lord, Thou knowest all things; Thou knowest that I love Thee* (John xxi. 17).

3. I have spoken now of the care of Christ for His servants, and of the mutual knowledge which exists between Him and them. I have yet one concluding reflection to suggest to you, drawn from the text itself, the last verse of the Gospel. And that is, *the special concern here indicated for the future extension, the successful gathering, and the final union, of that Church which is the blessed company of all faithful people.*

And other sheep I have; have already, in foreknowledge and purpose; *which are not of this fold,* this nation of Israel, to which the ministry of Christ, while He was Himself upon earth, was to be limited.

Them also must I bring: must, because so it is written of me; *must,* because my love, even as that of the Father who sent me, is not bounded by local or national restrictions; *must*, because *God so loved the world, that He gave His only begotten Son, that whosoever believeth in Him should not perish but have everlasting life* (John iii. 16). *Them also must I bring: I;* for, if I do it not, none else can: the work of saving one soul, as well as that of *gathering together in one the children of God that are scattered abroad* (John xi. 52), is beyond the power of any human messenger, and, except I work, from heaven, in the hearts of them that hear, no one man, to the very end of time, can be turned from darkness to light. *Them also must I bring: bring;* leading, not driving them; drawing them gently forward, by the persuasion of my Spirit within, out of the waste wilderness of sin and self into the *green pastures* and *beside the still waters* (Psalm xxiii. 2), out of the wretchedness of a life of cares and vanities into the joy and the peace which belong to my redeemed.

And they shall hear my voice. They shall recognize, one after another, in distant lands, in successive generations, the voice which addresses them as they are, and which offers them what they want; the voice which speaks the universal language, touches the universal wound, and heals the universal woe; the voice which whosoever hears within finds himself at once calmed, emancipated, and illuminated; the voice which whosoever patiently follows will find himself led onward from strength to strength by a wisdom not his own into a happiness of which he dreamed not.

Y

And there shall be one flock, one Shepherd. One flock, consisting of all those who accept Christ as their Saviour, under *one Shepherd*, that Saviour who casts out none that come to Him (John vi. 37).

My brethren, no passages of Scripture ought to be more attractive to us than those which, like this, show that our Lord Himself had from the very first our particular case in view. It was no after-thought, still less was it any accident, but a plan arranged by Him and declared from the beginning, which brought the Gentiles, which brought us of this land and age, into the flock and fold of Christ. Of us He thought when He was upon earth: for us He has made provision from His throne in heaven: in our behalf He sent forth that *great company of the preachers* (Psalm lxviii. 11), spoken of in the language of Prophecy, which has been ever since gathering new generations and new races into the Gospel fold: in our behalf He Himself uttered that memorable prayer in the same night in which He was betrayed, *Neither pray I for these,* my first disciples, *alone, but for them also which shall believe on me through their word; that they all may be one; as Thou, Father, art in me, and I in Thee, that they also may be one in us; that the world may believe that Thou hast sent me* (John xvii. 20, 21).

One flock, one Shepherd. Yes, such was Christ's will and Christ's promise. *That they also may be one in us.* Yes, such was Christ's prayer and Christ's ordinance. Has it been fulfilled? Is it in course of fulfilment? Yes, that also we doubt not. But, to look on, from the level of earth and of things present, upon the community of His professed people, we might well ask, Where is the sign of unity? where is the one flock? where is the one Shepherd? where is the saying, *That they all may be one?* It is sad to see divisions where there ought to be peace; men believing in one Saviour, seeking one rest and one home, and yet all differing about the means by which that end is to be won! Let us be careful not to add to such divisions. Let us be resolute to see Christ's people in all who own Him as their Saviour. Let us never doubt that there may be a unity of spirit in diversity of form, even as there certainly may be a diversity of spirit in unity of form. *They shall hear my voice:* let that be for ourselves, let that be (so far as it is necessary) for others, our test of unity. Are we, are they, listening to Christ's voice, and living, day by day, as He taught, as He teaches? Are we, are they, *fearing God and working righteousness* (Acts x. 35)? Are we, are they, doing all that can be done to set forward holiness and godliness on this sinful earth? Are we, are they, acknowledging Christ's Word as the rule of faith, and Christ's example as the rule of practice? Then are we already one in Him. Then may we be quite sure that, whatever differences of form may seem to divide us, these belong rather to the circumstances amidst which, than to the spirit in which, we are living here below. *If in anything ye be otherwise minded, God shall reveal even this unto you* (Phil. iii. 15). Many things which now appear to us to be almost or quite essential to Christianity may hereafter perhaps fall off from us as we pass through the dark river or through the golden gates beyond. Let us all *hold the Head* (Col. ii. 9), derive every day our own strength and grace from Him, and, be well assured, we shall find ourselves at last—much, it may be, to our surprise— to have been *all one in Christ Jesus* (Gal. iii. 28).

SERMON XIX.

THE EXPECTATION OF THE CREATION.

EPISTLE FOR THE FOURTH SUNDAY AFTER TRINITY.

ROMANS VIII. 18—23.

18 *I RECKON that the sufferings of the season which is now are not worthy in comparison with the glory which is about*
19 *to be unveiled unto us. For the earnest expectation of the*
20 *creation is waiting for the unveiling of the sons of God. For to vanity was the creation subjected, not willingly, but be-*
21 *cause of Him who subjected it, on [a footing of] hope, because even the creation itself shall be liberated from the slavery of corruption into the liberty of the glory of the children of God.*
22 *For we know that all the creation groans together and is in*
23 *travail together until now: and not only so, but even ourselves, having the firstfruit of the Spirit, even we ourselves groan in ourselves, waiting for an adoption, the redemption of our body.*

SERMON XIX.

THE EXPECTATION OF THE CREATION.

ROMANS VIII. 19.

The earnest expectation of the creature waiteth for the manifestation of the sons of God.

SINCE I last addressed you, the great Festivals of the Christian Year have ended, and we have entered now upon that long course of Sundays after Trinity which stretches through the whole of Summer and Autumn. That long succession of outwardly unmarked Sundays has been not unaptly compared to the Dispensation itself under which we are living. For many centuries God has ceased to deal with men by special interpositions. He is as really present, as really acting, as really saving and judging, as He ever was: but He does not carry on His works by visible or audible signs: men may, if they will, go on their way and forget Him. No one now *comes to us from the dead:* we are left with *Moses and the Prophets*, we are left with the written Word of Christ and His Apostles, and it is our business to *hear them* (Luke xvi. 29—31).

If we do not that, let us be well assured that we should not really have been profited by a different system. We often say to ourselves, If only some direct message could come to us from God Himself, we should be aroused, we should be convinced, we should be converted and live. But what saith the answer of God to us, as it is repeated in our hearing (perhaps with this very design) at the beginning of this unmarked portion of our year? *If they hear not Moses and the prophets, neither would they be persuaded though one rose from the dead*[1]. Startled we might be, terrified we might be; stirred, perhaps, for the moment to anxiety, agitation, and alarm: but it is not thus that permanent changes of life are effected in any: if at all, they must come from the inward working of God's Spirit, who can use as His instruments the commonest incidents of the most uneventful life, nay, whose presence is never indicated by the wind, the earthquake, or the fire, but is then first manifested when all these are finally followed by the *still small voice* (1 Kings xix. 11, 12).

The proper business of this season of the Christian Year, even as the proper business of lives spent, like ours, under the tranquil Dispensation of the Spirit, is the pondering of Revelation; the letting our hearts be penetrated with God's Word; the diligent hearing of Moses and the Prophets, still more of Christ and the Apostles; the steady, earnest, daily study of what God has taught, that so we may have a safe-

[1] Gospel for the first Sunday after Trinity.

guard within against the deadening influences of the present, and be enabled to anticipate, with unshaken unswerving faith, the great events which, whether we see their signs or no, are certainly to come upon the earth, and to bring with them, for each one of us, consequences of everlasting moment.

I know not that, in this point of view, I could select a more serious or a more profitable subject of reflection, than that which is presented to us here in the text and in the context, and which forms the Epistle for this day. May God give to each one of us an ear to hear it!

St Paul has been speaking of the Holy Spirit as bearing a concurrent testimony with that of our own spirit to our being sons of God. And he has added that the relation of sonship towards God involves in it the prospect of an inheritance; an inheritance to be received from God, and in which we shall be associated with Christ. *Heirs of God*, he says, *and joint-heirs with Christ; if so be that we suffer with Him, that we may be also glorified together.* As he says elsewhere, *If we died with Christ, we shall also live with Him: if we suffer (endure), we shall also reign with Him* (2 Tim. ii. 11, 12). The condition of our future union with Christ in glory, is, our being united with Him now in patient endurance.

Then he proceeds to say that it is worth our while to submit cheerfully to this condition. *For I reckon that the sufferings of the season which is now are not worthy* of mention or consideration *in comparison with the glory which is about to be unveiled unto,* so as to affect, and reach, and come upon, *us.* You observe how he speaks of the present life; as *the present season, the season which is now.* There is great seriousness, there ought to be great comfort, in the expression. We are apt to regard life as a long, undefined, purposeless expanse of time: St Paul calls it *a season:* and that word includes in it two notions; a limit, and a design. A season means a portion cut out of time, by One who sees its end as well as its beginning; and it means also, an opportunity for something, something to be done, or something to be gained, within those limits. Such is life, to our race as a whole, and to each one of us.

Now then this limited and designed period is one which contains sufferings. *The sufferings of this present season.* If we live long enough, we shall all find it so. There will be many things which thwart inclination, which try feeling, yes, which harass, which distress, which afflict us. No life is too young to have had some indications of this already. The sufferings of childhood are small when viewed from maturity, but never are sufferings more keen than when they come upon inexperience.

St Paul had great experience of suffering. *I die daily,* he once said of himself (1 Cor. xv. 31). He was a good judge therefore of one side at least of the case, when he instituted the comparison presented in the verse before us. He had entered, he tells us, into a sort of calculation. Was it worth while to

The Expectation of the Creation. 331

suffer as he did? to suffer, we add, as all persons must in a degree suffer in this life; as Christian persons must expect to suffer in an especial manner? What is there to be set against these sufferings for Christian persons? There is a glory, he says, to be hereafter revealed, and which is to come even to them. Glory: what is that? It is a vague word to many of us. But this passage may serve to clear it up. Glory is the manifestation of excellence. Applied to God, as in the phrase so common in Scripture, *the glory of God*, it means, the manifestation of what God is, whether in power, or wisdom, or goodness, or in all of these together. Applied to men, to Christian men, in the sense here designed, it means, the manifestation hereafter of what they are, not in themselves—for that could only be the exhibition of weakness, faultiness, and sinfulness—but in their relation to God as His children, to Christ as His redeemed, to the Holy Spirit as His dwelling-places and His temples. This manifestation is, as the next verse tells, the glory which is to be revealed.

And the passage would not be fully explained without a single word of comment upon that last expression, *revealed*. It is properly, *uncovered, unveiled*. The glory is there now, there already: Christian people are already children of God, already redeemed by Christ, already inhabited by the Holy Spirit: but there is a veil over the glory: men who pass by them do not see, are not aware of it: the world judges them often contemptuously, and, even if it could perceive their true dignity, their direct connection with God Himself, would scarcely think the better of them. But the glory which already exists veiled, will hereafter be uncovered, unveiled, revealed.

These brief hints must suffice as an introduction of the great subject before us to your view. You will remember the words noticed, and their meaning: a *season*, the season that now is; *sufferings; glory; revealed;* and the *calculation;* sufferings set against, weighed against, glory; and St Paul's unhesitating, triumphant, estimate of the preponderance of the latter over the former.

And now he says that, however indifferent the world may be on the subject, this future revelation of the Christian's glory has those who are deeply interested in it.

For the earnest expectation of the creation is waiting for the revelation (the unveiling) of the sons of God. This is the uncovering of the at present veiled glory of the Christian, of which I have already spoken. A very remarkable turn is here given to the subject.

Paul, with the eye at once of a poet and of a prophet, discerns in the present scene of created being tokens of a state of expectation. *The creation* here is a word of large import. It includes even the irrational, perhaps even the inanimate, portions of God's handywork on earth. The whole earth in its present state; the world of nature; the brute creation, as well as the human creation above and the material creation below it; all indicate a condition of imperfection, of suffering, of decay; all express, unconsciously where not consciously, a sense of want, of deterioration, of distress; all are, oftentimes, in many aspects, not what they would be, not what they were as they came fresh from the organizing hand of God; all denote, to one who looks on with the sympathy of humanity, much more with the reflection and discernment of one taught of God, a position very far removed from that which once they occupied, from that which they were designed to occupy, from that which they yet must occupy, under the sway of One as infinitely merciful as He is Omnipotent, Omnipresent, and Eternal. St Paul does not hesitate to say—and we know also that *he had the Spirit of God* (1 Cor. vii. 40)—that this degenerate, this suffering, this sin-contaminated world, expresses by signs not to be mistaken a longing and a yearning for those *times of restitution of all things*, those *times of refreshing from the presence of the Lord* (Acts iii. 19, 21), which shall accompany the *fulfilment of the mystery of God* (Rev. x. 7). The creation, he says, is *watching as with outstretched head* (such is the force of the original language) for the future unveiling of the sons of God.

For to vanity was the creation subjected. There is one Book in the Bible which forms, almost throughout, an inspired commentary upon this expression. You all remember the opening of that Book to which I refer. *Vanity of vanities, saith the Preacher, vanity of vanities; all is vanity* (Eccles. i. 2). And you know well the sort of topics with which that Book abounds.

The vanity of which it complains is not the frivolity of fashion, not the conceit of self-complacency, but rather the restlessness, the emptiness, the frailty, the disappointment, the unsatisfactoriness, the nothingness, alike of natural phenomena and of human circumstance; the weariness and the painfulness, the waste of effort and nugatoriness of endeavour, which belongs alike to man, and to nature as affected by man; the ceaseless round of labours issuing in no result, destitute of all hope, and fruitless of all abiding consequence. Such is the pregnant meaning of the word *vanity*, as here borrowed rather than originated by St Paul. Such is that condition to which he describes the creation, in all its parts, rational and irrational, animate and inanimate, as subjected, *not willingly*, not by any choice or act of its own, *but because of Him who subjected it;* that is, owing to the appointment of Him who, for man's sin, inflicted that judgment of subjugation to the power of corruption and decay; subjected it, however, not finally and for ever, but *on* a footing of *hope*, the hope of an eventual restoration and reconstruction, *because even the creation itself*, not man only, so far as he consents to the terms of the Gospel, but the inferior creation also, *shall be liberated from the slavery of corruption*, of suffering, of disease, and of decay, *into the liberty of (which belongs to) the glory*, the manifested perfection, *of the children of God*. The Fall of man involved the inferior creation also in some of its disastrous consequences: the introduction of the *new heavens and new*

The Expectation of the Creation.

earth, wherein dwelleth righteousness (2 Pet. iii. 13), shall bring with it the reversal of that derived doom.

For we know that all the creation groans together and is in travail together until now: the former expression denoting simply the suffering, the latter the hopeful prospect which is opened to that suffering (John xvi. 20—22). *And not only so,* not only the rest of God's creatures, *but even ourselves,* though *having the firstfruit of the Spirit,* that is, the firstfruits of our inheritance, namely, the Holy Spirit dwelling in us in this life, *even we ourselves groan in ourselves, waiting for an adoption, the redemption of our body.*

My brethren, the whole of the passage which I have thus brought before you speaks of an expectation. *The earnest expectation of the creation. Subjected the same in hope. We ourselves groan within ourselves, waiting for (expecting) an adoption.* The creation is expecting: Christ's servants are expecting; it is one of their two characteristics as elsewhere given; they have *turned to God, to serve* Him, *and to wait for* something, for some One (1 Thess. i. 10). Are there any then who are not expecting, who are waiting for nothing? Yes, there are: there are many who have no serious expectation at all; certainly none of the particular event, the particular change, of which St Paul is here writing.

The creation expects; even the irrational, even the brute creation, even inanimate nature herself, expects and waits. And the Church, the true spiritual Church of Christ, expects; yea, groans within itself as with outstretched head it watches and longs for an appearing. But the careless and the worldly wait not, expect not. They furnish indeed a sign to others: the things which happen to them, their eager covetings, their bitter disappointments, their hopeless despairings, their faithless suicides, all swell the chorus which rises from a sin-stained earth, telling the oft-repeated tale of a subjugation to vanity itself, yea, echoing that dismal world-wide sound, *Vanity of vanities, vanity of vanities; all is vanity*. But they, themselves, though their history may all go to intensify the general expectation, yet they themselves expect not. They stand aloof, as it were, from the two bodies of expectants, shamed not only by the example of the Christian indeed, but by the very spectacle of the beasts that perish: they rise not to the redeemed glory of the one; nay, they sink below the level of the instincts of the other.

It is not that any one lives and expects nothing. We are all looking forward; none more so than the man or the woman whose all is in time. We are all looking forward, with but too much confidence, or but too much eagerness, as the case may be, to something, yes, to many things, in prospect; to some things which may, to many which will never, come. But the great question is, What? What are we expecting? Is it the right thing? Is it the true thing? Is it the thing which is sure to come, because God has foretold it? Is it the great thing? Is it that consummation, that restitution, that rectification, that revelation, that unveiling, to the certainty of which St Paul here bears witness?

It becomes us all to look well into this matter. It is very disgraceful to be expecting nothing but that which is bounded by the limits, and involved in the chances, of time. And it is very affronting to God to take no pains to understand the particular thing which He has declared to be His will, to be His purpose, concerning us. Let us try, let us pray, to enter into it.

The creation is waiting for the unveiling of the sons of God; waiting for its own deliverance from the bondage of corruption into that liberty which belongs to, and which is to accompany, the glory, the manifested perfection, of the children of God. This is all somewhat mysterious. It seems to say that in the renovated earth, purged by the last judgment of fire, there shall be room for other existences besides redeemed souls: there shall be a face of nature too, and a race of inferior creatures too, and a life of freedom for the one in the enjoyment of the beauties and the bounties of the other: it seems to say this, and it is a very bright and pleasant picture for one who has suffered in this life with the sufferings of irrational animals, and wondered by what inexplicable links their destiny can have been fastened to the destiny of man. But these things, though pleasant ideas, and scarcely to be excluded from the passage on which we have dwelt, may be thought to savour more of poetry than of religion. Let us see then—if this be what irrational, what inanimate nature expects—what it is which the other class of expectants is looking for; that class which is directly lighted by knowledge from on high, and whose expectation is distinctly warranted by the word which cannot deceive.

We, we who have in this life the presence of the Holy Spirit as the firstfruits of our inheritance, what are we waiting for, when we groan within ourselves in the agony of a hope long deferred? We are waiting for our adoption. Is it not ours? Are we not already sons of God? Does not the Spirit within us already cry to God as our Father (Rom. viii. 15, Gal. iv. 6)? Yes; but we have heard already that, though sons, there is as it were a veil over our sonship; though adopted, we are not yet owned; though heirs, we are not yet possessors; and the world and the devil are leagued together to make it out that we never shall be. What we look for is the manifestation, the revelation, the disclosure, the unveiling, of the sons of God. And that, as St Paul here, and as the Scripture elsewhere, teaches us, is associated in God's purposes with another event, the redemption of our body.

Already are we adopted, and already we are redeemed. But the one is not yet individually avowed; and the other is not yet in every part completed. Christ's work and suffering has indeed perfected redemption; it has secured it in all its parts: it

The Expectation of the Creation. 339

contained in itself, potentially, its final fulfilment. Already in this life is the soul of the Christian redeemed: not only in right and power, but in act and reality, is the soul set free to know and to serve God, and to dedicate to Him in daily service that life which the soul regulates. However many the deficiencies, however many the faults, of a Christian, still, if he be earnestly striving, if he be devoted to his Saviour, they touch not the reality of his redemption, though they make a heavy demand upon him for increased energy and humility, faith and self-abasement. But there is one part of him which in this life is wholly unredeemed; his body. Not that the body is any longer allowed to indulge its sinful desires: it is held in check by the redeemed soul: it is made to offer *a living sacrifice* of active obedience (Rom. xii. 1). But there it still is; kept under, brought into subjection, regulated, mortified; yet withal a material, a fleshly, a corruptible, a dying thing, and *flesh and blood cannot inherit the kingdom of God* (1 Cor. xv. 50). That body which has been carrying about with it for years the seeds of disease and of decay; that machine which is wound up for its appointed time, but which is ever gradually wearing out, till at last it ceases to move, and refuses to execute the mandate of the directing will; must first perish before it can put on immortality; must first, with the exception of that one generation which shall be alive upon earth when Christ comes in glory (1 Cor. xv. 51, 52), be laid in the dust to undergo the process of dissolution and corruption, before it can be changed into that spiritual body, independent of the wants and incapable of the accidents of the life that now is, which alone can enter into the kingdom of God, or be at once the temple and the instrument of the redeemed soul through the ages of an eternal life.

St Paul thought much, spoke much, and wrote much, of this redemption of the body, which is resurrection. He had suffered much in the body, through the body, and from the body, and he longed to lay aside this daily drag and burden. On the other hand, he was a man of great and determined energy in God's service. He did not wish to cease from activity. He knew that a soul is but half a man; well qualified for the repose of the intermediate Paradise, but incapable of the resumed work for God which is to be the glory (though we know not its nature) of the reconstructed man in heaven. Therefore he desired, as he says, not to be *unclothed*, but rather to be *clothed upon* (2 Cor. v. 4); not to be divested finally of his bodily frame, but rather to have it so transformed and so remodelled as that it should possess at once a spiritual freedom and an unwearied strength. This was St Paul's conception of heaven, and of this the resurrection of the body was an indispensable condition.

We, my brethren, have too much lost this *hope of Israel* (Acts xxiii. 6. xxviii. 20); this special expectation of the resurrection of the dead. Therefore it is that we confuse the departure with the glory; make no distinction between the paradise of the soul and the heaven of the man; and scarcely enter into the vital importance of the promise, that *the same Jesus who was seen to ascend shall be seen in like manner coming* again to the earth (Acts i. 11).

And yet we need the doctrine, every day, of the resurrection of the body. We need it for hope; we need it for encouragement; we need it, most of all, for warning and for exhortation. If these bodies are thus honourable; if death itself shall only temporarily divide us and them; if the hope of the Christian is the resumption of the body, transfigured indeed and spiritualized, but still a body, and still the same body; O how careful should we be to keep the body in this life in all honour (1 Thess. iv. 4)! how earnestly should we remember the solemn words of the same Apostle of the resurrection, *Know ye not that your body is the temple of the Holy Ghost which is in you, which ye have of God; and ye are not your own, for ye are bought with a price: therefore glorify God in your body* (1 Cor. vi. 19, 20).

SERMON XX.

GOD THE SANCTUARY OF MAN.

EPISTLE FOR THE FIFTH SUNDAY AFTER TRINITY.

1 Peter III. 8—15.

8 [BE ye] all harmonious, sympathizing, brotherly, tender,
9 humble; not giving back evil for evil, or railing for railing, but on the contrary blessing; because unto this were ye
10 called, that ye might inherit a blessing. For he that would love life and see good days, let him stop the tongue from evil,
11 and the lips that they speak not guile; and let him swerve from evil and do good, let him seek peace and pursue it:
12 for the eyes of the Lord are upon righteous men, and His ears unto their prayer; but the face of the Lord is upon
13 men doing evil things. And who [is there] that will harm
14 you, if ye become imitators of the good? But if ye should even suffer because of righteousness, blessed [are ye]. And
15 their fear fear not, nor be troubled; but sanctify Christ [as] Lord in your hearts.

SERMON XX.

GOD THE SANCTUARY OF MAN.

1 PETER III. 15.

Sanctify the Lord God in your hearts.

ST PETER'S first Epistle has ever been a favourite book of Scripture with all Christian people. It affords a beautiful example of the inseparable union, in true religion, of feeling and conduct, of doctrine and practice. Nowhere do we find a more touching outburst of Christian trust and love, than in the opening of this letter. *Blessed be the God and Father of our Lord Jesus Christ, who according to His abundant mercy begat us again unto a living hope by the resurrection of Jesus Christ from the dead...whom not having seen ye love; in whom, though now ye see Him not, yet believing, ye rejoice with a joy unspeakable and full of glory* (1 Pet. i. 3, 8). And then how immediate is the practical inference! *Wherefore gird up the loins of your mind, be sober, and hope to the end for the grace that is to be brought unto you at the revelation of Jesus Christ; as obedient children, not fashioning yourselves according to the desires which were before in your ignorance; but according to (after the likeness of) the Holy One who called you, be ye yourselves also holy in every* part of your *behaviour; because it is written, Ye shall be holy, because I am holy* (i. 13—16).

By degrees the Apostle passes on into separate particulars of duty, into which we must not now attempt to follow him. But in the 8th verse of the Chapter now before us, the commencement of this day's Epistle, he turns from special addresses to give this general charge, in close connection with which the text will be found to stand.

Finally, be ye *all harmonious, sympathizing, brotherly, tender, humble; not giving back evil* in exchange *for evil, or railing for railing; but on the contrary blessing; because unto this were ye called, that ye might inherit a blessing.* If it is your hope as Christians to enter into the happiness of God's blessing; of having good words spoken of you (for that is the meaning of the original expression), words of forgiveness, comfort, and grace, by Him whose blessing is life; take heed that you be not guilty of the inconsistency of those who show a harsh and resentful spirit towards men, while they expect a merciful treatment from Him against whom they have sinned.

And then the Apostle illustrates and enforces his charge by a quotation from the Book of Psalms. *For he that would love life,* he, that is, who would fain enjoy life, *and see good days*, days of tranquillity and happiness, *let him stop the tongue from evil, and the lips that they speak not guile*. These things have a direct tendency to embitter life; not for others only, against whom our lips may utter words of unkindness or injustice, but, by a righteous reaction, for ourselves also. They have, besides, the displeasure of God upon them, and, where God's blessing is not, there is not and cannot be happiness. *Let him swerve from (shun) evil, and do good; let him seek peace, and pursue it*, as an object of the greatest value: if peace does not come to him, let him go in quest of it; if it seems to be escaping from him, let him pursue till he overtakes it and brings it back. These are amongst the most elementary of all rules of life: but do they not embrace also all that really makes life good and sound and happy? And then a motive is added, from the same passage of the Old Testament. *For the eyes of the Lord are upon righteous men, and His ears* are *unto*, that is, are open to, *their prayer; but the face of the Lord is upon men doing evil things.* The word is the same in either case; *upon* righteous men, *upon* evil doers: the sense supplies the difference: in the one case it is with approval, in the other it is with displeasure. In the Psalm itself, a clause is added: *The face of the Lord is against them that do evil, to cut off the remembrance of them from the earth* (Psalm xxxiv. 12—16).

There the quotation ends: then St Peter goes on to ask, *And who* is there *that will harm you, if ye become (prove yourselves) imitators of the good?* whether *of that which is good*, or *of Him who is good*, does not appear from the word employed. To do good has a direct tendency to preserve from wrong. One who consistently follows the example of Him who *is good and doeth good* (Psalm cxix. 68) will, as a general rule, provoke no hostility. *But if ye should even suffer for righteousness' sake, blessed* are ye. In a Christian estimate, to suffer for welldoing is to be like Christ: it is a token of His approval, and a pledge of salvation. *To you of salvation, and that of God* (Phil. i. 28). *To you who are troubled rest with us* (2 Thess. i. 7).

And their fear fear not; be not afraid of the intimidation of your enemies; *nor be troubled.* The quotation is now from the Prophet Isaiah. *But sanctify Christ* as *Lord in your hearts.* The passage in Isaiah stands thus, *Sanctify the Lord of hosts Himself;* and then adds, in further elucidation of the sense, *And let Him be your fear, and let Him be your dread; and He shall be for a sanctuary* (Isai. viii. 12— 14). Do not fear your earthly enemies, but fear God: sanctify Him in your hearts, and you shall find Him your sanctuary.

These are the words which I propose for your especial consideration this morning. May God by His Holy Spirit unfold them to us in their wisdom, in their comfort, and in their strength!

Dwell for a moment upon St Peter's form of the quotation. *But sanctify the Lord Christ*, or rather, *Christ* as *Lord, in your hearts.* It is only another proof, were it needed, of the place which Christ occupied in the faith and the reverence of His first disciples. His name might be substituted at will for that of God Himself in any passage of the inspired Scriptures of the Old Testament.

Sanctify then *God*, or *Christ*, or (to combine the two readings) *God in Christ, as the Lord, in your hearts*. God in Christ is to be the Sanctuary of His people.

I will say a few words on two parts of this subject. First of the consecration, and secondly of the use, of this sanctuary. A more instructive or a more delightful meditation could scarcely be proposed to us.

1. Elsewhere we are ourselves called temples. *Know ye not*, St Paul says to the Corinthians, *that your body is the temple of the Holy Ghost which is in you, which ye have of God* (1 Cor. vi. 19)? But the metaphors of Scripture are not to be tied down to one application. We are temples, or sanctuaries, of God, because of His Holy and Divine Spirit dwelling in us. But here we read of a temple within a temple. In that sanctuary which, in one point of view, we ourselves are, there is yet an inner shrine. Within the tabernacle itself there is a veil, and beyond that mysterious veil there is a Holy of Holies, a Most Holy Place.

The text tells of the consecration of this inner temple. *Sanctify*, St Peter says, that is, *consecrate, God in Christ as the Lord in your hearts*.

We have all of us, I dare say, witnessed the consecration of a Church. We have seen the fabric growing from its foundation. We have seen the first stone laid with much ceremony, amidst many hopes and with many prayers. We have passed the place daily, or visited it from time to time, in the interval between that laying of the first stone, which was the dedication of the ground, and that solemn act of inauguration which was the consecration of the finished building. We have seen the walls rise, the arches gradually spring upwards, the roof framed and at last covered, the windows carefully shaped and then filled perhaps with bright colours. All this time the workmen busied themselves within, as they might have done in the construction of a common dwelling. No one thought it irreverent to enter with his head covered: the time for such scruples was not yet. At last the day of consecration arrived. A religious service, of unusual ceremony and devotion, set apart the building for ever to the sole use of God's worshippers, and invoked the perpetual blessing of God Himself upon all who should there assemble in that character to the end of time.

This illustration, far as it sinks below the glory of that which is here spoken of, may yet help us to enter into the meaning of the first part of St Peter's charge, *Consecrate the Lord in your hearts*. Consecrate that inmost shrine of all, which is the very presence-chamber of God Himself in each living man.

Many of us have as yet no sacred place within. Their heart is not yet, in any part of it, shut off from all profane and common uses, and dedicated to a special worship and service. Every part is open. The world may come in. The flesh, with its affections and lusts, may come in. The devil, with his thousand malignities against God and man, may come in and go out at his pleasure. There has been no Consecration-Service yet. The heart is empty of any Divine presence: all is common, all is (in the most correct sense of the term) profane: no Deity yet owns it, to the exclusion of that which is alien to God or hostile.

And with many of us the sacred place within is wrongly tenanted. We have set up an idol, or many idols, in our hearts. One greater idol, self—and many lesser idols, of ambition, of covetousness, of worldliness, of passion, of lawful affection exaggerated, or of unlawful affection indulged—these things have entered in, and occupied the Most Holy Place with another than the Most Holy One; so that, in reality, if not empty, it is even worse than empty; God is not there: His temple has either never been consecrated, or it has been subsequently defiled.

To these two classes of persons—and does not the present Congregation contain examples of each? St Peter here says, Consecrate God, consecrate Christ, in your hearts. And what then is the particular thing, the particular act, denoted by this expression? I think we may briefly describe it as the inviting of God in Christ to come and dwell in us. According to our Lord's own saying, *We will come unto Him, and make our abode with Him* (John xiv. 23).

I can scarcely say anything new upon this all-important topic. But, though not new, what we say may by God's blessing be a word of truth. We have used a human comparison; that of the building of a Church, and its gradual preparation for the day of consecration. I am sure we all feel, instinctively I may almost say, that we are so made, in mind and soul, as to have great capacities for receiving God into us. All the various departments of our inner being, like the aisles of one of our great Cathedrals, point towards, and lead up to, one solemn and sacred end: they are not separate and isolated, they are not self-contained and self-completed, they are but parts of a whole, they have an ulterior prospect and a designed connection, they tend towards something, and they can be satisfied with nothing else. I am only expressing the universal feeling, when I say that neither intellect by itself, nor power by itself, nor wealth by itself, no, nor affection by itself, can at all still the tumult or fill the void of our nature: we want rest; we wanted it before, we want it still; and we find that it is one kind of rest, and only one, which we yearn after or can accept; we want something to lean upon which is all-supporting, we want something to grasp which is unchanging, we want something, nay, we want some One, to reverence, who is absolutely perfect, we want something, nay, we want some One, to love, who is altogether lovely. And until we have found this, until we have grasped this, until we have access

God the Sanctuary of Man. 353

to and communion with and incorporation in this —this thing, this Person—we must hunger and thirst, we must pine and sicken and at last die; nature cries out for it, because He, the God of Nature, first made us and formed us for Himself.

Now therefore let him who has not yet found this find it now. The Church is erected: its walls have risen to their full height, its pillars and arches are stately, its aisles duly guide eastward, its pavement is smooth and bright, its windows are tinted with storied colour: all is spacious, all is beautiful: the workmen have withdrawn, the work is accomplished: but to what purpose? here is a Church closed against the worshipper, and here is a Church actually desecrated to some other, some common, use: here (to drop the figure) is a man without religion, living altogether without God in the world; and here is a man making idols for himself of the creature; worshipping self, the meanest of deities, or worshipping the world, the most variable and the most cruel: my brethren, these things ought not so to be. Arise, while yet you may, and consecrate your temple! Arise, call upon God, who is even now nearer to you than the very soul within: tell Him your need, tell Him your disappointment, tell Him your sense of vanity and emptiness and nothingness, and invite Him to be your God: invite Him into the empty or else the desecrated temple, yea, *consecrate the Lord God in your heart!*

I am persuaded, my brethren, there is more in

these inward acts of religion than we often dream of. In pressing upon you this special, this solemn consecration, I urge a very real thing, and one without which the second charge to be addressed to you can scarcely find place. Enter into a very close questioning with your own hearts, secretly in your chamber, this day; and, if you perceive that God in Christ is not yet known to you personally as your very present help, as your Father and Saviour and Comforter, do not despise the counsel which bids you solemnly and earnestly invite Him to become so, invite Him into the heart which is empty of Him, invite Him into the heart which He has prepared for Himself, and which without His presence must be a wilderness, or worse, for ever. It is out of these deliberate acts of self-dedication, or (which is the same thing) of Divine consecration, that the new life has sprung in many of those whom the Church of Christ now looks back upon as its chief examples and guides. They have been in all ages the original starting-points of Christian lives; the landmarks, and the resting-places, and the occasional reparations, of such lives, in their onward course. So may it be with you! God waits but for the turning of the heart: He listens ever to the cry of that heart which asks Him to become its sanctuary.

2. And now let me briefly speak of the consequence of this act of consecration. Sanctify, consecrate, God in Christ, in your heart, as its shrine,

God the Sanctuary of Man.

its most holy place: that is the first point. *And He shall be for a sanctuary:* that is the second.

He shall be for a sanctuary. The words sound sweet and encouraging. To have God for our sanctuary seems as if it must be a comfort and a privilege. Let us draw out its meaning in two very simple particulars. A sanctuary is, first, a place of worship: and a sanctuary is, secondly, a place of refuge.

(1) A place of worship. God in the heart is the Christian's place of worship. Some persons are superstitious in their notions of the sanctity of place. They think their prayers are more acceptable to God in a Church than in a room. And of course in one sense they are so: that is, a person who despises the worship of God in the Congregation is guilty of a great sin, and can scarcely be expected to worship acceptably anywhere. And we know also that an especial blessing is promised to prayers offered where even two or three are gathered together in the name of Christ. It is not of these things that we speak as superstitious. We are thinking now of a different matter. And we would notice, as St Peter teaches us, that there is always a fear of our having no place of real worship, no sanctuary which is God Himself, in our own hearts. Many, we fear, worship, at the very best, as it were in an unconsecrated or else a desecrated place within. Many worship, whether in their private or in their public prayers, as it were out of doors, in a place which is not particularly God's, a place not set apart for Him in their hearts by an act of consecration, a

place which is open to any profane use, or else actually tenanted by an idol deity.

It is difficult, perhaps, to give full expression to the idea contemplated. In prayer we ought to be able to feel ourselves in God's very presence. He must have a place in our hearts, before we can find Him there. And then, having invited Him into our hearts by an act before described as one of consecration, we must ever be meeting Him there, going to Him there, speaking to Him there, as a Person not at a distance, not with a gulf fixed between us and Him, not doubtfully or precariously or accidentally present, but known and felt and often before found to be abiding with us, to whom, whenever we will, we may turn as in a moment, and be quite sure to have access by an immediate, a direct communication. This is one of the uses of that sanctuary which St Peter bids us to consecrate. It is a place of worship for us within the heart. Those of us who have known the dreariness of that state in which the prayer of each day is offered in hesitation, at a venture, as if to some one in another place or another country, some one who might perhaps, but only perhaps, be within hearing or inclined to hear; a state in which each particular prayer begins and ends with itself, as a separate act of duty, a separate and too often a reluctant exertion of will; can appreciate, at least by contrast, the happiness of him who has God for his sanctuary within, who carries about therefore with him the very shrine of his worship, and has only to enter it, on each particular occasion, as a familiar place, to which he has always a ready access, and in which he is ever certain alike of a ready welcome and of a gracious answer. Let us claim this privilege, each one of us; and be well assured that of God's free grace it will in due time be granted to all who ask it.

(2) *He shall be to you for a sanctuary.* We have spoken of the sanctuary within as a place of worship: we have still to speak of it as a place of refuge. It is probably in this latter sense that the prophet Isaiah in the passage quoted, and the Apostle Peter in the verse read as the text, especially used the expression. A sanctuary is an asylum. Such was the use made of the temple of old, when, to take one familiar example, *Adonijah feared because of Solomon, and arose, and went, and caught hold on the horns of the altar* (1 Kings i. 50). Such was the promise made to the rebellious nation in the days of its distress and captivity, when, as was said in the name of the Lord by the Prophet Ezekiel, *Although I have cast them far off among the heathen, and although I have scattered them among the countries, yet will I be to them as a little sanctuary in the countries where they shall come* (Ezek. xi. 16). A sanctuary is a place of refuge.

Be not afraid of their terror, neither be troubled; but sanctify the Lord God in your hearts...And He shall be for a sanctuary.

Is any one here present suffering, in any sense, for righteousness' sake? made to feel himself or herself the object of reproach, or of suspicion, or of coldness and indifference, because of a deeper sense than that which others possess of the importance of eternal things? More than this we can scarcely have to dread in these days: but even this little is not little. *A man's foes* may be *those of his own household* (Matt. x. 36), without one act of open violence or of direct persecution. Perhaps the art of opposition to Christ's cause in the world was never better understood than it is now. Softer times have introduced softer weapons: the sneer, the hint, the scarcely breathed insinuation of a wilful or a self-righteous singularity, not to mention the more flattering devices by which it is sought to draw the Christian into an acquiescence with the world, answer the purpose far more effectively than a rudeness which would disgust, or a severity which must alienate. The real *offence of the Cross* (Gal. v. 2) has not yet ceased, nor will it cease in this life ever. Most important is it, for all who would be Christians indeed, that they be raised above the fear of man by a deeper and a more impressive fear within.' And yet, next to the importance of being independent of the fear of man, stands the importance of being so in a right spirit. Much harm has been done to the cause of Christ's Gospel by an unchristian Christianity; by a regard to His service not shown in His spirit; by a perverseness, or by a self-will, or by an irritation, or by a harshness, most alien, in each instance, alike to His teaching and to His example. Now the secret of boldness, and the secret of charity, both lie in the charge before us. Have the Lord for your sanctuary. When man would make you afraid, enter your asylum. *The name of the Lord is a strong tower: the righteous runneth into it, and is safe* (Prov. xviii. 10). *Come, my people, enter thou into thy chamber,* the secret place of thy heart where God is enshrined, *and shut thy doors about thee: hide thyself as it were for a little moment, until the indignation be overpast* (Isai. xxvi. 20). Then wilt thou come forth, having learned the twofold lesson, of courage and of charity, of independence and of Divine love.

And is any one here present suffering not from opposition, but from anxiety? Is the care of life heavy upon you? Is anxiety, for the wellbeing, in soul or in body or in circumstance, of another, or for your own, weighing down the spirits, and tracing the lines of care upon your countenance? *O cast thy burden upon the Lord,* be it what it may, *and He shall sustain* even because *He careth for thee* (Psalm lv. 22. 1 Pet. v. 7). Let Him be thy sanctuary: run into it, into the shrine where He dwells within, and be safe, be strong!

Or is it sin that makes you afraid? sin past, burdening the conscience; or sin in prospect, weakening the energies by which it should be met and conquered? Is temptation powerful, and faith weak, and hope dead within? Is the enemy whispering, It is in vain: I am stronger than thou—evil, in thy case at least, more powerful than good? Brother, sister, remember what the Apostle says here, Consecrate the Lord in your heart, and let Him be your sanctuary. *What time I am afraid, I will trust in Thee* (Psalm lvi. 3). To the horns of the altar, to the place of the one sacrifice once offered, yea, to the mysterious mercy-seat where He, the God of grace, dwells within the veil, thither flee: thither can neither the accuser nor the tempter follow thee: abide there, and thou art free from condemnation: abide there, and thou art free from sin. And that place, that safe place, that blessed, that peaceful place, is within thee: thou leavest it not when thou comest forth: it is within thee still. Only let thy heart be God's, and He will keep thee. Where thou goest, He will go: where thou restest, He will rest: consecrate the Lord God in thy heart, and He, wherever thou art, will be to thee for a sanctuary.

SERMON XXI.

WISDOM TOWARDS THOSE WITHOUT.

COLOSSIANS IV. 2—6.

2 *PERSIST in prayer, being wakeful in it in*[1] *thanksgiving;*
3 *praying at the same time also concerning us, that God might open to us a door of the word, to speak the secret of Christ, for*
4 *which I am even bound, that I might manifest it as I ought*
5 *to speak. Walk in wisdom towards those without, buying*
6 *up the opportunity. Let your word be always in*[1] *grace, seasoned with salt, so as to know how ye ought to answer every one.*

---

[1] *Amidst*, as the very element or atmosphere in which the action is performed.

SERMON XXI.

WISDOM TOWARDS THOSE WITHOUT.

COLOSSIANS IV. 5.

Walk in wisdom toward them that are without, redeeming the time.

IN these words, taken from the second Lesson for this evening, we have first a rule, and secondly a principle. Each of the two is expressed a little more fully, in the parallel passage in the Epistle to the Ephesians. *See then that ye walk circumspectly, not as fools, but as wise; redeeming the time, because the days are evil* (Eph. v. 15).

But even in its briefest form, and within its narrowest limits, the charge before us has more in it than one Sermon can exhaust. A few practical remarks upon it can never come amiss.

Walk in wisdom toward them that are without. The rule respects the conduct of persons described as within a certain space, in relation to other persons described as being on the outside of it.

We all see what is meant by this description.

The enclosed space spoken of is the Christian body; the community of Christ's disciples and servants, as distinguished from that larger community which, though redeemed by Him as all the world is, yet is not at present His by the appropriation of that redemption.

It is easy to see what the meaning of this distinction would be to the Colossians who are here addressed. In those first days of the Gospel, a false profession of Christianity was so rare—had so little to make it a temptation, when to be a Christian was to be despised or to be persecuted—that all who worshipped God through Christ Jesus might be spoken to as sincere in that confession, and, however faulty, however far from the full stature of Christian perfection, still real partakers of the Divine Spirit and real heirs of the Divine glory. In those days therefore *they that were within* included all baptized and professing Christians, and *they that were without* meant the Jewish or the heathen world surrounding the Christian society.

Thus the duty of Christians in reference to their intercourse with one another and with the world must have been then clear and comparatively easy. I need not say that the case is greatly complicated for us. The world itself has now become nominally Christian. And we have no right, as individuals, to sit in judgment upon the right of others to the name and privileges of a Christian. Every baptized person, not excluded from the Church by a formal act of excommunication such as that denounced by St Paul in his first Epistle to the Corinthians (1 Cor. v. 3—5), or practically from Christian society by some proved or notorious crime of his own, is entitled to be regarded by us as a brother, whatever may be his real condition in the sight of God as to the depth of his convictions or the consistency of his feelings with his professions. We have no right to say that we are within, and that others, equally Christians by profession, are without, the pale of a Christian brotherhood. Notorious sin, in one calling himself a Christian, furnishes a sufficient reason for refusing his acquaintance, for avoiding his society: St Paul himself, in the chapter just referred to, tells us so (1 Cor. v. 11—13): but he tells us also that it is because he calls himself a brother, because he is a Christian by profession, that it is necessary thus to discountenance him: he does not become one of those without—a heathen, that is: he is still one of those within, and, because he is so, it is necessary that those within should mark their disapproval of his guilt.

No one will deny, my brethren, that these distinctions are important for us all, living in an age and a land of wide-spread profession. There is no practical question which more often comes before us than this; as to the proper mode of dealing with persons whose life and conversation indicate a want of real religion, without lying under any suspicion of actual immorality. We all know that society is largely composed of such persons. It would be affectation to suppose that the majority of those with whom we mix on occasions of business or relaxation are persons walking in the love of God or in the comfort and strength of His Holy Spirit. We perceive in them no sign of those dispositions or of those tastes which would certainly accompany such a life. And we know how they would be dealt with by many Christians. We know that it has been made by many Christian teachers and by many Christian people a first principle of true religion to live only amongst the truly religious; to shun the society of less serious persons as they would that of the avowed enemies of Christ; and to apply to all such, without further hesitation, all the terms used in Scripture with reference to a world of unbelievers and of idolaters.

My brethren, we have not so learned Christ. We cannot thus confound things that differ. We cannot thus obliterate the mark of Christian Baptism, or anticipate the disclosures of God's final Judgment. We doubt not indeed that God could judge even now between man and man in this Congregation, who are His in heart, and who are His only in name: but we are quite sure that this is not given to us, and that it is against His most solemn warnings if we attempt it. We see that to attempt it is full of evil on both sides; full of self-righteousness and uncharitableness on the one side, full of discouragement and actual injury on the other.

Has then the charge, *Walk in wisdom toward them that are without*, no application now? Yes, my brethren, like all the words of Scripture, it has its just, its important, its Divine lesson: and may God give us grace to understand and to receive it!

There are those around us every day, perhaps very near us, perhaps amongst our most loved and loving friends, certainly amongst our common associates in public and in private, who have not yet found, themselves being the judges, the comfort, the peace, the strength, or the hope, which Christ's Gospel offers and which the Spirit of Christ communicates to those who truly believe. There is nothing uncharitable in saying this. We say it only of those who would say it of themselves. There are some who do not yet feel their need of these things. There are some who find in a daily round of business or of amusement such satisfaction as at least makes them indifferent to a higher. There are some who are deferring serious thought till a more convenient season. There are some who persuade themselves that spiritual religion, if not a dream, is at least a special gift; the privilege of a few, not the necessity of all. And of course there are some of yet lighter or more prejudiced minds than these: some who talk slightingly or jestingly of devout men or of holy things; and some who in the disappointment of their own higher aspirations have acquired a perceptible bitterness of tone towards persons more successful in their pursuit of the life of God, and speak of religion in terms almost of disparagement, only because they think of it as a blessing denied to themselves.

These are examples of various kinds of character which meet us in the daily contact of life. We may well add to them those whom we should describe as simply well-disposed; enquirers, with more or less of earnestness, after the way of truth; young persons, not yet fixed in principle, not yet finally set in the way in which they are to go; amiable persons, full of kindly impulses, and in some danger of mistaking the natural for the spiritual; candid persons, open to conviction, and exercising a quiet and an intelligent judgment upon points of opinion and conduct which are presented to them in the intercourse of daily life. And surely we may add to these, yet again, a large class of persons consciously inconsistent; persons with some piety of feeling, but troubled also by some special root of bitterness, some perverseness of spirit or temper which daily interferes with it in practice; persons, too, who once perhaps seemed nearer to God than they now are; persons who have fallen more or less into acts of folly or sin, and who are bitterly accusing themselves of a want of resolution, of decision, of earnestness, in returning finally and for ever into those paths of virtue and watchfulness from which they have allowed themselves to turn aside.

I think that we are uttering no libel upon social life, or even upon family life, in thus describing the sort of characters which are to be found in each. St Paul, I do not doubt, would have considered all these cases as lying not without but within the pale of Christ's Church: the worst of them he would have described rather as brothers or as sisters walking inconsistently, than as persons to be dealt with as strangers or enemies, between whom and us there can exist no bond but that of an original humanity.

And yet it can scarcely be doubted that towards all, even the very best, of these, Christians to whom a greater measure of light and peace has already been vouchsafed have a very serious duty to perform, and one to which in a certain sense the rule is applicable, *Walk in wisdom toward them that are without.* Upon the conduct, upon the language, upon the spirit, of any one of us, in the daily intercourse of the family or of society, much may depend, for persons like those whom I have described, as to their being helped or else hindered in rising to a higher grace and at last reaching the very kingdom of heaven.

Walk in wisdom towards them. Can we not readily think of some ways in which this rule may be applied or else neglected?

Wisdom, in its practical working, is shown by the adaptation of right means to a right end.

Now what, as true Christians, should be your end? the object for which you live? The question might be variously answered. *That they who live should not live unto themselves, but unto Him who died for them and rose again* (2 Cor. v. 15). That would be a very comprehensive answer. St Paul chooses it as the briefest and clearest statement of a Christian's aim. He lives unto Christ. *Whether we live, we live unto the Lord; and whether we die, we die unto the*

Lord (Rom. xiv. 8); that is, in relation to Him; having Him in our view, and referring every word and act to Him, regarding each as it bears upon, as it affects, Him, His will, His glory.

But, in explaining our present subject, we may adopt a slightly different form of expression, and say, that our aim, as true Christians, ought to be, to glorify God, not only by serving Him stedfastly ourselves, but especially by drawing others, as opportunity is given us, towards Him and so towards their true happiness. In entering into society, as well as in the more private intercourse of family life, our object ought to be this; not so much to bear a testimony to our own convictions, as we might do in the presence of persons who were hopelessly set against truth and against the Gospel, but rather, to help these persons, in their various characters and states of mind, towards that which will make them happy, towards that one point of rest, towards that one living and loving Person, in which and in whom they will find the satisfaction of every want and the dismissal of every evil.

Does this seem an exaggerated, an enthusiastic, an unreal view of so common and so unromantic a thing as family or social intercourse? I do not think that it is. It may well be that the best and truest of Christians may mix for a long time in society, and yet not be able to point to any one definite instance in which he has been permitted to effect so great a result as the changing of a single character.

But yet, so subtle and so secret are the workings of man's soul, that He who knows them all may be aware of many instances, wholly unsuspected by the human instrument, in which the observation of the deportment, the words, the conduct, of one who has steadily kept in view the object which has been stated, may have been the means even of *saving a soul from death* and of *hiding* in the blood of Christ *a multitude of sins* (James v. 20). Only let it be our aim. That is the first and chief thing. Let it be our aim, to draw others towards their true happiness. This is the beginning of the wisdom spoken of; to have an object, and the right object, in view.

But then as to the means of effecting it. *Walk in wisdom* means, not only, Aim at the right object, but also, Take your aim truly. And I am sure we all see how untruly, that is, how injudiciously, many persons aim even at the highest and best object.

Observe—it is the key to a great part of the matter—the object is to attract, to win, to persuade. It is not to bear testimony and there leave it. That is a poor object. It is almost a selfish object. That is a testimony against, but we want a testimony to, attractive to, influential with, those of whom we speak. Then the first thing will be, to guard against repelling. It is very easy to repel. Persons in any of the moods before described will easily be repelled from good. If you are morose, if you are contemptuous, if you are harsh in your judgments, if you are intolerant of differences of opinion, you will not be walking in wisdom, however you may discharge your conscience. Let it be seen that you are just, let it be seen that you are charitable, let it be seen that you are open-minded, let it be seen that you are large-hearted, let it be seen, almost above all, that you are happy, and then the first point will have been gained: not only will you have had the right object in view, but you will, in one respect, have taken your aim rightly. The first thing to guard against is repelling when you would attract.

But there is a further point. St Paul says, *Let every one please his neighbour*—but he does not end there: indeed he says in another place, *If I yet pleased men, I should not be the servant of Christ* (Gal. i. 10) —therefore he adds, *Let every one please his neighbour, for his good, to edification* (Rom. xv. 2). So would we say here. It is not enough to attract: it must be towards truth, towards happiness, towards God. It is comparatively easy to attract; to make people like and approve your tolerant spirit, your calm judgment, your indulgent charity. But the question further is, To what end? Will they be the better for these things? Did you desire that they might be so? If so, you will have kept a watch over the door of your lips, that nothing inconsistent with the will of God may come forth out of them; no approval of worldly maxims, no acquiescence in unchristian principles, no admiration of wrong, no jesting at sin: your cheerfulness must not degenerate into levity, nor your charity into indifference. The object must have been not only proposed to yourself once, but steadily kept in view: to attract men towards God, not to attract them towards yourself.

These are difficult things, my brethren; very difficult, when we try at all to act upon them. It is so easy to make society a thing altogether apart from our religion, to regard it as a mere relaxation, a mere pause in the Christian life; and it is so easy to seek applause in it, to make agreeableness its object, the receiving of pleasure and not the doing good; that we can scarcely wonder at those who have turned aside from it altogether for the higher object, though it might not be wisely sought, of saving their own souls alive. Let us impress deeply upon our hearts the great end of all Christian intercourse: let us be on the watch, not only to avoid defeating it, but to find opportunities for promoting it: let us not be satisfied with doing this generally, by the maintenance of a Christian spirit in the sight of others, but let us also be watchful and thankful for every opening, given to us or made by us, for a more close access to the heart and soul of another, with the hope of fostering some good inclination, or of removing some doubt, some difficulty, some discouragement: and thus, in all ways, let us make it our object to seek God's glory and the welfare of His redeemed; remembering, in the last place, the principle which is here appended to the rule—

Redeeming the time.

There are two words employed in Scripture to

express our one word *time*. One of these words denotes time vaguely; mere duration, mere extension, of time: the other, which came before us last Sunday, and which occurs to-night in the clause now under consideration, expresses a portion cut out of time, limited consequently in extent, and designed to answer an object. This latter term therefore contains the idea of each of our two expressions, *season* and *opportunity*. Last Sunday we spoke of it in the words, *the sufferings of the present season* (Rom. viii. 18): to-night we must briefly indicate its meaning in the phrase, *redeeming the time*, or rather (to give it very literally) *buying up the opportunity*.

When, in the Book of Daniel, the Chaldeans had said, in answer to the king's demand that they would tell him both his forgotten dream and its interpretation, *Let the king tell his servants the dream, and we will show the interpretation of it;* we read that *the king answered and said, I know of certainty that ye would gain the time, because ye see the thing is gone from me* (Dan. ii. 7, 8). The words rendered, *ye would gain the time*, are, in the Greek Version of the passage, the very same here employed, and their use there explains their meaning here. *Ye would gain the time*, is, more exactly, *ye desire to buy up the opportunity;* that is, like merchants eagerly possessing themselves of the whole of some valuable commodity, you are trying to make the very most of the opportunity which my forgetfulness of the dream gives you for concealing your real want of skill in the art of the diviner.

Redeeming the time, is, in like manner, *buying up,* as a very precious kind of merchandise, and so, making the very most of, turning to the very best possible account, *the opportunity.*

Life is not only a certain duration of time: it is also our opportunity. It has an object as well as a course; an object which must be gained during it, or it cannot be gained ever; it is our opportunity—regarded as a whole, it is our one opportunity—of reaching, of attaining, of effecting, of becoming, something, which, if we reach not, if we do not, if we become not, while life lasts, we must forego, we must forfeit, we must lose, for ever.

Therefore buy it up. Make the very most of it. *Walk in wisdom toward them that are without, buying up the opportunity.* Soon will these lips be silent. Soon will others be in your dwelling. Soon will a new generation arise, which knows you not. At present you are upon the earth: soon will you sleep below it. Take heed to *occupy* while you can (Luke xix. 13). When your Master returns for you, let Him find your work done. See that some shall have been the better for your day on earth. See that some have cause to bless God for your having had life given you. Let the next generation of your family find it not less but more easy to remember God, for your having gone before them. *Brethren, the time is short* (1 Cor. vii. 29). Already God sees your life as a whole, and is judging it. Already—it is a happier thought, and not less true—already God has had mercy upon you, and accepts for Christ's sake every act that you have done, every word that you have spoken, as for Him. Do you not wish that others should be partakers with you in the benefit, in the *unspeakable gift* (2 Cor. ix. 15)? O bless God that He has so made and so endowed you as that you can do something—little it may be, for are we not all dust of the earth when weighed in the balances of eternity? yet something still, in making Him better known, more regarded, more loved, on this earth on which in its turn each generation frets itself and sins and suffers.

Buy up the opportunity. Yes, say not in your heart, Life is long and tedious: a day lost is nothing in such a reckoning. Each day is an integral part of the great opportunity: lose one day, and the whole must be defective. Lose one day, and the chances are greatly against your redeeming the next. Let each day have its work done, as it has its work assigned. Let the account of each be sealed, before the next be opened. Let the omissions, let the shortcomings, let the negligences, let the indolences, let the timidities, of one, be well confessed and consciously forgiven, before you enter upon the next. And O, amongst these, will not the want of wisdom toward them that are without, will not the indifference shown toward the souls of others, will not the faint-heartedness, will not the coldness, will not the self-indulgence, of our intercourse with others, occupy a large and a tear-blotted page? May God forgive us all, and help us all, for His Son's sake! It is good for us to be sorry. The time was short, and we have made it shorter. The opportunity was precious, and, instead of buying up each fragment of it, we have squandered of it whole days, whole weeks, whole years! *Enter not into judgment* with us, O Lord (Psalm cxliii. 2)! Give us Thy grace of repentance: give us Thy grace of contrition, and of soberness, and of watchfulness, and of godly fear! Grant that the future, if it be short, be well used! Grant that the past, for Thy Son's sake, may not rise against us in judgment! Happy will that day be, when we shall receive the final seal of forgiveness, and shall rest in hope. We would not prolong our days here, but we would end them peacefully. We would see our work finished. Then would we bathe it in the tears of repentance: we would wash it white in the blood of the Lamb. In Thy forgiveness would we find peace: *in Thy light* alone would we *see light* (Psalm xxxvi. 9).

SERMON XXII.

THE MAN OF SIN.

1   AND we beseech you, brethren, by[1] the presence[2] of our
2 Lord Jesus Christ and our gathering together to Him, to the
end that ye be not quickly shaken from your understanding
nor disturbed, either through spirit or through word or
through letter as if through us, how that the day of the Lord
3 is instant. Let not any one deceive you in any way: for[3],
unless there have come the apostasy first, and the man of
4 sin have been unveiled, the son of destruction, who opposes
and exalts himself exceedingly against every [so] called god
or object of reverence, so as himself to have taken his seat in
5 the temple of God, displaying himself that he is God——Remember ye not, that, while I was still with you, I used to
6 tell you these things? And now ye know that which re-
7 strains, to the end that he be unveiled in his own season. For
the secret of lawlessness already works: only he who now
8 restrains [will do so] until he be taken out of the midst: and
then shall be unveiled the lawless one, whom the Lord will
consume by the breath of His mouth and destroy by the mani-
9 festation of His presence: whose presence[2] is according to the
operation of Satan in all power and signs and wonders of
10 falsehood and in all deceit of unrighteousness for[4] them that

   [1] Literally, *for*, that is, *for the sake of*.
   [2] That is, as often elsewhere, the *coming*.
   [3] The sentence, after being extended by the enumeration of particulars in verse 4, is interrupted by the question of verse 5, and
not resumed.
   [4] *In relation to, towards.*

perish because they accepted not the love of the truth to the end that they should be saved. And for this cause God sends them an operation of error to the end that they should believe the falsehood, that all might be judged who believed not the truth but took pleasure in unrighteousness. But we are bound to thank God always concerning you, brethren beloved by the Lord, because God chose you from the beginning unto salvation in consecration of[5] the Spirit and belief of the truth; whereunto He called you through our Gospel, unto acquisition of the glory of our Lord Jesus Christ. Só then, brethren, stand fast, and hold the transmissions which ye were taught whether through word or through letter of ours. And may He Himself, our Lord Jesus Christ, and God our Father, who loved us and gave everlasting encouragement and a good hope in grace, encourage your hearts and establish them in every good work and word. 11 12 13 14 15 16 17

[5] That is, *by*.

SERMON XXII.

THE MAN OF SIN.

2 THESSALONIANS II. 8.

And then shall that wicked be revealed, whom the Lord shall consume with the spirit of His mouth, and shall destroy with the brightness of His coming.

THE course of our Services has brought before us once again this evening the Chapter from which the text is taken. The sound of its words has been often in our ears. We have occasionally perhaps heard what is commonly called a controversial Sermon upon it. More often we have passed the Chapter by, and observed that our Ministers did so, as a portion of God's Word difficult of interpretation, and waiting for its full elucidation till a time still future.

Shall we endeavour, my brethren, to draw from it to-night something which may be instructive, interesting to us all, and edifying? We will try to look into it with a calm and unprejudiced mind, bringing to its examination as little as possible of preconceived opinion, dismissing as far as possible all that we may have before imagined or accepted as to its meaning and its application. So reading it, I think we shall gain some good to our hearts and souls, and God will bless us in the humble effort to walk in His light.

The time will not be wasted if I first read the words to you once again, with some closeness and even baldness of rendering. It is especially necessary in such a case to throw out of our way anything of merely human appendage, and to arrive at the exact language of the blessed Apostle himself.

And we beseech you, brethren, by the presence, the future presence, or *coming, of our Lord Jesus Christ, and our gathering together to Him*—as described in the former Epistle to this Church—*to the end that ye be not quickly shaken from your understanding,* that is, from your calm and right judgment, *nor disturbed, either through spirit or through word or through letter as if through us*—by any supposed testimony, whether in the form of a spiritual gift, or an inspired utterance, or an epistle purporting to come from us your Evangelists—*how* (stating) *that the day of the Lord is instant,* absolutely impending and imminent. *Let not any one deceive you in any way: for* that day comes not *unless there have come the apostasy first, and* unless *the man of sin have been unveiled, the son of destruction,* or *perdition:* the very term applied to Judas in the prayer of our Lord to His Father (John xvii. 12): *who opposes and exalts himself exceedingly against every so called god*—the expression is borrowed from the Book of Daniel (xi. 36)—*or object of reverence, so as himself to have taken his seat in the temple of God, displaying himself that he is God.* Remember ye not *that, while I was still with you, I used to tell you these things? And now ye know that which restrains, to the end that he be unveiled in,* and not before, *his own season. For the secret of lawlessness, of wickedness,* or *disobedience, already works: only he who now restrains* will do so *until he be taken out of the midst: and then shall be unveiled the lawless (the wicked* or *disobedient) one, whom the Lord will consume by the breath of His mouth, and destroy by the manifestation,* the *Epiphany, of His presence,* or *coming: whose presence,* or *coming*—that is, the coming of the wicked one—*is according to (by) the operation of Satan, in (amidst) all power and signs and wonders of falsehood, and in (amidst) all deceit of unrighteousness,* every deceit and trickery that wickedness can practise, *for (in relation to,* that is, practised upon) *them that perish (that are in process of destruction) because they accepted not the love of the truth to the end that they should be saved. And for this cause,* because they would not love the truth, *God sends them,* in judgment, *an operation of error, to the end that they should believe the falsehood; that all may be judged (condemned) who believed not,* while they could, *the truth,* but took pleasure in unrighteousness. But we are bound to thank God always concerning you, brethren beloved by the Lord, because God chose you from the beginning unto salvation in (through) consecration of (wrought by) the Spirit, and belief of the truth; whereunto,* to which state or result, *He called (invited* or *summoned) you through (by means of) our Gospel,* our message of good tidings, *unto acquisition of the glory of our Lord Jesus Christ. So then, brethren, stand fast, and hold the transmissions,* the doctrines transmitted to you, *which ye were taught whether through word,* when we were with you, *or through letter of ours:* the reference is to his former Epistle. *And may He Himself, our Lord Jesus Christ, and God our Father, who loved us, and gave,* once for all, *everlasting encouragement and a good hope in grace,* through His free favour, *encourage your hearts and establish them in* the maintenance of *every good work and word.*

Now let me, in the next place, express in a very brief paraphrase so much of the substance of this passage as involves no doubtful interpretation.

I hear that there is an unsettlement of mind amongst you, arising from an impression that the great day is close at hand. I pray you to correct that impression. I thought that I had guarded against it. You surely remember what I told you, when I was with you, as to the necessary preliminaries to the great end of all. Many things have to be accomplished before the great drama reaches its close. The apostasy—does not that word recall to you a whole train of predictions? The man of sin, with all his blasphemous pretensions, his claim to preeminence above God Himself, his power and signs and lying wonders—where is he? Is he yet manifested? Nay, is there not still in existence, as you heard from me, an impediment to his manifestation; an impediment which must be removed out of the way before that manifestation can be complete? I remind you of these items of doctrine: it is needless, I am sure, to detail them. Be prepared then for delay in the coming of the Lord. Space must be given, first for the subtle working, already begun, of the mystery of iniquity. That must go on, underground as it were, or at least amidst checks and discouragements, so long as the obstacle of which I have spoken shall remain in force. Next, when this is removed, there shall be an unveiling of the wicked one. He shall take to himself all his power; he shall surround himself with signs and portents, fallacious indeed, but not the less deceptive; he shall deceive, if it were possible, the very elect; he shall lead captive in an easy and willing thraldom all those who, at the season of his manifestation, shall not have received into their inmost hearts the love of the truth. It shall be the punishment of all these, to believe the lie. And then, upon this developed Antichrist, this enemy of God, this seducer of man, at the very height of his triumph, in the very hour of his fancied security, there shall burst the light of Christ's presence: the Son of Man shall be seen, descending even as He once ascended, and the very breath of His mouth, the very brightness of His coming, shall consume, shall destroy, shall smite with instant discomfiture, him who but now seemed to have succeeded in obliterating God Himself from the earth which He created. I thank God for you, beloved brethren, that you, when that last deluge sweeps the world, will be secure in an ark which can safely ride the waters. You have listened to the call of Christ's Gospel: you have *believed the truth: you have been made holy by an indwelling Spirit: you therefore have the sign of God's choice upon you, you shall be amongst those who obtain the glory. Only stand fast. Hold the traditions. Guard zealously the good deposit: and may God your Father keep you evermore in His peace and in His strength, even as He has already loved you, and given you the encouragement of an eternal hope.*

I could not bear to leave such a Chapter, my brethren, in that region of obscurity and almost of repulsiveness in which I am sure that for many of us it has heretofore lain. Let us turn now from its general aspect to consider a few special points in it.

1. And, first, you will observe that it teaches us a lesson of humility. And this in two senses.

(1) First, there are limits to our knowledge.

Even in the Book of God's Revelation there are things which we cannot explain. In the Chapter before us a reference is made to certain things which St Paul had told the Thessalonian Christians when he was with them. *Remember ye not, that, when I was yet with you, I told you these things?* How natural, how like the general character of the Apostolical writings, which are incidental not formal, letters not treatises, that he should leave that reference unexplained! Those to whom he wrote understood him: that was enough. God's Providence indeed, and therefore God's design, caused the Epistle to have a wider use than its writer foresaw for it: but this wider use was not to affect its composition: that which it was unnecessary to explain to the Thessalonians, because they already knew it, was not to be explained for others into whose hands, after them, the Epistle was to fall. Everything essential to faith or practice has been taught us in some place or other of those Holy Scriptures over which God's care for His Church has so marvellously and so effectually watched: but many things may have been told, by word of mouth, to Churches which the Apostles were planting, and not, in every single particular, to those who were to possess only the correspondence by which the later wants of those Churches were from time to time supplied. It is one part of our trial to be required to content ourselves with imperfect light. St Paul says to the Thessalonians, *When I was with you, I told you what withholds, what restrains, the manifestation of the wicked one. Ye know what it is.* They knew, and therefore were not told. We know not, and yet are not told. Conjectures as to the meaning have been abundant. But we want certainty, not conjecture: and if we cannot have certainty, we must be content to wait. It is no business of the preacher, and it is no business of the expositor, to tell us what he thinks, when what we want to know is what God says. Here is a point on which we are not instructed, and (what is more trying) on which others were. And yet I had far rather be told to wait, than conjecturally enlightened. It is easy to guess what may have been in St Paul's mind when he thus wrote. Speaking as he is of a future manifestation of evil, in a form and with a virulence unknown before, we may imagine that by an obstacle to that manifestation he may have intended some coercive and therefore salutary power like that by which the organization of the great Roman Empire in his time, or of the civil government of nations in all times, held or holds in check the unbridled license of impiety and crime. It may be so. But where the language of Inspiration is silent, we do well to be silent too. And we learn from the silence of Inspiration a lesson not wholly negative. It reminds us of the ignorance of nature: it should make us thankful for even a partial illumination: it should stimulate our desire for the full light of the future: it should repeat to us the words of St Paul as written to another congregation, *Now I know in part: but hereafter I shall know, even as also I am known* (1 Cor. xiii. 12).

(2) Thus we learn, in the first place, a lesson of humility as to the boundaries of our knowledge. But there is also a lesson of humility, specially suitable to this Chapter, as to the right and the wrong estimate of the importance of our own age.

It is a natural feeling, and I know not that it is altogether inoperative for good, which prompts us to overvalue, by comparison at least, both the magnitude of the events, and the characteristics (for good or evil) of the persons, occupying the stage of the world while we are among its spectators. Every age has its own importance: and of some periods it may perhaps be predicted, even at the time, that they will fill a large page in history. The effect of that belief, so often recurring, if it be not always more or less prevalent, in the minds of men, that their own is such a marked period, ought to act beneficially in various ways. It ought to awaken a keener interest in the course of events—in other words, in the procedure of God's Providence—outward and inward, social and mental, at home and abroad. It ought to stimulate to more active energy every faculty and every power vouchsafed to us, that we ourselves lag not behind in a race so ardent, or prove ourselves unsuitable to a crisis so momentous. We can never be wrong in exalting the importance of our own times, if we draw from that exaltation the right inference, and turn it to the right account. But it is otherwise when we begin to apply the language of Revelation, and more especially the language of inspired Prophecy, to the days in which our own lot is cast. That which was useful as a stimulus to energy may become vain and even mischievous when it is made the criterion of judgment. Examples will occur to all my hearers in which particular events and particular persons have been for the moment invested by hasty interpreters with a dignity of praise or blame which a few years later those very interpreters would have been compelled greatly to modify. We can all see, as we look down a common chart of history, how prophecy would be interpreted, if we know not how it was interpreted, at particular epochs, by persons reading its language through the medium of contemporary feeling. And possibly the fault, so far as it was not caused by the mere passions of the moment, may have lain, not so much in applying as in restricting; not so much in saying, This is a legitimate use, as in saying, This is the designed and the only meaning, of such or such a particular prediction contained in the word of Revelation. We can understand that a certain principle may have been involved in such or such a contest, or exhibited in such or such a character; and that, as far as it was so, it may have fallen within the scope of a certain warning of danger or a certain prophecy of judgment; and yet that it would have been both unjust and irrational to tie down that prophecy to this one sole use; a disproportionate and therefore false view of the inspired declaration; a dishonour done to Infinite Wisdom by a misreading of existing facts under the influence of an excited and therefore shortlived feeling. We can all imagine, if we are not all cognizant of, applications of the very prophecy before us made some fifty years ago, which all would repudiate now, nay, which some might be inclined to replace by another, equally narrow, erroneous, and transient. We cannot attempt these things with safety. We cannot trust the human judgment which would attempt to pass God's sentence upon the present. We cannot tell how He regards it, if only because we know not how we shall ourselves regard it fifty or even five years hence. Upon the moral character of actions—our own first of all—God's seal of righteous approval or disapproval is set visibly and legibly. If we know a deed done, know the whole of it, with its circumstances and its motives; or if we really have the materials for estimating a whole character—and, again I say, most especially with reference to our own—we can declare even now that the one is either right or wrong, the other either good or evil. But we dare not say what place that right or wrong deed, that good or evil character, holds relatively to the whole of time, or to the entire counsel of God. We look on, with interest, with anxiety, with awe, upon events as they pass, upon men who rise, and rule, and make war and peace, and foster or oppress God's truth and God's servants: but we do not presume to say that it is of this man or of that man particularly that God has spoken, any further than that it is He who ruleth above all at all times in the kingdom of men, and that He weighs both high and low in the balance of an infallible and an impartial judgment. That humility which we would learn with reference to the boundaries of our knowledge, we must learn also, in the second place, with reference to our inability to estimate correctly the place which our own times shall eventually hold in the scale of a relative and a comparative importance.

2. Yet, after this first lesson has been thoroughly learned, we shall find that enough is left to us in this very Chapter to quicken every energy of our minds into an earnest looking after those things which are coming on the earth. What does the Apostle here

seem to say? If we read his words for the first time, before controversy had usurped them, should we not all gather this from them—can we doubt that the Thessalonians, unless strongly guarded against it by some earlier communication, must have gathered this from them—that St Paul, writing by the inspiration of God, predicts a very incarnation of evil before the end comes? Listen once more: *That day shall not come, unless the man of sin, the son of perdition, be first revealed ... who opposeth and exalteth himself against all that is called God or that is worshipped, so that he, as God, sitteth in the temple of God, showing himself that he is God....And then shall that wicked one be revealed, whom the Lord shall consume with the breath of His mouth, and shall destroy with the brightness of His coming; even him, whose coming is after the working of Satan with all power and signs and lying wonders.* The words seem to point all one way; to some concentration, some impersonation, some incarnation, of evil. Surely, if not to one living man in whom the very power of Satan himself is embodied and developed, yet at least to some system, some combination of living agents, to which a personal appellation could be affixed without a violent abuse of terms, some open antagonism against truth, against holiness, against the Gospel, against Christ, against God Himself, upon which shall speedily, if not instantly, descend the yet more crushing might of good, nay, upon which or upon whom shall burst the appalling revelation of Christ Himself from heaven, with a decisive stroke of discomfiture, with a consuming thunderbolt of judgment. Need I say, to any one here present, that such a person, or such a combination, thus openly hostile to God, and (yet more) thus instantly visited by the return of Christ for judgment, has never yet been realized on the earth? Unchristian, ungodly, violent, cruel men—unchristian, supersitious, foolish, immoral systems—these there have been: single rulers, like Nero, Diocletian, or Julian, who set themselves to trample out the Gospel from the earth; combined powers, such as that of the Papacy, which have distorted Christianity into a caricature offensive alike (so far as its distinctive features go) to reason and to Revelation; social systems, like that of the first French Revolution, which have done despite to God Himself, and worshipped openly as their deity the vilest passions of a fallen nature: types, all of these, of that wicked one, of that man of sin, that son of perdition, of whom St Paul has here written, but no one of them satisfying the prediction, no one of them fulfilling its terms, and no one of them finally overthrown by the very coming of the Lord from heaven. That still remains: and we may well doubt whether, amidst all the wild confusions of thought and action in these marvellous times, we have yet seen the birth, or at least the maturity, of that man, or that power—call it which we may—in whom or in which the mystery shall be accomplished, and whose ruin shall be consummated by the Epiphany of Christ's presence. Therefore I say that the eye of Christian expectation may well be strained to the utmost, and the wings of human imagination stretched as for a boundless flight, in waiting and watching for those last signs of all, which shall prognosticate the actual Coming, and introduce the end of time. We desire not to be wise above what is written: but we must guard the written Word itself against mean and grovelling applications: we must refuse, until the last close shall refute our conclusions, to believe that St Paul wrote thus when he meant something infinitely less, infinitely different, or when in reality he had no message to convey, beyond that which the instincts of his own reason could have dictated apart from God.

There is room, I say, for the operation of curiosity, of wonder, of awe, yes of fear, as to those scenes which have yet to be played out upon the stage of this earth. We can see nothing incredible, and nothing unworthy, in some such manifestation (before the time of the end) of the wicked one in human form, and in the fullest exercise of all that malignity, all that subtlety, all that cruelty, and all that hatred of God, which is characteristic of him, as shall bring into a definite compass the great struggle between good and evil, shall compel men to take an open side with the one or with the other, and make the second Advent of Christ the direct intervention of a Deliverer and a Conqueror. Such was the expectation of the Church in its early age: I am far from thinking that the change which has come over it within the last three centuries has been altogether a change to the more reasonable or the more true. The restriction—I do not say the application in a modified sense, but the restriction—of this prophecy to the errors or the mischiefs, the sins or the crimes, of one particular perverted form of Christianity, has savoured quite as much of the party-spirit of man as of the immutable wisdom and jealous truthfulness of God. Let every form of error be assailed with the weapons which befit it: there may be some such weapons in this Chapter, as certainly there are abundant weapons in other parts of Scripture, with which to meet the aggressions and to humble the pretensions of the Church of Rome. But that the prophecy before us neither begins there nor ends there, I am deeply convinced. It points still onward, onward still; and then only will it have received its last, its highest fulfilment, when it has met with that particular developement of evil, be it what it may, which, in the first place, contains in it no element whatever of a true faith and no possibility whatever of a Christian practice, and which, in the second place, is proved by the event itself to be that special and culminating wickedness which brings down upon itself the actual interposition of Christ for judgment.

3. I have drawn from this prophecy a lesson of humility, and a lesson of expectation. Let me add, in the third place, a lesson of vigilance. Let me remark upon the necessity for personal watchfulness, arising out of the indications already perceptible of a

preparation for the last outbreak of evil. *The mystery of iniquity*, St Paul said even in those early days, *doth already work*. The iniquity spoken of is *lawlessness*: the wicked one predicted is *the lawless one*. The great characteristic of the man of sin is his exaltation of himself against every thing bearing the name of God, against everything claiming the reverence or awakening the awe of man. Need I say how descriptive this language is of the times in which our own lot is cast? National prosperity may prevent outbursts of violence: the respectability as well as the humanity of rulers may present few points on which misrepresentation or disaffection can fasten. This is well while it lasts: we may thank God for it. But never was there a time in which obedience, as such, was rarer or more exceptional: family obedience, civil obedience, ecclesiastical obedience. Everything is canvassed; and, where respect is rendered, it is given, not to authority, but to tried and approved authority; rendered not as a duty but as an act of will. Perhaps it is more valuable so: certainly it is good for the superior to feel that without merit he cannot win respect. But I fear we do not err in seeing a spirit of lawlessness even in these its less dangerous workings. And when we turn to that part of the prediction which regards the relations of man towards God, I much fear that we see a yet stronger feature of resemblance to our own times, and one for which we cannot plead the same excuse. In religious opinion there is a lawlessness now which it is vain to repress by claims of authority, but which yet is leading men every day further and further from the simplicity of the faith of Christ. There is a want of reverence abroad amongst us, which makes it scarcely an exaggeration to say of us that we exalt ourselves, as censors and judges, above everything that is called God or that is worshipped. Enquiries conducted in a reverent spirit, with prayer for light, amidst habits of devotion, with watchful and holy lives, will never end, as we believe, but in faith and wisdom: but is that the spirit in which all our theological writers, all our candid and profound thinkers, carry on their researches into Divine truth? We ask the question, but we cannot answer it. And, alas! for the multitude of men, high and low, educated and uneducated, who in these days sit in judgment on every mystery of doctrine and on every form of worship, how can we dare to hope that any spirit of inward reverence presides over their speculations, or that any iota of the faith will be the residuum of their (so called) mental processes? Too truly may we say, in the words now before us, *The mystery of lawlessness doth already work:* and, when that which now checks it shall be removed; when men's minds shall have become habituated to a freedom of speculation which but a few years ago would have been called impiety, and it shall have come to be regarded as an old-fashioned prejudice, to hold in its integrity the simple faith as it was once delivered to the saints; then can we understand how readily he may strip off his veil who is to come amongst us as *the lawless one*, how instant an acceptance he may gain for his lying wonders, how speedy may be the transition, in minds thus prepared, from holding truth in suspense to exchanging it for *the lie*.

4. And therefore I would add, in the fourth and last place, to the lessons of humility, of expectation, and of watchfulness, a lesson also of discrimination; drawn from the observation of two opposite characters here presented to us; of the persons who in the last great conflict shall side with the Wicked one, and of those who in the same crisis of their faith shall remain faithful to their Lord.

Of the former two things are said: that they *believed not the truth*, or *received not the love of the truth;* and, that they *had pleasure in unrighteousness*. Of the latter, that they *believed the truth*, and were *sanctified by the Spirit*.

My brethren, this brings us back from any flights of imagination, from any investigations of abstruse doctrine, from any general reflections upon the state of opinion now or upon the prospects of our race as revealed to us by Prophecy, and fixes our whole attention on the two personal questions, Have I believed the truth? and am I following after holiness? Strange that it should be needful to ask the former of these questions! What are we? Are we not Christians? Do we not believe in Christ as our Saviour? Do we not worship Him, weekly, daily, in public, in private, as our Redeemer, our Propitiation, our Lord?

Yes, we do all these things: but I must ask, yet again, Have we received the love of the truth? Is the Gospel real, is it comforting, is it strengthening, to us—that Gospel, I mean, that true message from God to sinners, which tells of sin put away by the sacrifice of Christ, of Christ ever living to be the Intercessor and the Life? Have we received the love of the truth? We all know that: do we love the revelation of *God with us?* do we love Him who is thus revealed? And, if we do, then are we seeking day by day the presence within us of His Holy Spirit, bringing every part of our lives, every corner of our hearts, into His bright and searching light, desiring that it may be shone upon, desiring that it may be transformed, by His immediate presence, by His quickening power?

If these things are true of us, then we shall be safe in the day of the revelation of the Wicked one. He will *have nothing in* us (John xiv. 30); no wavering, no reluctant faith, glad to take refuge in the lie; no inconsistent, no crooked life, glad to be excused from the effort after holiness. To us it will be no satisfaction to be offered something more rational than a crucified Saviour: to us it will be no comfort to be told that we may sin and not die. The delusion may be strong, the apostasy may be general: but we shall have a safeguard within; the same Presence which has raised us out of sin, which has cheered us under sorrow, which has often lightened our darkness and made our weakness strong. We know that voice too well to mistake another's for it: we have waited for that coming too long to accept in its stead another hope. *A thousand may fall beside us, and ten thousand at our right hand* (Psalm xci. 7): but the infection shall not come nigh us: He whose we are will turn aside the poisoned arrow from our heart, and at the moment of our sorest need we shall *look up, and lift up our heads,* and behold *redemption,* yea, the Redeemer Himself, at last *drawing nigh* (Luke xxi. 28).

SERMON XXIII.

THE WAGES OF SIN AND THE GIFT OF GOD.

EPISTLE FOR THE SEVENTH SUNDAY AFTER TRINITY.

ROMANS VI. 19—23.

19 *I SPEAK a human thing because of the weakness of your flesh. For as ye did present your members [as] slaves to uncleanness, and to lawlessness unto lawlessness, so now present your members [as] slaves to righteousness unto con-*
20 *secration. For when ye were slaves of sin, ye were free [in*
21 *regard] to righteousness. What fruit then had ye then [of things] at which ye are now ashamed? for the end of those*
22 *things [is] death. But now, emancipated from sin, and enslaved to God, ye have your fruit unto consecration, and*
23 *the end eternal life. For the pay of sin is death: but the free gift of God is eternal life in Christ Jesus our Lord.*

SERMON XXIII.

THE WAGES OF SIN AND THE GIFT OF GOD.

ROMANS VI. 23.

The wages of sin is death; but the gift of God is eternal life through Jesus Christ our Lord.

THE whole Gospel is summed up in this contrast. What we are by nature; what we should have come to, if we had been let alone; what we shall come to if we let ourselves alone: on the other hand, what we are by grace; what God has done for us, and in whom; and where it is to be sought, and how it may be found: all these things are contained in the brief verse read as the text, and our work will only be to open it by God's help, so that its contents may be seen, apprehended, and appropriated by us all.

The verse before us is the last verse in a Chapter. It is also the close of an argument.

St Paul has been making a very strong statement of the blessings into which Christ's Redemption admits all who believe. The foregoing Chapter has ended with these emphatic words. *But, where sin abounded, grace did much more abound: that, as sin reigned in death*, as the field of its manifestation, the arena of its triumph, *so also might grace reign through righteousness unto eternal life through Jesus Christ our Lord* (Rom. v. 20, 21). So broad a declaration of the conquest of sin by grace might seem almost to make the existence of sin a matter of indifference. May not sin itself redound to God's glory in forgiving and in outdoing it? Such is the question with which the Chapter before us opens. And it needs indeed a scribe well instructed (like St Paul) in the mysteries of the kingdom of heaven, rightly to combine the two halves of the true doctrine; the inexhaustible store of pardon, and the sinfulness of that sin which has to draw upon it. Some men cramp and fetter the freedom of the promise: other men leave it open to an almost inevitable abuse. Not so did the inspired Apostle. He first declares plainly the freedom of the promise; and he then shows, not where it fails, not the case which it is inadequate to meet, but the utter incongruity of a life of sin with a state of grace, the utter impossibility of one who has died with Christ, and risen with Christ, and ascended with Christ—of one who is united to Christ, as every Christian is united to Him, by a union dating from the individual appropriation of Redemption in Baptism—continuing earthly and carnal and sinful, dead in sin while Christ is alive with God, the creature of time and sense while the Saviour with whom he is one has passed through the heavens into the cloudless light, into the eternal life, above.

The time would fail us to pursue the argument through all its details. Enough for our present purpose will be found in the verses immediately preceding the text. They contain a recapitulation and an application of the whole.

I speak a human thing—I use a human comparison, repeated in the words which follow—*because of the weakness of your flesh;* because of that infirmity in apprehending spiritual things which is inseparable from your condition as persons still in the body. *For*—I repeat the same comparison which I have already employed to illustrate my meaning—*as ye did* formerly *present your members*, the members of your body, and the faculties of your natural mind, as *slaves to uncleanness, and to lawlessness unto (to work) lawlessness; so now present your members* as *slaves to righteousness unto consecration*. The comparison employed, from the 16th verse onwards, is that of a master and a slave. St Paul tells us, humbling as it may be to human pride, that we cannot, any one of us, be absolutely free: we must have a master, and we cannot have two masters: but we have a choice. We cannot be free, but we may, and indeed must, exercise one power of freedom, that of choosing our service. On the one side, bidding, as it were, for our allegiance stands Sin; that great tyrant, who knows well how to deck out his yoke with gay colours; nay, how to represent that it is no yoke at all, but a mere self-pleasing, a mere regard to what is pleasant, to what is easy, to what is natural, agreeable to inclination in each particular point; but who, none the less for this, is a tyrant, and a stern and cruel as well as powerful tyrant, over all who yield themselves to his direction.

This is one alternative. Sin: personified here as a living power, a real person, to whom we are invited to surrender ourselves, our bodies and minds, the members of the one, the faculties of the other, to be his instruments, the implements of his service. Sin, the antagonist of God; Sin, the self-will, as opposed to God's will; Sin, the contradiction of duty; Sin, the personification of the fallen as opposed to the original nature. On the other side stands Righteousness; personified also; called in a former verse *Obedience;* that is, obedience to the rightful authority, the authority of God Himself; Righteousness, which is the will of God; Righteousness, which is the constant reference of everything, and in everything, to what God would have us to be and to do. And the charge is, that, as we once gave ourselves up to sin, whatever the particular direction in which it turned us, so now we should surrender ourselves, in word and act, in body and mind, to Righteousness: *unto consecration;* to live, that is, as God's consecrated ones; in all the peace and in all the dignity of persons set apart by God Himself for His immediate use and service.

The following verse dwells once again upon the direct contrariety and antagonism which exists between the one life and the other. *For when ye were slaves of sin, ye were free* in relation *to righteousness.*

The Wages of Sin and the Gift of God. 409

You cannot serve both at once. You were once serving Sin; obeying, we may briefly say, inclination in all things. While this was so, the other master, Righteousness, the will of God, had no hold upon you. You were free in regard to it. That sounds like an advantage. Freedom is a great object with us all. *What fruit then*, the Apostle adds, what advantage, what profit, *had ye then*, at that time, of (from) things *at which ye are now ashamed?* He bids them reflect upon their life out of Christ. Was it a happy life? was it a remunerative life? did it repay you? Scarcely so: *for the end of those things*, of a life of self-pleasing and sin, is *death*. While you are living in it, it may at times be a life of enjoyment, as it certainly is at other times a life of conscious weariness, disappointment, and disquiet: but look to the end: certainly its end will not be blessed: *the end of those things*—they may last for fifty or sixty or seventy years—but *the end of those things*, of such a life, is *death*.

But now, having been *emancipated*, as by one act of decisive liberation when you became Christians, *from sin, and enslaved*, subjugated, *to God*. Be not afraid of that expression. To be God's slaves is as delightful a thought as to be slaves of any one or of anything except God is degrading and repulsive. *Enslaved to God* means the being entirely His; His property, His charge, His purchased possession; those whom He has thought it worth while to make His own twice over, first by creation, then by the blood of His Son; those whom He designs to employ as His ministers and His instruments; those for whose well-being He is responsible, and who never, by any act or any violence, can be plucked out of His hand. *Servants of God* may quit Him, may part from Him: but *slaves of God* are His for ever. This was the chosen title of Apostles themselves. *Paul, a slave of God* (Tit. i. 1). *Paul, a slave of Jesus Christ* (Rom. i. 1). *Paul and Timotheus, slaves of Jesus Christ* (Phil. i. 1). *James, a slave of God and of the Lord Jesus Christ* (James i. 1). *Simon Peter, a slave and an Apostle of Jesus Christ* (2 Pet. i. 1). So it is here. *Emancipated from sin, and enslaved to God, ye have your fruit unto consecration, and the end eternal life.* The advantage of your new service is a consistent and successful consecration to God: and its end is, not, like that of the service of sin, death, but, on the very contrary, immortal, everlasting, eternal life. *For the pay (wages) of sin is death: but the free gift of God is eternal life in Christ Jesus our Lord.*

The subject thus proposed for special consideration to-day divides itself for us into two parts. First, *the wages of sin is death.* Secondly, *the gift of God is eternal life in Christ.*

It lies on the surface of the text to remark that there is a contrast here, as between the nature of the two results, so also between the terms of the two services. Sin gives wages: what God gives to His servants is a gratuity. Let us dwell a little upon this thought.

The word here rendered *wages* is the same

The Wages of Sin and the Gift of God.

which is used in Scripture for a soldier's pay. *Be content with your wages* (Luke iii. 14), was the charge of John the Baptist to the soldiers who asked of him their duty. *Who goeth a warfare at any time at his own wages* (1 Cor. ix. 7), that is, for pay furnished by himself? was St Paul's question to those who would grudge to a minister of the Gospel his right to *live of the Gospel.*

But, whether in its application to the pay of a soldier or to the wages of a servant, the whole point of the expression lies in this; that certain work done has a right to a certain remuneration. *The wages of sin*, in like manner, will be, the remuneration which sin gives for work done in its service.

My brethren, it is a sad and a solemn subject, but not on that account is it the less needful that it be sometimes brought before us in the congregation: how sin repays those, who, in the alternative presented to each of us as to our choice of a master, have been unhappy enough to make the wrong choice; to have chosen the service of sin and not the service of God.

Let us not forget that Sin is a word of wide import. We can all assent to the truth of the statement before us, if it be restricted to the case of great excesses of wrong-doing; to the case of the dishonest, the intemperate, the grossly profligate, who reap the fruit of their evil deeds in bodily disease or in civil punishment. Great cause indeed have such persons to say to themselves, In serving Sin, I have served a very just master. For each one of my dishonest acts, for each one of my sinful lusts, Sin, my master, has given me a definite and a very exact equivalent. I squandered my money in riotous living, and I have come to penury. I neglected my health, I despised the warning of the physician, I deemed myself exempted from the common conditions of the bodily frame; and I am now a wreck of what I was, every organ disarranged, and the whole existence a burden and a curse. I gave no heed to the voice of conscience, I treated as a dead letter the terrors alike of man and God, I went on as though none would ever see, as though the Judge Himself were in league and concert with the criminal; and at last I found that, in deed and in truth, God is, and is a just God: Sin paid me my wages, and, behold, they were exactly counted, and short neither in tale nor weight! *Be not deceived: God is not mocked: for, whatsoever a man soweth, that shall he also reap* (Gal. vi. 7). There is a sowing and a reaping: there is also a working and a wage!

But, though less obviously, it is not less really true, in reference to cases far short of criminal excess.

We see it in the way in which sin pays in kind. A man neglects prayer, neglects his Bible, neglects the Sunday, once: that is sin; it is a contradiction of the known will of God. He supposes himself free to resume any of these intermitted habits when he will: he is his own master, he thinks, and what he has to-day willed one way, he may to-morrow will the other. But Sin is standing over him, and mocking his vain calculations. He has done a piece of work for Sin to-day, and Sin will pay him his wages in inclining him to do the same to-morrow. To-morrow it will be easier to him to sin. To-morrow the voice of inclination will be stronger, and the voice of conscience weaker, and thus he will do again as he has done once, and find it far less difficult and at the time far less remorseful.

That is sin, which contradicts the will of God. No sin can be really more sinful, by whatever name it may disguise itself, than that of a predominant ungodliness; an habitual living without God, apart from Christ, in a world which God has created, which Christ has redeemed. I am sure I need not say how this sort of sin repays its service. I am sure I need not say how retributive, how strictly retributive, is that consequence which follows such a life; how very dreary it is in dark days to have no light above; how very lonely it is in times of bereavement to have no Friend in heaven; how very formidable it is in seasons of danger, in the approach of death, to have no guiding hand, no experienced care, no trusted love, to which to commit the keeping of the life and of the soul.

And here we approach the question, What are sin's wages? *The wages of sin is death.*

This is true in every sense in which the word *death* is found in Scripture.

It is true of natural death. Though not the wages of individual sin, in all who undergo it, yet even natural death, the death of the body, is the consequence of sin. But for sin, there would not have been death. Every funeral which passes us in our streets, every loss which occurs in our families, should remind us of sin; and, though it be not the punishment of the particular sin of him who dies, yet it should awaken in our hearts the remembrance of sin generally, and of our own individual participation in that universal defilement.

And yet, my brethren, natural death is the least part of sin's wages. Natural death, if that were all, might be for us, as it has been, we believe, for countless thousands, the gate of life. It is otherwise with the second kind of death, spiritual death; the death of the soul. If the life of the soul be union with God, the death of the soul is separation from God. The words are soon spoken: separation from God. But O, my brethren, let us reflect upon the thing spoken of! Who that has known the struggle of getting back to God, can be insensible to the darkness, to the misery, to the all but hopelessness, of that state which makes such a struggle necessary? Nothing but long familiarity with that condition could make it tolerable to any of us. *Without God in the world* (Eph. ii. 12): what can be more dreadful? We can imagine what it would be to carry about a dead body with us: what must it be to carry about everywhere with us a dead soul? O, there is a pain in it, be quite sure; though it is that sort of dull pain which we can just endure so long as we feel it to be inevitable. But let a chance of escape come, or even let one gleam of real light shoot in upon our darkness, revealing it to us as it is, and indeed we shall see that the death of the soul is no light matter; we shall see that the wages of sin are not all future, not all waiting till a future state for payment, but already in course of payment, already, not threatening only, but preparing for, a payment in full.

The full payment is a third kind of death mentioned in Scripture; what is there called *the second death* (Rev. ii. 11. xx. 6, 14. xxi. 8). It would be presumptuous, as well as most painful, to dilate upon that dreadful thing which is thus described. But I fear we must say that it is the consummation, the certain and inevitable consummation, of a life spent on earth either in sin or without God; the state into which entrance is given by the reunion of a dead soul with its reanimated body; the state of one who would not have God for his Father, and died in that refusal, and whose day of grace has at last issued in an eternity of darkness. *Knowing therefore the terror of the Lord, we persuade men* (2 Cor. v. 11).

But let me hope that the thought of this painful truth has disposed some hearts in this Congregation to listen to the gracious revelation which accompanies it. *The wages of sin is death: but the free gift of God is eternal life in Christ Jesus our Lord.*

The free gift of God. God does not give wages. He gives something far better: for who has made God his debtor? *When we have done all that is commanded us*—and when will that be, for any man?

at last we must say, *We are unprofitable servants: we have done but that which it was our duty to do* (Luke xvii. 10). God has a right to our entire obedience: if ever it were entire, still there would be nothing over; no room for claims of merit, or for rewards of extra-service.

And He waits not for these. He begins by giving. No one can serve Him till he has first received. The service of God does not consist in a number of definite disjointed acts, but in a certain spirit, a certain mind, towards Him, prompting a certain kind of life which has been as simply as beautifully described in the three words, *companionship with God*. This spirit, with all which precedes and all which results from it, God must give, God alone.

I say, with all which precedes it. Because the spirit itself, which is God's gift, is procured by something else, the gift of Christ. First, a free forgiveness, wrought out for us by Christ bearing our sins: then the belief of that forgiveness, the fleeing for refuge into the harbour of God's love in Christ: then the spirit of the child breathed into our hearts, crying *Abba, Father:* and then the daily endeavour, in the strength of the Divine Spirit within, to live as God's children should live in the midst of a world which still too much lies in wickedness. These things, these four particulars, may all be considered as entering into the composition of that whole for which we give thanks, when we say with St Paul, *Thanks be unto God for His unspeakable gift* (2 Cor. ix. 15). *The gift* of God is eternal life in Christ Jesus our Lord. God hath given to us eternal life: and this life is in His Son (1 John v. 11). *This is life eternal; that they might know Thee, the only true God, and Jesus Christ whom Thou hast sent* (John xvii. 3).

Life, life eternal, is union with God, through faith in Christ, by the Holy Spirit.

We can never too often remind you how very near to us this *life* is. *Go, stand and speak in the temple to the people all the words of this life* (Acts v. 20). That was the charge given to the Apostles, when the Angel by night opened the prison-doors, and brought them forth to resume their ministry. And it is still as much as ever the one business of Christ's ministers to endeavour to make that message audible; to endeavour, God helping them, to speak to their people all the words of this life, this eternal life, which God has given to us in His Son. We do not like the language of reproof; we think that God has taught us a more persuasive language: but we do not disguise from ourselves, and we must not disguise from you, that dead souls are often found in living bodies, and that there is but one way, for any of us, of finding life for our souls, even in coming to God through Christ, and continuing with Him, when we have thus come, by a true and earnest faith; that sort of faith which looks upward, in prayer, in watchfulness, in earnest longing, and sees, behind the cloud which forbids the entrance of the eye of sense, One who is invisible indeed but far more real than anything that is seen; One who lives and acts, who loves and may be loved and bids us love Him, One who upbraids us not with the past if only we will cast it away and take refuge from it in Him, One who will never leave nor forsake us till He has carried us safely over the waves of this troublesome world into the still calm waters of an everlasting haven.

Eternal life in Christ Jesus our Lord. No man cometh to the Father, but by Me (John xiv. 6). No man can abide in God, but He who rests in Christ. *He that hath the Son hath life: and he that hath not the Son of God hath not life* (1 John v. 12).

My brethren, if there is anything between you and God, any cloud, any veil, any barrier, any gulf, be quite sure it is something in you, not in Him. And be quite sure, whatever it is, that you cannot too quickly or too resolutely cast it aside. It will not make you happy. It may give you wages, but it will never make up to you for the free gift. How many—alas! we fear, a multitude which no man can number—are just missing, all through life, the enjoyment, yes, the attainment, of that one thing which would make them happy, which would give them peace, and which lies, all the time, O how near them! only just out of their sight; close by their path; directly above them; yea, as St Paul expresses it (Rom. x. 8), in their very mouth, so far as the profession of it is concerned; in their very heart, so far as the intellectual knowledge of it can profit them! O that they could be induced—God alone can do this, but He is ready to do it for any one of you—to put out their hand to receive God's free gift! It is a simple thing; it is an easy thing: men who have done it marvel how they could have lived so long without doing it; how they could have endured the blank, the dreary blank, of being without it. Only believe the love that God hath to you in Christ (1 John iv. 16): and then, according to your faith, so shall it be to you (Matt. ix. 29).

SERMON XXIV.

THE MATURITY OF CHRISTIAN EXPERIENCE.

8 BE not therefore ashamed of the testimony of our Lord, nor of me His prisoner; but suffer with the Gospel according to
9 a power of God, who saved us and called us by a holy calling, not according to our works, but according to a purpose and free favour of His own which was given us in
10 Christ Jesus before eternal times, but was manifested now through the appearing of our Saviour Jesus Christ [as] having abolished death and brought to light life and in-
11 corruption through the Gospel, unto which I was appointed
12 a herald and Apostle and teacher of Gentiles. For which cause I suffer even these things; but I am not ashamed: for I know Him whom I have trusted, and I am persuaded that He is able to guard my deposit unto that day.

SERMON XXIV.

THE MATURITY OF CHRISTIAN EXPERIENCE.

2 TIMOTHY I. 12.

I know whom I have believed.

WE have passed, between last Sunday and this, from one of the two earliest, to the very latest, in point of time, of all the Epistles of St Paul. There is something proverbially interesting in last words. The voice which speaks, or the hand which writes, for the last time on earth, may well be heard or read with more than common feeling. Such is the impression which ought to be made upon us, and which, I think, almost insensibly is made upon us, by this second Epistle to the beloved and faithful Timotheus. There is one touching passage in it, which speaks directly of the approaching end. *I am now ready to be offered, and the time of my departure is at hand. I have fought a good fight, I have finished my course, I have kept the faith. Henceforth there is laid up for me a crown of righteousness, which the Lord, the righteous Judge, shall give me at that day* (2 Tim. iv. 6—8).

But, independently of this marked allusion to the

coming close of his labours, does there not run throughout the whole Epistle a golden thread of pathetic feeling, as well as of matured experience, which renders it peculiarly affecting, as well as peculiarly instructive, to its readers in every age?

This is a very different thing from saying, as some have said, that the doctrine of St Paul was modified by lapse of time, or that the language of his Epistles to the Thessalonians is of a different character altogether from that of his Epistles to the Ephesians, for example, or the Colossians. Such remarks are a straining of facts to suit a theory. St Paul, when he wrote to the Thessalonians, was as much an inspired man, as much a commissioned and divinely enlightened Apostle, as he was when he finished the volume of his letters with the fourth chapter of this Epistle to Timothy. He had had nothing, on his own part, from first to last, to retract or to unsay, he had nothing even to re-word or to modify—though he may have had misconceptions of his meaning by others to repudiate and to remove—throughout the whole course of his ministry from his conversion to his martyrdom.

Indeed, we have in the Epistle before us, as if for the very purpose of precluding such an idea as that of a change of spirit or of doctrine in the course of his writings, one passage standing in the most obvious agreement with his language to the Thessalonians examined last Sunday. Those *perilous times* which, as a later chapter of this Epistle tells us, are to *come in the last days*, what are these but the full developement of that *mystery of iniquity* which the other Epistle tells of as *already working*, and destined to a final revelation before the second coming of the Lord from heaven? The later and the latest testimony sets its seal thus distinctly to the earlier and the earliest.

I know not whether there may not be something to be learned, in this connection, from that one clause which falls somewhat harshly upon the ear towards the close of this Epistle, *Alexander the coppersmith did me much evil: the Lord reward him according to his works* (2 Tim. iv. 14). May we not see here, what has often been noticed elsewhere in Sermons from this place, a sort of final indication of the naturalness of St Paul's character; how, even to the last, there was a zeal about his work, and an impetuosity of eagerness as to its success, which showed itself, in some of the latest lines which he ever wrote, by an appeal to God in its behalf against its adversaries, which modern feeling might almost accuse of a severity barely compatible with charity?

From first to last he sets himself before us as one man not many: from his first conversion to Christ till the very eve of his death for Christ, he is seen real and the same; an instrument of service as wisely selected for what he was by nature, as marvellously adapted and polished by a process not of nature but of grace. For let us never forget that the God of grace and the God of providence is one God: the endowments of nature are never overlooked, in the choice of His servants to do His work, though they need to be disciplined, consecrated, and transformed, by the higher influence of His Holy Spirit acting upon each *severally as He will* (1 Cor. xii. 11).

The doctrine then of St Paul, and the natural character of St Paul, were the same from first to last: there was no change in the one, there was no obliteration of the other. But what shall we say of the course of his religious character? Was there any gradual formation, was there any such thing as weaker and stronger, lower and higher, observable in his history as a man of faith, as a child of God? It has been supposed so: and, within certain limits, we may well admit it. It is not very often in his writings that he alludes to what is passing in his own mind, as distinguished from that in which he regards those to whom he writes as participating. But there are at least three passages in which the personal thought is predominant. And they occur in this order; each separated from the other by a considerable interval of years. There is first the passage in which he says to the Corinthians, *I keep under my body and bring it into subjection*—and the expressions in the original are stronger still, and yet more remarkable—*lest that by any means, when I have preached to others, I myself should be a castaway* (1 Cor. ix. 27). The words are those, not of a combatant only, but of a combatant who can at least conceive the idea of defeat. They indicate, not only a struggle with the flesh, and with the carnal mind within, but also a struggle which any relaxation of effort would render doubtful, and which an abandonment of effort would render desperate. There is, again, the passage written to the Philippians during his first imprisonment in Rome, in which he speaks of himself, not, as before, under the figure of a combatant, having his own body for his antagonist, but still as a runner, with a long race set before him, a race tasking every energy and demanding an entire absorption in its success, a race not yet completed, though its goal is in full view, and its prize almost within reach of the hand which is to grasp it. *Brethren, I count not myself to have apprehended: but this one thing I do; forgetting those things which are behind, and reaching forth unto those things which are before, I press toward the mark for the prize of the high calling of God in Christ Jesus* (Phil. iii. 13, 14). The struggle is still going on; but the words which speak of a possibility of defeat are now, whether accidentally or purposely, withdrawn. Years again pass between: and then we reach the language of assured hope with which this Epistle abounds: not the words only, already quoted from its last chapter, which tell of a crown of righteousness reserved for him against the day of the great account, but those also of which the text forms a part, *For the which cause I also suffer these things: nevertheless I am not ashamed: for I know whom I have believed, and am persuaded that He is able to keep my deposit,* that which I have committed into His hands, my hopes, my life, my soul, my present and eternal being, *unto that day*.

I know whom I have believed. Or, yet more exactly, *I know Him whom I have trusted.*

I would not exaggerate the progressive character of St Paul's faith. I do not doubt that he could have said from the first day of his surrendering himself into the hands of Christ at Damascus, *I know whom I have believed.* St Paul was not, like so many of us, a man of morbid self-consciousness, always looking for something within at the very time when he was professing to renounce all such confidence and to look wholly for salvation to One without. He was not a man of half-convictions: he did not leave the great question of the way of salvation in suspense, for himself any more than for others. While he was in his ignorance, he was strong in that ignorance: when he was once enlightened, he was strong in that enlightenment. Up to a certain time, he was earnestly protesting against what he regarded as the fatal error of the new religion: in his zeal for the truth, as he then regarded it, he was vehement to the length of cruelty: he would save men's souls even at the cost of their lives: *he made havoc of the Church* (Acts viii. 3), yea, as he says himself at a later time, *beyond measure he persecuted the Church of God, and wasted it* (Gal. i. 13). In the same way, when conviction at last came to him, it came decisively. He had seen Jesus Christ (1 Cor. ix. 1); he had heard Him speak, and speak to him (Acts ix. 4); he had received a message from Him, offering pardon, offering salvation, yes, offering work also, offering the commission of an Apostle, with all its responsibility and all its glory (Acts ix. 17. xxvi. 16): did not these things bespeak a real Person, a living and exalted Saviour, once dead, now alive again? and could he question, ever again, whether what he had seen and heard, what had been given to him and forgiven, was true, was a fact, was certain, or, if certain, then unchangeable too? Therefore I do not doubt that St Paul would have said, as soon as Ananias left him in the house of Judas at Damascus (Acts ix. 11), *I know whom I have believed, and am persuaded that He is able to guard my deposit,* that which I now and here commit to Him, soul and body, life and hope, things present and things to come, *unto that day,* the day which I now know of, the day for which henceforth I shall be evermore looking, the day of *His appearing and His kingdom* (2 Tim. iv. 1).

We must never, in our zeal for the advantages and the privileges of a long-tried and established Christian, forget the possessions, the very birthright and inheritance, of the mere babe in Christ. There is not one of you, my brethren, who, believing in Christ with all his heart, if it be to-day for the first time, may not say with all truth and with all assurance, *I know whom I have believed.* It is the habit of fixing a remote date for the security and the comfort and the happiness of being a Christian, which keeps many persons back, humanly speaking, from ever being

Christians at all. You have only to lay hold on the offer of Christ, you have only to believe what He has done for you, you have only to see that He died for your sins and rose again for your justification (Rom. iv. 25); and, behold, *all things are yours* (1 Cor. iii. 21); forgiveness, peace, strength, as you need them, received, day by day, out of His hand, in yours, even till the day when you shall want no more!

But, though this is true, and though it must never be lost sight of in the endeavour to enhance, whether with reference to St Paul's case or our own, the later position on earth of Christ's true disciples, yet it is quite just, and very encouraging also, to dwell from time to time on some of the ways in which we may expect to *increase and go forwards*, even upon earth, *in the knowledge and faith of God and of His Son by the Holy Spirit* (Ordination Service); some of the senses in which the words may be made good to each of us, even before death, *They that sow in tears shall reap in joy* (Psalm cxxvi. 5).

Is it not, too often, a *sowing in tears* for us all? How very difficult do we find it even to realize our own convictions! There is so much against us. So much against us in the very attempt to approach Christ. Such a difficulty in that one little step from the seen to the unseen. Such a sense, too often, of unreality in the things that we pray for, in the words in which, yea, in the Person to whom, we pray. And then, when we have prayed, and prayed earnestly; when for a moment we have, as it were, *seen the heavens opened and Jesus standing on the right hand of God* (Acts vii. 56) as our Intercessor and our Life; O how transient is that glory! O how soon does it fade from us, only to be recovered, if at all, by an effort as great, by a patience as unwearied! And, as to living according to the prayer; as to *enduring*, in the trials, less or greater, of daily life, of an actual home, of public or private duty, by *seeing Him who is invisible* (Heb. xi. 27); as to being able to keep in mind the things taught, and to have them always ready, always available, for word and act, when the opportunity, when the temptation, expected or unexpected, actually arrives; and this, day by day, through perhaps a long life, without flinching, without denying Christ, without drawing back unto perdition; O how can these things be? Tell us how it can be done! Tell us, if you can, that it shall not be quite always so; not always quite so difficult; not always quite so discouraging; not always, as now, a perpetual beginning; but some day also a going forward, a getting on, yes, an advancing and an arriving!

When St Paul, or any experienced Christian person now, says, *I know whom I have believed*, what may we understand him to mean, beyond what the same words could possibly denote for us, mere beginners perhaps in the life of Christ?

The difference intended is not that between believing and knowing. St Paul does not say, Once I believed in Christ, and now, instead of believing, I know Him. Knowledge itself is belief; belief of that which is true, and on sufficient grounds. Those two conditions are satisfied in the Christian belief. The Christian's belief in Christ is a belief of that which is true; and it either is, or it ought to be, a belief based on sufficient grounds. He ought to be able to *give a reason for the hope that is in him* (1 Pet. iii. 15), a reason for believing. Certainly St Paul could have given such a reason. And therefore we do not understand him to say, Once I believed—now I know. His belief had always been knowledge. He believed in Christ because he had seen Him, because he had himself been dealt with by Him—apprehended, instructed, commissioned—and because he could not therefore be mistaken in declaring that He who once died had also risen and was alive. What he says is rather, *I know Him whom I have trusted.* In putting my trust in Christ, I am following no slight or flattering imagination; I know Him, and, because I know, I trust. I cannot be deceived: I cannot be disappointed: for I know Him in whom I have trusted.

Many things might be said in elucidation of these words, and in their application to the maturity of the Christian life. But the time will only permit me to mention very briefly two considerations.

1. First, the increased confidence of Christian faith, in the later days of life, arises out of a prolonged experience of what I may call the explaining power of the Gospel.

It is usual for persons in mature age to speak with fond regret of the supposed happiness of youth. Every one agrees to speak of the early days of life as the brightest. And no doubt God has mercifully apportioned our burdens to our strength, and has spared the period of growth, bodily and mental, from that weight of oppressive care or sorrow which must have stunted or crushed it. And yet I greatly doubt whether the advance of life does not bring with it more than a compensation for anything which it takes away. I am sure it does so to the Christian. I am sure that the light heart of youth can well be dispensed with by one who has received in its stead the abiding comfort of the Spirit. Let such a person compare with his later experience his earlier recollections. Will he not say, When I was a child or a young man, I was at the mercy of a thousand fears and doubts, a thousand anxieties and caprices, from which I now find myself set free? What a puzzle is life itself to the young! How confusing, how perplexing, the labyrinth in which they find themselves involved! Has it indeed a clue? Apparently so uncertain, has it any scheme? so mysterious, has it a key? so unsatisfying, has it a rest? so shadowy, has it a substance? Yes, as age advances, it is found to have each and all of these in Christ.

In all sciences, the observation of facts is the test of truth. If a supposed law is found to satisfy all the phenomena which occur within that portion of the field of nature to which it refers, it is accepted by a sound induction as unquestionably true. Now the same thing may be said with regard to Christ's

Gospel. He who has it in his heart possesses the key to human life as a whole and in its parts. If the Gospel be true, the phenomena of this world are all intelligible.

The Gospel says, *From within, out of the heart of man, proceed evil thoughts* (Mark vii. 21), and from evil thoughts evil acts: that is the account of men, apart from Christ, without the power of the Holy Spirit within. Is it not verified? The Gospel says, *There is nothing covered, which shall not be revealed* (Luke xii. 2): *God shall bring every work into judgment, with every secret thing* (Eccles. xii. 14). Do we not see Him already doing so; already revealing, already judging, in the earth, every day? The Gospel says, No amount of natural gifts, intellect, knowledge, education, health, abundance, affection, or whatever else may have been vouchsafed to a man, can be depended upon either to make him happy; or even to keep him safe from folly, sin, or shame: nay, these things may, without God's special grace, only aggravate danger, and make ruin easier as well as more disastrous. Is it not thus? do we not see it to be thus every day? The Gospel says, The sum of life, without God, is *vanity and vexation of spirit* (Eccles. i. 14): *there is no peace to the wicked* (Isai. lvii. 21): there is no safeguard against misery, there is no antidote to despair, except in Christ: and which of us can say that we have either found or seen any such, or that the words which thus warn us are not as true as they are explicit?

On the other hand, the Gospel says, This life is not your all: there is an immortality beyond, in which all the inequalities of this life shall be rectified, and all the distresses of this life done away, for all who will listen to Christ's voice now: this life is but a small part of the whole of man's being: God is not unrighteous in allowing His servants to suffer here; nor is He indifferent to human happiness, as He might be thought to be if this troublous state were either of His causing or were the whole of man's existence: even now Christ has opened a refuge for you: He says, *Come unto me*, all ye that are unsatisfied, all ye that thirst, all ye that are unhappy, yea, all ye that are grieved and wearied with the burden of your sins, *and I will give you rest: ye shall find rest unto your souls* (Matt. xi. 28, 29): *the blood of Jesus Christ cleanseth from all sin* (1 John i. 7): *the Spirit of life in Christ Jesus* shall *set* you *free from the bondage of sin and death* (Rom. viii. 2): it is not by Him therefore that you are forgotten, it is not of Him that you are miserable: *hear, and your soul shall live* (Isai. lv. 3). And is not the experience of life, on these points also, clear and decisive? Are there not those in the world, and numerous enough to make good the saying, who have evidently found rest to their souls in Christ? Are there not cases—not as many in number as we would there were, but enough to establish the promise—in which lives have evidently been changed, in habit and in destination, so that they who were one thing are now another; another in point of usefulness, another in point of devotedness, another in point of holiness, another in point of happiness? Are not these things matters of experience, even to one who looks on as a spectator? Is it not found that there is an amplitude, as well as a versatility, in Christ's Gospel, which makes it at once large enough to satisfy all wants, and minute enough to minister to all symptoms? Is there any case to which that Gospel is not found applicable, if there be only the will to apply it? And, where there is the will to apply it, is it not the testimony, the eventual testimony, of all and of each, that it was comforting, that it was salutary, that it was powerful; that it came home to the heart in a way which nothing else did, and awakened there aspirations, impulses, and at last hopes, such as nothing else could either emulate or simulate?

Often indeed has the Christian, in the course of life, slackened his own speed in running the heavenly race, and then he has been taught, by an opposite experience, to appreciate the blessedness of living close to God. Often, again, has he sought, and sought earnestly, to bring home his own experience to the heart of another, and has found himself baffled, in doing so, by the coldness, by the prejudice, by the hardheartedness or the faintheartedness, of man. Yet even then he has seen the Gospel exemplifying itself by its refusal as much as by its acceptance: he has recognized here the very picture of man's heart as drawn by the Gospel itself, and has bowed himself in deep submission beneath the disappointing as beneath the wonder-working hand of God.

Thus, in all ways; by observation and by experience; by what is given and by what is withheld; by mercy and by judgment; by the revelation of man and by the revelation of God; there grows up around his path, as he moves onwards toward the goal, such a multiplied and such a varied evidence of the truthfulness of the Gospel, as constrains him to say with tenfold conviction, *I know whom I have believed:* His Gospel is the key to human life: there is not a chamber, not a lurking-place, in it all, which that key cannot unlock and open.

2. But certainly this experience of what we have called the explaining power of the Gospel would be most incomplete if it were not accompanied by another experience; that of the directing and supporting power of Christ Himself.

I know Him whom I have believed, if it means nothing else, at least means this: I know Christ as a man knows his friend, and I can trust Him with the future because I have found Him trustworthy in the past.

We begin perhaps by an approach to Him, timid, feeble, hesitating, tentative. It is a mere peradventure that He may help us. We *have heard of Him by the hearing of the ear*, but our *eye has* not *seen Him* (Job xlii. 5). We are in sorrow, or we are in difficulty, or we are in anxiety, or we are in temptation, and we want a strength and a comfort not our own. Therefore we come to Him. But so dim is our light, so feeble our strength, in doing so, that it is as if faith preponderated over unbelief but by one small grain; as if it must be all but an affront to Christ Himself to approach Him at all with such a heart. And yet He hears. *Lord, I believe: help Thou mine unbelief* (Mark ix. 24): that prayer was accepted once; it is accepted always. This was the beginning. Thus faith grew. Sometimes an answer was felt to come when we prayed: then we were encouraged. Sometimes no answer seemed to come when we prayed: then we were quickened to greater humility, to a deeper self-knowledge, to a more godly fear. But by degrees we began to expect an answer. Prayer was emboldened, hope fostered; and in the same degree life brightened, and courage grew. At last we were able to depend upon an answer. We began to perceive that Christ listened, and that He was strong to save. Then we could treat Him with more confidence It was a mighty change for us when we really felt what it was to know Him whom we believed. This could only be by experience; the experience of much mercy, the experience of real help, the experience, first and last, of great patience. We have found Him to be near: we have found Him to be within hearing: we have found Him to be concerned in us: we have found Him to be all-wise: we have found Him to be Almighty: we have found Him to be *very pitiful and of tender mercy* (James v. 11). Then at last we shall be able to say, *I know Him whom I have believed; and am persuaded that He is able to keep that which I have committed unto Him against that day.*

SERMON XXV.

THE SPIRIT OF BONDAGE AND THE SPIRIT OF ADOPTION.

EPISTLE FOR THE EIGHTH SUNDAY AFTER TRINITY.

ROMANS VIII. 12—17.

12 *BRETHREN, we are debtors, not to the flesh, for the pur-*
13 *pose of living according to flesh. For if ye live according to flesh, ye are about to die: but if by spirit*[1] *ye are putting to*
14 *death the actions of the body, ye shall live. For as many as*
15 *are led by a*[2] *Spirit of God, these are sons of God. For ye received not a spirit of slavery again unto fear, but ye received a*[2] *Spirit of adoption, wherein we cry, Abba, Father.*
16 *The Spirit itself beareth witness together with our spirit*
17 *that we are children of God: and, if children, heirs also; heirs of God, and fellow-heirs of Christ; if at least we suffer together, that we may also together be glorified.*

[1] *By spirit;* that is, by means of, under the power, the direction and dictation, of spirit. When *spirit* is thus opposed to *flesh*, it expresses the renewed mind of a Christian; the soul of man as quickened and inhabited by the Holy Spirit: whatever is done therefore by *spirit*, is done by the agency of the Holy Spirit: the difference is but one of expression. Sometimes, as in verses 16, 26, &c., the Holy Spirit is introduced directly and personally: sometimes, as here, mediately, through the human spirit, which He animates, and *as* so animated by Him.

[2] A careful comparison of passages seems to show that the absence of the definite article with *Spirit* (when the Holy Spirit is the subject) expresses a *communication* (*gift, agency, operation*, &c.) of the Holy Spirit; the presence of the article marks the Divine Person, *the Holy Spirit Himself.* See note on Romans v. 5 (3rd Edition).

SERMON XXV.

THE SPIRIT OF BONDAGE AND THE SPIRIT OF ADOPTION.

ROMANS VIII. 15.

Ye have not received the spirit of bondage again to fear: but ye have received the spirit of adoption, whereby we cry, Abba, Father.

I KNOW not where we could have found a more fitting close (if such it be for some of us) for the Christian instruction of the present season, than in the words thus brought to us in the Epistle for this day. Their very sound says to us, It must be a delightful thing to be a Christian indeed. Their very sound says to us, That self-examination to which duty alike and prudence calls me, as to the reality of my participation in Christ, can be no doubtful or difficult matter, so long as I have the test here proposed to me to direct and to decide it. The spirit of bondage or the spirit of adoption—the spirit of a slave, or the spirit of a child, towards God—if the question be only, which of these two? let conscience speak, and let there be silence for her answer, and assuredly I shall know for certain which of the two conditions is at this moment mine.

A very brief glance at the context must prepare us, as usual, for bringing home more closely to our hearts the searching yet (I would hope) not depressing question of the text. I read from the 12th verse.

So then, brethren—if this be what the flesh does for us; if the carnal mind, the mind of those who mind the flesh, is, as we have above declared, death; if the carnal mind is enmity against God; if they who are in the flesh cannot please God; if no one who has not passed out of the state of flesh into the state of spirit, by the possession of the Spirit of Christ, really belongs to Christ, or is interested in the hope of the future quickening of his dead body in resurrection by the operation of the indwelling Spirit—it must follow from all this, that *we are debtors, not to the flesh, for the purpose of living*, that we should live, *according to flesh.* Surely we are under no obligation to this thing which works nothing but condemnation, nothing but wrath, nothing but exclusion from all bright hopes and from all present consolations. The *flesh* is the body, with all that belongs to it; its passions, its appetites, its ambitions, its jealousies, its vanities, its selfishnesses. It is the body *with its affections and lusts* (Gal. v. 24). It is that through which the world acts upon us. It is that which the devil uses as his instrument of temptation. It is that of which St Paul complained when he said, *O wretched man that I am! who shall deliver me from this body of death* (Rom. vii. 24)? It is that of which St Paul spoke as his own chief antagonist, when he said, *I therefore so run, as not uncertainly; so fight I, as not beating the air: but I buffet my body, and bring it into servitude, lest that by any means, when I have preached to others I myself should be a castaway* (1 Cor. ix. 26, 27).

Here therefore the same Apostle writes that we are under no obligations to the body. What has it ever done for us—that is the thought suggested—what do we owe to it for favours received, that we should live according to it, should submit to its dictation, and make its promptings our rule of life?

For if ye live according to flesh—if ye follow the inclination of the body, when the selfish principle, acted upon by it, says, Do this, or forbear from that; if that is the life you are living—*ye shall die; ye are about* (or *destined*) *to die:* the death of the body will be your death: they who have *sown to the flesh* must expect to *reap corruption* (Gal. vi. 8): they who have known no life here but that of sense and of self, can expect no happy life hereafter, but rather a state of living death, when all that survives will be Divine and spiritual.

But if ye by spirit are putting to death the actions of the body, ye shall live. If your present life is one of treating the body as if it were already dead; a life of union with Christ as having died and risen again, exercised by constantly living above earth even while still in it (Rom. vi. 3, &c. Col. iii. 1, &c.); a life of refusing to gratify natural inclination when it bids you to indulge yourself, to yield to sloth, to pamper appetite, to court the world, to humour vanity, to make things present your aim, your treasure, your idol; if this be your life now, and if in living such a life you are not merely casting out one evil spirit by another, as indolence by ambition, or sensuality by pride, but really seeking and following the guidance of the Holy Spirit of God and of Christ within; then indeed *ye shall live:* even now you shall enjoy that true life of man which is union with God, and hereafter you shall be admitted into that nearer access to Him which is to be the happiness through eternal ages of all who have come to Him through His Son.

This must be: this eternal life must be the portion of true Christians: *for as many as are* habitually *led by a Spirit of God, these are sons of God;* and sons of God must be partakers of the immortality of God. All who are connected with God by a true bond of relationship must live, like God and with God, for ever (Luke xx. 37, 38). And such, the Apostle proceeds, is indeed your glorious position. *For ye received not,* in becoming Christians—he refers their thoughts, here as always, to the time when the Holy Spirit was first communicated to them as believing and baptized converts—*ye received not a spirit of slavery again,* a second time, like that which you had before received from a fallen nature or from a dispensation like that of the Law, *unto fear,* so that your feeling should be one of slavish dread towards God: *but ye received a Spirit of adoption, wherein,* in virtue of which Spirit, *we cry, Abba,* that is, *Father.* The same Hebrew form of the word *Father,* and combined, as here, with it, is familiar to us all in our Lord's prayer in the garden of Gethsemane, *Abba, Father, all things are possible unto Thee; take away this cup from me; nevertheless, not what I will, but what Thou wilt* (Mark xiv. 36); and again in a passage in St Paul's Epistle to the Galatians, *And because ye are sons, God sent forth the Spirit of His Son into your hearts, crying, Abba, Father* (Gal. iv. 6). To the sense of the verse we shall return immediately, after just adding the conclusion of the paragraph.

The Spirit itself beareth witness together with our spirit that we are the children of God. In prompting this feeling towards God, this cry of our hearts to Him as our Father, the Holy Spirit ratifies the assurance of our own spirit that we are indeed God's children; *and, if children, also heirs; heirs of God, and fellow-heirs of Christ; if at least we suffer together* with Him, *that we may also together* with Him *be glorified*. The relation of children towards God involves in it the expectation of a future inheritance; of an inheritance in which we shall be associated with Christ. The train of thought is exactly that of a passage just referred to in the Epistle to the Galatians. *Because ye are sons, God sent forth the Spirit of His Son into your hearts, crying, Abba, Father: wherefore thou art no more a servant, but a son; and if a son, also an heir of God through Christ* (Gal. iv. 6, 7); or, according to another reading of that clause, *also an heir through God*, by God's gift and operation. And then the last words of the paragraph remind us, in accordance with other like exhortations of St Paul, that our entrance into the future inheritance depends upon our willingness to share in this life Christ's sufferings; to be made like Him in patiently bearing disappointments, trials, and sorrows, as God shall appoint, to be more than compensated hereafter by *a far more exceeding and eternal weight of glory* (2 Cor. iv. 17). But this thought having been dwelt upon on the first Sunday of the month, in considering the Epistle for the Fourth Sunday after Trinity, we will turn now to the contrast more particularly chosen as this morning's subject, *Ye received not*, in becoming Christians, *a spirit of bondage again to fear: but ye received a Spirit of adoption, wherein we cry, Abba, Father.*

1. *Not a spirit of bondage.*

Last Sunday, commenting upon an expression in the Epistle for the day, *enslaved to God*, I tried to show you the comfort and the dignity of that position which Apostles claimed for themselves so earnestly and so frequently, the position of a slave of God. This was one view of the term: to belong to God, to be His property, His charge, His purchased and now inalienable possession, is one thing: but to have the spirit of a slave towards Him, to receive for the second time a spirit of bondage unto fear, that is quite another.

The words themselves seem to indicate, as already noticed, that a spirit of bondage towards God is our natural feeling. Ye received not *again* a spirit of bondage. And is it not so? Is not that our own experience?

What is a spirit of bondage, or slavery, towards God? What are some of its elements? some of its characteristics? some of its workings? We shall perhaps almost be anticipating, in endeavouring to reply to these questions, the second part of our subject, that which is to place in contrast with the spirit of a slave the spirit of a child: but nevertheless let us take the two parts as they come, and, while appealing to your consciences as to the one, endeavour to interest your hearts in the consideration of the other.

We read in the Epistle to the Hebrews, that it was the object of Christ's coming into the world in human nature, and dying in that nature for us, to *deliver them who through fear of death were all their lifetime subject to bondage* (Heb. ii. 15). The fear of death, and of the terrible possibilities (at least) which must be faced just beyond death, lies, no doubt, at the root of that spirit of bondage which oppresses man in life. The feeling that we are in another's hands, powerless alike over the duration and to a great extent over the circumstances of our own being, is a very formidable thing in itself. If we add to this, that the Person in whose hands we thus are is either unknown to us or supposed to be unfriendly, we have suggested a consideration which has exercised more influence than any other upon the religion, and through it upon the history, of the world. Hence all manner of superstitions: a powerful Being, absolute over our destiny, yet unknown to us in character, in will, and in intention, must be propitiated by such offerings as we possess or can discover, if perchance He may be induced to use His power for protection and not for destruction. Thus the spirit of bondage is the very religion of the heathen.

But is it necessarily changed by the possession of a revelation? a real revelation, accepted by the understanding and respected by the conscience?

It is a great thing, no doubt, to possess the revelation of a Divine Father, a most merciful Saviour, and an indwelling Comforter, Perhaps in the worst of cases this revelation is not wholly inoperative upon the minds of those who possess it. There lies, no doubt, under many an inconsistent life, under many a rebellious will, under many a defiled conscience, just a peradventure both of faith and hope; just that little spark of good which, however neglected, however smothered, however all but extinguished, yet makes it possible, in this life, that a change may come; possible that, in some day of darkness, there may be an arising and turning as to a Father, a prayer for a forgiveness known about if not known, a cry for mercy which could not have risen from a heathen heart, because uttered in the name of a Redeemer whose very existence is the secret of the Gospel.

There is this, in the very worst of us, to counteract the spirit of bondage. But may I not go far above the very worst, far above persons of evil life and hardened conscience, and yet say that the spirit of the slave may be predominant? Yes, we see it, we have all probably felt it, if indeed any feel it not now, in every dealing of the natural heart with God, in every relation of the natural heart to God's worship and to God's service.

We have learned, my brethren—the experience of life has taught us—to be thankful for any sort of regard for God which may be cherished or manifested in men. We find much less of it than we might have expected. We believe that the tendency of these later days of the world is to get rid of superstition without replacing it by religion; to have the fear of God cast out, not by the love of God, but by indifference, by hardihood, yes, by audacity towards Him. That formula which was inserted into indictments for murder—*not having the fear of God before his eyes*—has a far wider application than to criminals and malefactors. It might be made the description of many a decorous life, if it could be read in the light of an infallible insight. It cannot be denied that God is put further off from us now than He was felt to be two centuries or two generations ago. Phenomena of nature which were once His witnesses are now silent concerning Him. They are referred now, one after another, truly it may be, to what are called laws, traceable by man or untraceable, but, in either case, in name at least, and to the popular apprehension, far removed from the direct agency of God Himself. It is not every one who stays to enquire what a law of nature means, what nature herself means, whether to the philosopher or to the Christian: the one, God's procedure, the other, God's rule: nature, God's agency in things outward; a law of nature, God's mode of conducting that agency. These things being left out of sight, the mention of these things having come to be regarded as obtrusive if not unphilosophical, no wonder if the advance of science exercises sometimes a malign influence upon the popular religion; if its tendency, most needlessly and most unworthily, has sometimes been rather to diminish the dread than to magnify and bring home the love of God.

I have mentioned one possible cause of what I cannot but regard as the diminished fear of God in these times, whether as a motive or as a check upon human conduct. If time permitted, or if the present subject warranted it, the enumeration of such causes might be greatly extended. We do not see around us, even in persons well brought up and on the whole well conducted, that prevalence of the fear of God as a reason for doing, and still more for not doing, which seems to have belonged to what I may call the same level of character in earlier times. But my business is now, rather to speak of the imperfection, than to exalt the value, of mere fear as a principle of religion. Fear is better than carelessness; any fear better than no regard; the very spirit of the slave better than the spirit of the rebel: but we are seeking to show how fear, at the best, falls below and comes short of the Christian standard; how unworthy it is of the place which it often usurps in our feeling towards God, whether as shown in His worship, or as shown in His service.

It is a matter which comes home very closely to us, and which nothing but personal enquiry will enable us to decide. Now therefore let me appeal to you, my brethren—and I would especially say, let me appeal to the younger members of this Congregation —as to the feeling with which they observe any forms of devotion which they may practise in private, and as to the feeling with which they come hither, Sunday by Sunday, to God's public worship. Is it not too much in the spirit of the slave? Is it not rather as a matter of necessity, of what I may call conscientious compulsion, than as a matter of privilege, an exertion of ready and joyful will? Do you not feel rather as if God would be angry with you, as if some judgment would overtake you, if you failed to perform this quota of service, than as if you were permitted, by God's special kindness towards you, to come and to speak to Him, to spend a little time with Him, and to be refreshed, revived, and reanimated by His gracious converse? You can scarcely imagine how much turns upon the aspect of these duties, upon the mere light in which you view them, upon the spirit in which you come to them. Treat them as duties; they will be such, and nothing more, to you. You will discharge them, and there it ends. You will imagine perhaps that you have done a good deed, and go away self-satisfied. Or you will feel that it was a very poor deed, full of infirmity, full of sin, yet required of you, and you will go away empty and perhaps murmuring. But in either case you have done it as a slave, of whom your Master exacted such or such a task-work. And thus, though it was right you should do it, and it would have been wrong not to do it, yet, not doing it in a right spirit, not doing it out of love, not doing it of free-will, not doing it cheerfully and thankfully, but of necessity if not grudgingly (2 Cor. ix. 7), you could scarcely expect to reap a blessing: it was done as a single disjointed act; it was done to satisfy God; it was not done out of love; it was not done as a child towards a Father, but as a slave towards a Master.

Let these brief hints, my brethren, not have been quite thrown away. See whether, by God's blessing, you may not give quite a new character to your acts of worship. Say to yourself when you kneel down in secret, say to yourself when you come hither to worship, God has been very good to me: He has redeemed me by the blood of His Son: He permits, nay, He bids me, to regard myself as redeemed, as brought nigh, as His Son: and now, at this time, I am coming to exercise this relation towards Him: I am coming to tell Him my wants, I am coming to tell Him my sins and infirmities, that the one may be supplied, and the other put away, by His direct act: yes, He is here, and I am come here by His gracious will, that I may commune with Him, may tell Him that I adore, that I trust, that I love, that I desire to serve Him, and may hear Him speak to my inmost soul the words of His forgiveness and of His love. See whether prayer will not become pleasant to you, when you cast behind you, in beginning it, the spirit of the slave, and claim as your right by God's gift the spirit of adoption, the spirit of a son.

Now I must not stay to urge the same enquiries, or to offer the same advice, with reference to God's daily service. What has been said as to His worship must suffice to indicate also what should be said as to His service: how, in each particular act, we are prone to regard ourselves as performing a task, something which must be done, which we shall be punished for not doing; how every act of charity is infected, and I may well say poisoned, by this feeling; how every duty of domestic, social, or public life is made to be, if a religious act at all—and I am speaking of those who try to make it so—yet at least an act not rising higher than the region of conscience, not springing out of the renewed soul, not the consistent and, if I might so express it, the natural working of the risen life, the life which is hidden above with God in Christ (Col. iii. 3), and which, in every pulsation, is derived from a vital union with that Saviour who dwells above at the very right hand of God in heaven. Here too, the way to cast out the spirit of the slave will be, to say to ourselves, day by day, and many times in each day, not so much, God requires of me this duty or service, but rather, God in His great goodness allows me to do this or this for Him; He is here, present with me in it, working in me both to will and to do; His Spirit can consecrate this the commonest act into a living sacrifice; His Spirit can strengthen me for this the most difficult act if I set myself to do it in His name; and thus, in all things, let me live both in God and unto God, counting it my highest happiness to be entrusted with anything that can be done for Him, as an expression of love, and with a view to His sole honour and praise. So living, we shall be happy. So living, it will be no revulsion, no revolution, but a mere change of circumstance, a mere developement of that which has been long known and done below, when we find ourselves transplanted from the wilderness of earth to the garden of the Lord in heaven (Isai. li. 3).

2. Not a spirit of bondage, but a spirit of adoption. We have combined the two points in the one. Yet let me not end without very briefly indicating four of those particulars in which the spirit of adoption will manifest itself, and by which, consequently, each one of us may judge of its presence in ourselves.

(1) The spirit of adoption is a spirit of reverence. Not of slavish fear, but of filial reverence. It is not without reason that I urge this first amongst its attributes. No man is absolved from this duty: let me rather say, no man can be happy without having some one to revere; some one whom, the more he knows of him, the more he reveres; some one towards whom that process of discovery which is inseparable from

prolonged intercourse is a process wholly of increasing reverence, insomuch that they who stand nearest to His throne in heaven veil their faces as they worship (Isai. vi. 2), and they who live nearest to Him on earth are ever found the most humble, the most self-abased, yea, the most full, of all men, of reverence and awe and godly fear.

(2) The spirit of adoption is a spirit of submission. The cry, *Abba, Father*, is the expression of an entirely resigned will. It was so used on earth by Him who, *though He was a Son*, yet condescended to *learn obedience by the things which He suffered* (Heb. v. 8). *Abba, Father, all things are possible unto Thee: take away this cup from me: nevertheless, not my will, but Thine, be done* (Mark xiv. 36. Luke xxii. 42). *If this cup may not pass away from me, except I drink it, Thy will be done* (Matt. xxvi. 42). Where is he in this Congregation who has no need—where, certainly, is he in this Congregation who will not one day have need—to learn that spirit, to pray that prayer? God grant us all betimes that spirit of adoption from which alone that prayer can rise heartily, or be heard with acceptance! Well may he who knows that he has indeed a Father in heaven, submit himself in all respects to His wise and fatherly will.

(3) The spirit of adoption is a spirit of trust. Submission runs on into confidence. The one is a readiness to bear even though the stroke were in anger: the other is the assurance that the stroke will not be in anger, or that, beneath the anger, even if

anger should be needful, will lie a deep purpose of eventual mercy. *Though he slay me, yet will I trust in Him* (Job xiii. 15): for even from the very depths of the grave I know that He can and that He will at last raise me up (Heb. xi. 19).

(4) And thus the spirit of adoption is, in the last place, and throughout, a spirit of love. It seems very wonderful that God should care for our love. But it is so. Not awe, not fear, not dread—not in these things is God glorified, but in that going forth of the human spirit to Him, as to One in whom alone it can rest and be satisfied; that return of love for love; that same yearning of the heart, after an affection unchangeable and inexhaustible, which upon earth, as directed towards a human object, is the source of all our deepest joys and of all our keenest sorrows; this it is which God would have turned towards Himself, and which, when once so turned, is as certain to be satisfied as it is in itself elevating and glorious. Herein is the spirit of adoption fulfilled. Reverence for God, submission to God, confidence in God, all meet and are consummated in the love of God. May He *who has prepared for them that love Him such good things as pass man's understanding, pour into our hearts such love toward Him, that we, loving Him above all things, may obtain His promises, which exceed all that we can desire* (Collect for 6th Sunday after Trinity), and *be filled with all the fulness of God* (Eph. iii. 19).

SERMON XXVI.

GOD SPEAKING IN HIS SON.

1 *In many parts and in many ways God having spoken of old to the fathers in the prophets, at the end of these days*
2 *spoke to us in a Son, whom He constituted inheritor of all*
3 *things, through whom He also made the ages; who, being an effulgence of His glory and an impress of His essence, and supporting all things by the word of His power, after making a purification of sins, sat down, at the right hand of majesty, on high.*

SERMON XXVI.

GOD SPEAKING IN HIS SON.

HEBREWS I. 1, 2.

God, who at sundry times and in divers manners spake in time past unto the fathers by the prophets, hath in these last days spoken unto us by His Son.

THE remarkable and magnificent opening of the Epistle to the Hebrews has in all ages been dwelt upon with admiration. Its very dissimilarity to anything else in the Scriptures has no doubt added to its interest. There is no other Epistle which does not begin with the name, or with some clear indication at least, of the writer. Here, whatever the reason, the writer entirely disappears. That he was not unknown to his intended readers, that there was no intentional concealment of the authorship, is clear from some intimations at the close of the fifth Chapter, and yet more from the last verses of the Epistle: *Know ye that our brother Timothy is set at liberty; with whom, if he come shortly, I will see you* (Heb. xiii. 23). But that which was remarked in reference to the subject, in commenting (two Sundays ago) upon the second Chapter of the second Epistle to the Thessalonians;

may here be said with regard to the authorship; namely, that there were things known to the early Church, or to some of its congregations, which are not known to us; doctrines delivered orally, and referred to afterwards in letters as remembered and therefore needing no repetition; or else letters written, as from a known person to persons well remembering him, but without happening to mention the name itself, and therefore left to later generations in the position of anonymous compositions, awakening a natural curiosity, and justifying all possible research and comparison, scarcely more by the treasures which they open than by the mysteries which they conceal.

Of this latter order is the great Epistle before us. That impetuous and often presumptuous positiveness which marks the dogmatism of human critics upon points which lie too deep for discovery, or else beside the mark of practical importance, is not shared by the Church as represented in her canon of Scripture or in her formularies of faith: where evidence is incomplete or indecisive, the authority of the Church bids us rather doubt than err, and is contented to assign a place amongst God's inspired communications to a treatise of which she dares not pronounce finally upon the human authorship. The Epistle to the Hebrews, as we must all have remarked, does not stand in our Bibles where it certainly would have been placed had its authorship been unquestioned. The Epistles of St Paul are not placed in chronological order in the Bible. Rather has an attempt been made to arrange them according to their importance; either with regard to the Church to which they were written, or with regard to the subjects of which they treat. Thus, and perhaps on both accounts, we have first in order the Epistle to the Romans, though in reality written not first but sixth of St Paul's Epistles; after the Epistles to the Thessalonians, the Galatians, and the Corinthians. On either principle of arrangement—with reference to the importance of its subject, or the importance of the Church addressed—the Epistle to the Hebrews could scarcely have failed to occupy a very early place. But we find it after the shortest and the most private of all St Paul's Epistles; after those to the smallest and least celebrated Churches; after those even to individuals, to Timothy, to Titus, and to Philemon. This is because the authorship of the Epistle to the Hebrews is not certainly known. Upon this point the Church has been wisely willing to suspend her judgment. She has named it the Epistle to the Hebrews: she has given it a decided place amongst the oracles of God: but she has not presumed to call it—though that title has gradually crept into our editions—the Epistle of Paul the Apostle to the Hebrews: she has rather sought to express the calm and instructive language of one of the greatest Christian writers of the third century, *Who wrote the Epistle, God knoweth.*

Yet I think we may say with truth that no Book contained in the Volume of Revelation bears on its face a more decisive stamp of Inspiration. What a majesty, what an eloquence, yet what a simplicity, shines throughout it! In one respect we owe more to it than to any other portion of the New Testament: it has given us the key to the Old. Writings, institutions, ordinances, lives, which we might otherwise have passed by in the pages of the Old Testament as belonging merely to the history of Israel, as possessing no value for us, and as never having possessed anything of vital or spiritual import even to those to whom they belonged, we here find to have had a meaning, and one of everlasting moment; to have sprung out of the very depths of the Divine Wisdom, and to be as instructive in their retrospect as they were enlightening and ennobling in their prospect. The Epistle to the Hebrews might well be entitled, The Gospel of the Old Testament.

But it is to its opening words that I must confine your attention this evening. I will read once again to you the first three verses, with a few brief words of explanation, and then draw from them three remarks upon the contrast indicated in the text.

In many parts and in many ways God having spoken of old to the fathers in the prophets, at the end of these days spoke to us in a Son, whom He constituted inheritor of all things, through whom He also made the ages; who, being an effulgence of His glory and an impress of His essence, and supporting all things by the word of His power, after making a purification of sins, sat down, at the right hand of majesty, on high.

My brethren, our object is instruction first, then exhortation. Bear with me therefore if I endeavour to say a word or two in explanation of difficulties in three of the most important verses in the whole Bible. I will make my explanations as brief as possible.

The words rendered in our Version *at sundry times and in divers manners*, are really, *in many parts and in many ways*. God's former revelations of Himself to man were made, as it were, in portions, not in whole. Here a little and there a little, as occasion required, He disclosed His character, His will, or His purposes, to man. It was done *in many parts;* never as a whole, never completely, never comprehensively.

Again, it was done *in many ways.* Sometimes by dreams or visions, sometimes in type and emblem, sometimes by a direct message, communicated to a living man to be communicated by him to living men. There was this variety in God's earlier revelations. Your own recollection of the Old Testament history and of the writings of the Prophets will enable you to verify the remark.

Then, this fragmentary and this various communication was made *in the prophets;* in the person and by the mouth of human utterers of Divine truth. A prophet, in Scriptural language, is not necessarily a predicter: some were and some were not such: but the title implies rather a forthteller than a foreteller: a prophet is one, not who divines, not who sees into futurity by some art or gift of his own, but one who utters in God's behalf a message which God first communicates for this purpose to him.

Such was the mode of revelation under the Old Dispensation. It was occasional. It was fragmentary. It was various in mode and form. It was always made through human utterers.

Now comes the contrast. *In these last days.* More exactly, *at the extremity of these days. These days* is an expression often found in the Scriptures—or something equivalent to it—in contradistinction to *those days. This age* is contrasted with *that age* (Luke xx. 34, 35); the period that is now, with the period that shall be, that is to come. The one is the period before Christ: the other is the period of Christ. It was not given to the Old Testament writers to know of two comings of Christ. It was not given even to the New Testament writers to know of the length of the interval between the two. This has always been one of the secret things which belong to the Lord our God. Therefore we often find in the Scriptures expressions which refer to times still future, future even to us, used with regard to the whole of that period which was introduced by the first coming of Christ, His coming in the flesh, and will be greatly affected by His second coming, in glory, in His kingdom. Here God is said to have spoken to us by His Son *at the extremity of these days;* that is, at the close of the Old Dispensation; at the end of the period which was prior and prefatory to the times of the Messiah.

God spoke to us in a Son. Such is the form of the

original expression. In one who was not a prophet but a Son. One who occupied that position, stood in that relation to God, which is essentially incommunicable to others, the position, the relation, of the very Son of God.

Whom He constituted inheritor of all things. To whom, as the reward of His humiliation, God *gave a name which is above every name* (Phil. ii. 9), a glory and a dominion—not as the original partaker of the Divine Nature, but as the risen and exalted Son— which is commensurate with the universe and irresistible in power.

He who is thus exalted after His humiliation for man, is the same Person *by whom* God originally *made the worlds.* The exact expression is, *by whom also He made the ages.* The word used is that which speaks of the universe not in relation to space but to time, and which is extended by the sacred usage (Heb. xi. 3) to include all the conditions and all the subjects of the present state; the whole stage on which, and all the beings by whom, the agencies of time are wrought and the destinies of eternity shaped.

The description goes further. *Who being an effulgence of His glory and an impress of His essence.* The *glory* of God is His perfection; His whole character; what we may describe as the aggregate of His attributes; God such as He is, in all His characteristics, of power, wisdom, truth, holiness, goodness, love. In Christ God's whole perfection shines forth for the illumination and for the salvation of man.

Christ is the sum of those rays which come forth from the central, the unapproachable Sun, for the enlightening, comforting, and fertilizing of the earth. He is *light in communication.* Thus is Christ the *effulgence of God's glory.* He is also the *impress of His essence:* that Person in whom the very nature of God is engraven, even as the letters of a name (such is the figure) may be cut upon the seal, or the features of a face upon a coin, with all the clearness and the indelible permanence of the art of the engraver.

And then, finally, it is added that He by whom at first God made the worlds is also the constant upholder of that existence which He gave. Just as it is expressed in St Paul's Epistle to the Colossians: *Who (Christ) is the image of the invisible God:* there is the *impress of God's essence:* then, *in Him were all things created ... all things have been created by Him* as the Agent, *and unto Him* as the Object, of all ... *and in Him all things consist* (Col. i. 15, &c.): He is not only the bringer into being, but He is also the upholder in being, the very condition of the consistence and coherence, of the universe of God.

He it was, even He, thus glorious, thus powerful, thus essential to the very existence of being, who first purged away our sins by the sacrifice of Himself, and then took His seat at the right hand of God, to carry on there the work of the Mediator and the Intercessor, until the time shall come, fixed in the counsels of God from the beginning, when He shall return even as He ascended (Acts i. 11), but in power and great glory, to be the Judge of quick and dead.

It is the very highest office of preaching, to set Christ Himself before men. That is our work. If that be done—so far as that is done—God will not leave us without witness. The object of this Epistle was to make Christ so great in the eyes of the Hebrew congregations, that they might be bold and firm in adhering to Him in days when their courage and constancy were to be put to a very severe test. In like manner would we, my brethren, urge upon you and upon ourselves, if it were in one last testimony from this place, the incomparable greatness of that Gospel which we believe God to have sent to us from heaven, and thus lay the foundation for that appeal which these same pages contain to the understandings and the consciences of men, *How shall we escape, if we neglect so great salvation* (Heb. ii. 3)?

We may see three chief considerations involved in the words now before us; in the fact that God in these last days has spoken to us by His Son. These are, in brief, the authority, the tenderness, and the finality, of the utterance.

1. It has come to be regarded, in these days—perhaps not for the first time, but there is something of novelty in it for us—as an entirely open question, what we will take, and what we will leave, of the Divine Revelation. We take the Book into our hands, and we sit in judgment upon its contents, as we would upon those of any human composition. Some

men will have nothing to say to the Old Testament. Because the Epistle to the Hebrews gives us a high estimate of the wisdom and of the glory of the Old Testament, therefore this too must be dismissed along with that. One part of the Scriptures is too mysterious, another too Jewish, another too historical, another too uncharitable. Thus the volume is pared and clipped until indeed a very small residue is left undamaged or unmutilated. Now I am far from saying that human criticism is altogether misplaced in reference to Divine truths. There are questions, preliminary questions, which must be settled, with regard to the canon of Scripture, and with regard to the text of Scripture, yes, and with regard to the truth of Christianity itself, which it is doing no honour to God, but the very contrary, to leave unsettled or to shrink from as unsettling. The love of truth is not only consistent with, it is essential to, a real love of the truth. Truth, and the truth, can never be at variance. But what is to be lamented is, that persons, professing at least to be convinced of the substantial truth of Christianity, should never be able to accept any part of it as coming to them with authority. If we do believe that Christ is more than man, if we do believe that God in these last days spoke to us by His Son, then surely our question should only be, what did Christ utter? what did God speak to us by His Son? And that which careful examination—it cannot be too careful— has satisfied us that Christ really said, by Himself or by His commissioned Apostles, ought not then to be tried over again, to see whether it is such as our own reasonings would have taught us without His saying it, before we receive it, and set ourselves to live by it, as an integral portion of the revealed truth of God. First be convinced of the historical facts of the Gospel: satisfy yourself that there was such a person as Jesus Christ once upon earth: satisfy yourself as to His life and death and resurrection, as you would satisfy yourself of any other historical facts resting upon human testimony: then satisfy yourself that the books which profess to be are really a record of His message: spend, if circumstances permit, all the care and all the skill which is at your command in ascertaining the fidelity with which the text of that record has been transmitted and preserved: but at last—let the time at last come . . . and life is short— its all-important work must not be for ever deferred . . . at last take the message as you have it, and believe—believe, for it is reason even more than religion which bids you to believe it—that God, who does nothing in vain, would not have spoken to you by His Son that which you could have discovered as well without Him; believe that there was a purpose and a use in that as in every other act of God; and, as you value your immortal soul, do listen to what Christ has said, and seat yourself, in heart, at His feet, to hear and to receive and to live His Word!

It is in this point of view that we would thank God for what He has here and elsewhere taught us as to the dignity and as to the greatness of His Son. He has spoken to us in these last days by His Son: who is He? My brethren, who is He? Who is the Son by whom God has spoken to us? I ask the question, not of unbelievers, not even of persons in suspense about believing; I cannot expect that they should answer it with the understanding or with the heart; but I would ask it of you who do believe, of you whose consciences and whose hearts have had some dealings with God on the basis of His Revelation, and I would bid you answer it, as you surely may do, out of the pages of that Revelation itself. I would bid you say to yourselves, He by whom God speaks in the Gospel is He by whom at first He made the worlds. It is He who upholds all things every day by the word of His power. It is He who is the effulgence of God's glory, and the very impress of God's essence. It is He whom He hath constituted heir of all things, and who now sits in heaven at the right hand of the majesty of God Himself. Be not afraid to say these things boldly. The very faith of the believer is in danger of being affected by the incredulity, by the doubts, yea, by the scorn of the unbeliever. But be not ye shaken. Grasp the truth of Christ's Divinity, of His eternity, of His power, of His work in creation, of His present existence, of His kingdom and glory, all the more tenaciously because others would rob you of it, because others would explain it away, would affect not to see it in the Bible, or would rather suffer it there than glory in it.

God speaking in His Son.

We need for ourselves, not for purposes of attack only or of defence, purposes of controversy or of orthodox confession, but for our own personal warning and quickening and even alarming, the true doctrine of the authority, the dignity, the majesty, the glory, of Him by whom God spake to us when He spake to us by His Son. Be afraid not to listen to Him. Yes, He appealed Himself to such motives, when He said on earth, in answer to the enquiry of His enemies, *Art Thou the Christ, the Son of the Blessed? I am: and ye shall see the Son of Man sitting on the right hand of power, and coming in the clouds of heaven* (Mark xiv. 61, 62). Ye shall see Him—O let us have heard Him first!

And, as for warning, so for comfort also, we need all the weight of that testimony which tells us of the dignity of the Son. We want a support for our faith such as nothing short of Divinity can supply. And we have that support. We have it here; in these few words. Do we use it? O, this is why our lives are so inconsistent, our aspirations so faint, our steps so tottering and so wandering; that we are afraid of leaning with our whole weight upon what God has testified of His Son. Say to yourselves, and let nothing ever tempt you to shrink from the avowal, *I believe that Jesus Christ is the Son of God.* I believe that He was from the beginning with God, and was God. I believe that He made the worlds. I believe that He upholds all things by the word of His power. I believe that all hearts are open to Him. I believe that He is present everywhere. I believe that He will come again to judge the quick and the dead. I will trust Him therefore implicitly. I will speak to Him as being all this. I will believe that it is God's purpose *that all men should honour the Son even as they honour the Father* (John v. 23), and I will not fear being condemned for doing so. He by whom God in these last days has spoken to me shall be to me, not my Lord only, but my God.

2. And thus the authority passes into the tenderness; which was the second consideration drawn for us from the text. *When He had by Himself purged our sins.* I know not that I could add anything which the very sound of those words has not suggested. He by whom God has spoken to us, being such as we have heard in nature, in power, in dominion and glory, took upon Himself our weaknesses, and in a human body died for our sins.

We see in the very greatness of the contrast an argument for its truth. There is something in it so transcendently above man's conception, and in the same degree so wonderfully like God. A greatness and a condescension, a majesty and a tenderness, so *far above* indeed *out of our sight* (Psalm x. 5), but, when suggested, when combined for us out of sight, so exactly satisfying our idea of fitness, our idea of what, if God acted at all, would be meet, would be becoming, would be Godlike! How truly is this the New Testament developement of that combination of greatness and of condescension, of which even in the Old we cannot read without emotion, *Thy way is in the sea, and Thy path in the great waters, and Thy footsteps are not known: Thou leddest Thy people like a flock by the hand of Moses and Aaron* (Psalm lxxvii. 19, 20). *Being the brightness of His glory, being the express image of His person, He, by Himself, purged our sins.*

And yet, my brethren, even before we reach that verse, we have read enough to make good the second point on which we are touching, when we find that God spoke to us *in His Son.* The Sonship of Christ is the proof of God's tenderness in speaking by Him. When the owner of the vineyard in the Parable, *having yet one son, his well-beloved* (Matt. xxii. 37), determined to send him also to the rebellious husbandmen, he said, *They will reverence my son.* When God sent His Son to us, it was as though He had said, not only, *They will reverence*, but also, *they will love my Son, when they see Him*, when they hear Him. Yes, considering from what Christ came, and to what He came; considering who He was, and how on earth He was dealt with; considering the glory which He had had with the Father before time began, and the humiliation and the shame and the pain and the death which was the very condition, the very object, of His Incarnation; we may well be touched when we think of the Father *not sparing Him, but delivering Him up* (according to the Scriptural expression) *for us all* (Rom. viii. 32); handing Him over, as it were, into unloving, unsympathizing, unfeeling hands, to be profaned, to be contemned, to be tortured, to be crucified! Yes, the tenderness has not all to be learned from the details of what Christ said upon earth, or was, as God's messenger: it is learned already in the thought of God's selecting Him as the messenger, and, in the foresight of all that was involved in it, choosing in these last days to speak to us in His Son.

3. But, leaving this deepest and most beautiful of all thoughts for your own thankful meditation, I must hasten to the third and last topic, that of the finality, arising out of the completeness, of God's revelation of Himself in the Son. God's revelations by the prophets were made, as we have seen, *in many parts;* one part of the whole of His truth here, another there; one part now, another then; and never pieced together; no clue given to the labyrinth of perplexities, of seeming contradictions, involved in the separate utterances; no harmonizing principle stated, which might reconcile, for example, the justice and the goodness, the mercy and the judgment; no manifestation of the whole of God's character, or of the manner of the coexistence of this part of His character with that. It was a succession of separate revelations, as partial in their character as various in their form.

Now place in contrast with this, His speaking to us by His Son. Here, you see, it was not only a word, or a number of words, spoken, but it was the speaking in a Person. The Person was the Word. The message was Christ Himself. God was brought to us, in the whole of His character, in the unity at once and the fulness of His attributes, because brought to us in Him who was the effulgence of His glory, and the living impress of His nature.

Now it is of the very essence of such a Revelation, that it should be final; that it should be the last of all. There is no other behind, because any other must be less glorious. When God has come to us in His Son, He can come to us in none greater. In the Son *dwelleth all the fulness of the Godhead bodily*. In the Son *are hid all the treasures of wisdom and knowledge* (Col. ii. 3, 9). *He that hath the Son hath life* (1 John v. 12); hath wisdom, hath the knowledge of God, hath God Himself. He who once spake *in many portions* hath now spoken in His Son, and spoken, in doing so, for the last time. *Then cometh the end* (1 Cor. xv. 24).

My brethren, if we are poor in Divine knowledge, the fault is our own. We are so slight, so perfunctory, in our study of God. We think we know all. We sit in judgment upon the Word, when we ought to be letting the Word judge us (John xii. 48). And therefore that solemn saying is made good against us, *Thou hast hid these things from the wise and prudent, and hast revealed them unto babes* (Matt. xi. 25).

Take then fully into your view the finality of Christ's Revelation. It is, in every sense of the words, *a dispensation of the fulness of time* (Eph. i. 10). Lose it not, for there is no other. God, in speaking by His Son, has spoken indeed for the last time.

But here is our comfort. God at last has spoken

to us in a Person. It is not so much the knowledge of truths to which He calls us: it is the knowledge of a Person. Of that there is no end. If we live with a human person, whom we fondly love, and who is in any sense worthy of our love, we all know that we do not exhaust that person, even so far as the knowledge of him is concerned, by any length of intercourse, nor by any devotedness of study. There is always something new; some new exhibition of character, drawn out by some new conjuncture of circumstances: and whereas the longest, the most interesting, or the most difficult, of human books would, in the course of years, be drained to its very dregs and cast aside as done with, it is not so with the living man; it is not so with the acting and thinking life; it is not so with the loving friend, in whose constant presence we have found comfort and repose.

If this can be so with human converse, how ought it to be for us all with that communion which is more than human? O, my brethren, God did speak once, but is He not still speaking, in His Son? God grant that that voice be not silent to any of us! Alas for those to whom it is only a matter of history that God spoke in Christ! What are they not missing? What have they in its stead? Whose voice are they listening to? Or whose voice are they listening for? There are some who pass all through life listening for, instead of listening to, a revelation; always expecting, never receiving; *ever learning, never able to come to the knowledge of the truth* (2 Tim. iii. 7). God grant that we be not of that number! Here, in this Book, He has spoken: but it is chiefly for the purpose of opening the inward ear, that He may speak to us personally in His Son. That voice is never silent to any who have the will to hear it. No new revelation: the volume of the written Word is closed now against additions: but the Voice which spoke speaks still; speaks to attract, speaks to warn, speaks to counsel, speaks to explain, speaks to comfort: takes the word from the dead silent page, and speaks it inwardly to the listening heart; makes it the word, not of information only, but of strength and peace and direction, saying, *This is the way, walk ye in it* (Isai. xxx. 21), when we are turning aside to the right hand or to the left.

There, in that presence, let us all meet one another day by day, walking in the light while we have it (John xii. 35), and looking forward, with one heart, to *that blessed hope, even the glorious Epiphany of our Lord Jesus Christ* (Tit. ii. 13).

THE END.

www.ingramcontent.com/pod-product-compliance
Lightning Source LLC
Chambersburg PA
CBHW051201300426
44116CB00006B/395